SOCIAL MEDIA MARKETING 2021

THE ULTIMATE MASTERY TO USE THE SECRETS OF DIGITAL BUSINESS AND BECOME AN INFLUENCER

THIS BOOK INCLUDES

INSTAGRAM, YOUTUBE, TWITTER, AND FACEBOOK MARKETING 2021

ANDREW PROCTOR

This collection includes the following books

FACEBOOK & TWITTER MARKETING 2021

YOUTUBE & INSTAGRAM MARKETING 2021

FACEBOOK & TWITTER MARKETING 2021

How to use social media for business and how to create a viral brand. Learn step by step the latest strategies, advertising and the secrets used by influencers

ANDREW PROCTOR

Table of Contents

Introduction

— — — — — ❧❦❧❦ — — — — —

Almost around a decade ago, television and print were considered to be the main modes of marketing and getting the message across to the consumer. With the advent of Facebook marketing in recent years, the competitive landscape has majorly changed. Companies now use Facebook as the main mode of communication between them and the consumer due to the many advantages that it offers to them.

This change has mainly happened due to the rise of social media usage and the effect that it has on consumers. People use Facebook excessively in the modern age, more so to connect with other people. However, as the usage of Facebook has increased tremendously, marketers have noticed that it allows them to reach consumers in a much better way – a way that is more engaging than conventional media. Facebook marketing not only allows marketers to get their messages across effectively but also allows them to form personalized connections with consumers. People share a lot of their experiences with a specific product or service on Facebook, which eventually does not only stay restricted to them but reaches a much larger and wider audience by the use of the social networks of those very people. People also share a lot of reviews, advice, warnings, and tips on social media that marketers can use to their advantage. This gives other people a lot of validation before choosing to buy a product or service. With conventional media, this was not really possible.

In addition to that, it is also of importance to note that it is much easier to reach a target audience through Facebook than it is to make a mark through conventional mediums. Statistics show that on an everyday basis, almost 684,478 pieces of content are shared on Facebook. This is a huge amount of data if you look at it closely. With this much amount of data circulating the internet every single day, marketers can make use of this, and they are absolutely doing so in the modern era. With a lot of filtering out of information and customization being available on Facebook, consumers also trust Facebook advertising way more than they trust other mediums. On Facebook, advertising does not only happen through the companies or company representatives but also through opinion leaders and other customers. Word of mouth is known to be a very strong and trusted medium of marketing and Facebook marketing does a very good job of generating word of mouth.

Twitter is a social media and microblogging tool accessed by users worldwide. The platform offers you an opportunity to exchange messages that are 280 characters long. It also allows you to follow other people's profiles as they follow you back.

The messages exchanged via Twitter are known as tweets. Most individuals share information and news on the platform with the hope that others will find the information useful. Besides interacting with other people, you can also use your Twitter account for blogging. You can also share other people's posts using a process known as retweeting.

When using Twitter, you can share your feelings, thoughts, and news in as many updates as you wish. When you create a profile on the platform, it becomes visible to other users across the world. However, you may decide to make your profile private and accessible only to a number of people.

Twitter is a popular platform because of the way it brings together people of diverse beliefs, locations, and interests. You can easily identify, track, and read posts from preferred individuals and groups each day. The limited number of characters in each tweet promotes sound interaction between individuals. Twitter has a large audience in terms of the people that use the platform. Most individuals have become popular through the proper use of the site to promote themselves.

Besides using the platform for personal interests, companies are now using the platform to market their businesses as well. The main aim of creating the platform is to help you answer the question, "what are you doing." Most companies have used it to reach out to new customers and grow their profits in unimaginable ways.

Chapter 1

------ ✂✂✂✂ ------

Facebook page

Once you have decided to add Facebook to your marketing campaign strategies, it is important to note that like every strategy, there are pros and cons and a knowledge of them will help you navigate through this journey in the best ways possible. While sticking to the pros (advantages) to determine your actions, you will be expected to dodge the cons (disadvantages) so that your campaign will not lead you to a place of self-destruction.

Before you launch your Facebook Marketing campaign, it is important to take the following facts into cognizance and determine if it is going to be worth it at the end of the day. Also, a knowledge of these facts will help you to know which strategies to stick with and which to avoid. That said, let us take a quick look at some of the advantages of Facebook businesses.

Pros

• Helps you reach a wider audience: as we have rightly stated earlier, Facebook has about 1.5 billion users of different age groups and sexes. A business page on this platform that is home to the world's largest community, however, means that you will be able to reach a wider audience. Since this is a place where your customers spend a lot of their time, it is only logical for you to reach them here. This is the largest audience that is interested in what you have to offer.

• Interact with customers before they become buyers: Facebook stands out when it comes to customer engagement, with its array of strategies that helps you interact with customers in all the stages of the buying cycle which include post-purchase. With reviews from existing customers on the page, you get the chance to announce your strengths to your potential customers and let them know if you are to be trusted or not.

• Tell your customers who you are: Beyond buyer to seller relationship, customers these days want to have a firsthand impression of who you really are, especially if they are to trust you with their money, or for you to provide quality goods or services. Your Facebook page is the best way to tell them all about yourself and your business, your tenets, and your goals. The best way to do this is through engagements. Since the platform gives room for photo and video sharing, you will be able to showcase your products and services to your audience. They, on the other hand, will get the chance to react to these products or services by liking and giving feedback through comments. They can also refer you to their friends by sharing your content with them. This is an easy way to sell yourself through the web.

• Easy access to information: The beauty of Facebook is that your customers are just a click away. With this platform, you can easily update information about changes and improvements on your products and services or even your brand in general. Do you see? With your Facebook page, you do not really need to issue a press release or do TV and Newspaper ads to pass information to your audience, unless in cases where it becomes absolutely necessary.

• A chance to prove your authenticity and transparency: So many of your customers have had their fair share of bad experience from scammers and fakes. Your page is your opportunity to show them that you are different and you are just the right brand to do business with. The more real you are, the easier it is for people to come close and transact business with you. You have to build a connection with your followers, as it is easier for them to do business with you when they feel they have a connection with you.

• Easy to measure results: The main aim of every business is to achieve measurable results. These results, however, will only make a visible impact if you are able to measure them in real time. This way, you will know if you are to push harder by sticking to that which you are currently engaged in or if you should change strategy. Facebook marketing makes it easy for you to measure your landmarks with page insights, which are always available to established businesses. It allows you to see the activities on your page and how far they are taking you.

•   Specific ad targeting: with Facebook ad automation tools, you will be able to target your ads to a specific audience. For example, if your products are more useful to those that domiciled in New York, you will be able to target your ads to those that have listed New York as their state of residence. What this means is that instead of your ads popping up all over the place without reaching those that it will specifically be useful to, you will instead be able to target it to a useful audience, with hopes that they will be converted into customers. You may also decide to break your ads down by different demographics like age and gender. While you are designing your ad, an estimated cost will also be shown to you so that you are aware of the cost of investment you are putting into the advert.

•   Generate leads and sales with ads: Facebook ads get targets at their comfort zones so it is easy to catch their attention. So, once you have the attention of these customers, it will be easier for them to follow up on leads and land on your page, and if possible, patronize your products.

Though Facebook strategies may be difficult to master, it is absolutely worth trying and investing in to get the best results for your marketing campaign.

Cons

Below, let's take a look at some of the features of Facebook that may prove a threat (cons) to your brand/business.

•   Demands a lot of investment: Starting up a Facebook page is absolutely free but it takes more than merely having a page to run a successful Facebook marketing campaign. First, you have to keep in mind that you are going to have to invest quality time in it to make it a success. Not only does it take time to build your Facebook page to a certain level, but it also demands quite a lot of money to run campaigns like Facebook ads and build human resources, which is someone/people that will interact with the community that you are trying to build. The person/they will have to spend a lot of time making comments and liking posts.

•   Slow progress: It takes time to build a Facebook page and if you are not the patient and dedicated type, you may find it discouraging. However, there are ways to increase the pace of the growth of your page. You can either do this by investing in resources or increasing your budget for advertising. Also, you can decide to run competitions and giveaways. One quick way to grow your followers is by getting people to get their friends to like your page as a way of winning the competition - by using the number of likes a person can generate as a measure.

• Content strategy is key: Your marketing campaign will not work if you do not have a solid content strategy that works. Content is the only way you can pass useful information across to your audience. You cannot do this successfully if you do not have a plan on how to execute evergreen content that will always get your audience to interact with your page in the best way possible.

• Pay to promote content: Unlike the way it used to be in the past, Facebook's algorithm has now changed in a way where you have to pay to get your content out there. Take note, however, that this content is different from ads. To get your posts to reach a wider audience, you have to pay to promote them. Posting contents on your page are only half of the job that needs to be done, as the other half lies in your decision to pay to promote your content.

• The success of a page is not determined by the number of likes: Over the years, businesses have spent a lot of money to grow the number of likes on their page. Unfortunately, a page's likes do not determine engagement/interaction on the page. This is because Facebook has shifted the focus of pages from likes to ads. The page will have to reach a good number of users to be able to generate engagement. If you have successfully grown the number of likes on your page over the years, it is now time to invest more in ads and promotions to increase engagement.

•   Serve as the face/voice of your company: In the past, many businesses have made the mistake of leaving the management of their Facebook pages to interns that don't have the full scope of knowledge to use Facebook effectively. This may be a grave mistake as whatever is put out there on the page determines the way people perceive your page. This, therefore, means that you may have to employ the expertise of a communications expert to represent your brand in a community of over two billion people. This is to help monitor the information that goes out about your company.

•   Manage your reputation: If you have succeeded in building a good reputation for your brand, congratulations. Beware, however, that merely building a reputation for your brand is not enough. It is more important that you should know how to manage this reputation because a single mistake can ruin it all for you and you may have to start from scratch over again. For this reason, you will need to have reputation management policies in place to handle difficult situations like bad reviews. Your ability to handle these situations will also go a long way to increase the confidence of your customers.

• A high amount of spam: Once you have built a great business with a good reputation, you will have to face quite a lot of spam. Forget the trolls, those ones are always all over the place to do what they know how to do best. Once your business becomes influential online, you will be surprised by the number of spam links and posts that your content may accumulate. Other businesses may also try to boost their own reputation by riding on your own. This is a major threat because restrictions may not be enough. All someone needs to do is to like your page and post their comments. This becomes particularly difficult as you are not able to easily differentiate between the genuine pages and the fake ones. This adds more work to the level of commitment that you have to put in to maintain the reputation of your page.

Chapter 2

— — — — — ❧❧❧❧ — — — —

Targeting your audience

Marketing and advertising are businesses in and of themselves. The idea of selling products is an age-old business that thrived long before the creation of social media. Marketing firms still exist and have traded lots of their advertising in newspapers and magazines for online ads. Still, it is necessary to have a marketing plan to capitalize on the needs of your audience and to capture your target market. Just because the medium has changed doesn't mean the content and timing need to fall by the wayside. Do your homework, find your target audience and play into their needs.

This book will read a little differently depending on the business. In general, any business is either out to sell a physical product or a service. The idea of service is very broad and could include anything from personal training in person at a brick and mortar location to providing information through a website, like a blog.

The goal for most bloggers is to put out information that is helpful and incites the desire to learn more, or change. For example, if a blogger is passionate about saving the rainforest, their primary goal will be to drive their followers to propel political change. Not every business is selling something for money, and that is a very important distinction to make. Just as well, not every business has money to spend on advertising, like a non-profit. Therefore, their marketing goals online will be much different.

The first step to a successful Facebook campaign will be discovering your target audience. Most likely, you have already started a page to promote your business. Facebook has a handy feature that will show you page statistics. Simply click on the 'Insights' tab on the top of the page toolbar. From here you can analyze each post and how well it performed. You will find stats on how many people the post reached, and how many people liked and engaged in the post. You will also find stats on how your page did as a whole through time.

The page has a list of each of your posts, how many likes and how many shares it received. What you want to pay attention to most is the organic reach. This is the amount of people who saw your post because someone they are friends with either liked or shared the page. When you think of organic, think of the growth of a thunderstorm. With the right conditions, like warm air and moisture, a giant cloud can form. With static electricity, the cloud produces lightning, thunder, and of course rain. Without these conditions, the cloud cannot form. This is your post. Like the cloud, your post must have the right combination of interest and relevance to attract followers that eventually form a cloud of Likes. On Facebook, more likes and shares lead to a bigger following, similar to the growing cloud.

Organic reach is a great indicator of interest because it shows how many people are interested in the post. The more Likes and shares mean that a post has traveled to a greater number of people in a relatively small circle, and hopefully, your target audience. A high organic reach shows that your followers liked the post, and then their friends liked the post, and so on. Use this information to develop future posts that could also grab the same attention. Organic attention is the best kind because it is essentially free advertising.

Since you have likely had an active Facebook account for a while, take some time to go through your insights and determine what posts did best, and how to build a marketing campaign from there.

Also, watch what areas of your business do best. For example, if you own a flower shop and you discover that most people are interested in your floral arrangements for weddings, play into that audience. You may find that your followers have no need for specialty balloons and other gifts, but the arrangements do well. Give your followers what they want and post more information about wedding flowers. This is good for one of two things. Your current followers will hopefully find what they are looking for in your business and provide an increase in sales, but they will also share the information with their friends and family, creating greater organic reach.

Use this information to coordinate sales and other brick and mortar marketing strategies as well. Popularity may change over time, especially during wedding season. If trends in sales can be seen online, you bet that will translate into your store as well. Test the waters and post periodically about your specialty balloons. If there is little interest and your in-store sales support that, it is likely time to rethink your inventory. Take the opportunity to pinpoint products that take up valuable shelf space and replace them with things that there is more of a demand for.

It doesn't matter what type of product you are selling; this strategy works with everything, including intellectual content which are websites and companies that do not sell a product but capitalize on information. For example, a blogger may like to post about camping. They realize that their posts on gardening and homesteading are getting much more attention lately. Topics trend and lose steam, and using page insights to determine the ebb and flow of trends can be used to your advantage. It may not be feasible to continue writing about the same topics if the interest isn't there. While many people create blogs for the fun of connecting and sharing information if you are a professional blogger who uses a website as a money making venture, keeping up with trends is valuable. Since Facebook and other social media sites are used exclusively to draw attention to these sites, gaining insight from the demographics information can be a priceless marketing tool.

Don't be afraid to ask your followers what they want. You can certainly rely on your stats and page likes to form marketing plans, but sometimes it is beneficial to be straightforward and ask your followers outright what they are looking for. This is beneficial for a number of reasons. First, you get the marketing information you are after. Second, it gives your customers the opportunity to voice their opinion and shows that your business cares and caters to the needs of its customers.

Promote your product showing its benefits and see how people respond. In your post, tell people you are considering carrying the product, and tell them you are trying to find out how to better meet their needs. Remember, most people relate better to a business that has a true human element, and most try to support local businesses when possible. Big box businesses have focus groups to tell them what products to carry. Small, local businesses have their target audience, so utilize it. Show them that you care about their opinion, and they will notice.

Try creating a simple post asking a question. Try to be specific, as the vaguer you are about the information you are requesting, the less useful the feedback will be. For example, if your business sells bicycles, ask what kind of things followers would like to learn more about. While that is sort of vague, include examples, or even multiple choice. Offer possible suggestions to prompt the conversation.

An interesting feature to Facebook Insights is "Pages to Watch." Here you can find business pages that are similar to yours and Facebook will help you compare your stats to theirs. This is useful in a number of ways. First, you can tell if a competing business has a better following than you. This can help you focus your marketing plan and will hopefully give you a boost in motivation to work harder in your business

The "Pages to Watch" feature also allows you to see post engagement for other pages for the week. Once you begin watching a page, look for sudden spikes and dips in their engagement, then compare what has been posted on their site that may have caused it. Not only can you get ideas for what is trending in your field of interest, you can see some of the advertising techniques that failed for your competition, also very beneficial information.

Let's go back to the florist example. This business owner has been monitoring their page insights but has recently been looking at their local competitors' stats as well. From their page, they determined that their specialty balloons aren't creating much interest. This created a problem in that they want to find a new product to fill the shelf space. Using a competitors' page to determine what works best for their business is a good way to find a new product that is driving business. This is very simple market research.

Regardless of your type of business, creating a solid marketing plan is vital to the success of the business overall, and overlooking social media as part of that plan is a big mistake. These tools are free online and should be taken advantage of. Creating a marketing scheme on a gut feeling will not work. Use the information at hand and make a plan that will be irreplaceable to your company.

Chapter 3

Page theme

Where there is the internet, there's Facebook. Due To this omnipresence, Facebook boosting is almost requiring if your picture will triumph online. The problem with this is fundamental: Facebook marketing is a massive subject with a good deal of moving components. You ought to consider a slew of variables to genuinely concentrate on a method, and that's the matter that we have to help you with. Whatever your organization or brand, we can help you with getting your Facebook showcasing methodology off the floor. What's more is in the event you're currently knee-somewhere down on Facebook, then we've got a couple of ideas for you which can take your advertisements out of exceptional to shocking. How about we start.

Starting with Facebook Marketing

To begin with, I want to understand that not every man is on Facebook for a personal link. The magnificence of drawing closer Facebook showcasing from a company standpoint is you can keep different sides of your life mostly totally isolated. As you cannot use Facebook covertly, you may have a listing where the critical individual data available is your title you select, and whatever else is linked to the company accounts. Here and there, maintaining those sides completely different will limit your capability to promote to certain socioeconomics, (by way of instance, Facebook parties and maybe Events); at any situation, it's all up to you on which would be the most critical areas of the stage.

As we journey through the various topics, we'll address which parts may use your profile rather than a company one. On the off probability that it is not listed, you should be shielded to anticipate your picture personality will be individuals in general facing character. Generally, we'll accept you'll have a profile using sensible protection settings to your record.

Phase 1: Create Your Facebook Account

On the off likelihood that you now have a record, do not be afraid to look down a bit. This development is signaling; it is effortless to start on Facebook itself.

You might be tempted to tap the Create a Page link at the bottom of the display. But bear in mind it is going to permit you to create a webpage for your picture fast, and the process hits a barrier as it asks that you sign up in. So we will push forward with creating a listing first and then producing the newest profiles we'll work. So press on the join button, you'll find an email to confirm you are genuinely you. Don't hesitate to put in the code to show you're just one.

At the stage when you press Continue, you will be taken to a clear path of events. The principal must-do thing today is repairing your security preferences. Regardless of if you use Facebook by and not, assessing your protection preferences is a wise notion. Click on the bolt at the upper-right corner and then select Settings to start.

After all is said, well done, we'll run under the presumption that you only let your pals see proper data, nevertheless increasingly touchy information is set to Just Me. That's merely the absolute minimum for safety. So, make sure that you have the entirety of these tabs at the left sidebar and then change them for your inclinations. We would, however, concerning feature the section titled Do you require web crawlers out Facebook to link to your profile? There are other numerous people ignorant of, so on the off possibility, you want to divert your profile out of open Google appearance, assess this container. These will, in turn, does not affect your picture character, by way of instance, Pages, Groups, or Events.

Stage 2: Produce a Facebook Page

The Facebook Page is your location; most of your marketing will occur. You may run promotions by your webpage, have events, stream live video, and speak with your group of audiences. Pages would be the center point of the majority of open facing associations. They could -- normally -- do whatever that an individual document can perform. Be as it might, without needing to talk who's the soul behind the marking.

Using a page to market lets you dole out a bunch of people to take care of your small business, and we'll discuss each of the tasks and consents a bit lower. Most importantly, how about we dip in on actually creating the webpage. To start, find the Pages join from the sidebar to a single side of your path of events.

You may, at this point, obtain a rundown of the significant variety of pages for you. This rundown will soon be empty on the off possibility you haven't done this before. From the upper-right of this toolbar, in your Pages tab, then you need to press on the Create Page button.

You currently select if your Page will Talk to a company or Brand (administrations and objects, by and large) or a Community or Public Figure (portrayed as linking and supplying to people, an institution, group, or collecting). For our reasons here, we'll go with Brand or Business.

You need to have a name chosen with this Stage (doubtlessly the title of your company or site or manufacturer itself --, as an instance, Elegant Themes). We do not suggest making another Page to get a solitary thing (by way of example, our Divitopic) because that may be a show under the umbrella of a more significant page, which has an additional reach and usefulness past that individual product.

In this progression, you may select a Profile Picture plus a Cover Photo. You have the alternative to bypass them to the moment to collect your assets afterward. Sooner or later, these are necessary

With that settled, you will visit your new page on the subsequent screen. It'll be with no substance and information today. However, that's the thing you're able to deal with straight away.

Period 3: Customize Your Page

Overall else up to customization, The @username you select is most significant. Just tick on the Create Page @Username link to one side of this display to get started.

Additionally, you receive a Facebook Messenger URL where your customers can lawfully instant message you personally, and these messages proceed straightforwardly for your Messages program (accepting you utilize it). With this particular set, it is a perfect chance to fill in your picture subtleties. These are the fast and dirty chunks of information your clientele and network should consider you. A depiction of what your individuality is, the best way to find you someplace else on the internet, where to find you face to face in case you have a client-facing facade or bodily place, menus, email documents, etc.

Page Description

Some of the most unmistakable is adding a page description. To incorporate a depiction, click where the Insert a brief Description link is beneath Welcome to Your New Page.

A modular will appear where you can include a 155-personality depiction. These are your elevator pitches. The minimal way you'll be able to portray your picture or company. For example, Elegant Themes' page gets the portrayal. Elegant Themes constructs incredibly lovely Premium WordPress Themes together with cutting edge usefulness and kind assistance. Simple and comes to the heart of the matter. At the stage when it's completed, another modular display up, asking as to if you would like to change the rest of your page information or hold until any other time. No time like the present, thus we should change this information.

General Page Info

An additional modular display up, now with three tabs: Contact, Location, and Hours. These might not link to your organization or brand. In the event you're an internet store, you may not have hours. That means that you can always select open. What's more, on the off likelihood that you don't have a street address or phone, you can access them, and they won't appear at all on your webpage. Whatever you do enter, in any circumstance, will show up on principle webpage for many visitors to view under your About section.

Free Facebook Page Tools To Create Your Business Easier Today

Facebook apparatuses were a piece of this advertiser's regular toolbox in 2018. We picked several unbelievable Facebook application production devices that could help you with producing custom Facebook pages. Each of them possesses a constrained free choice that does not lapse, and they do not call for a good deal of tech skills to use.

Here are the free Facebook apparatus Available to acquire your basic Facebook demonstration page prepared for action.

1. ShortStack

ShortStack is a Facebook program Creation tool that permits you to create Facebook greeting cards, software, and conflicts without adapting any fresh thoughts. ShortStack includes a free arrangement with very striking highlights:

Endless Campaigns

Share usefulness

Promotions

Export drives/passages

5,000 Campaign Visits per 30 times

25 drives/passages

25,000 Facebook enthusiast remittance

ShortStack functions with the mainstream Phases:

Facebook -- conduct challenges on your webpage, Direct lovers to subtitle a picture for a chance to win. Give them more opportunities to acquire on the off possibility they input again by way of the Facebook program. Collect information from the challenge: photos, enjoy, and opinions.

Twitter -- increment the virality with ShortStack's sharing highlights to create Twitter challenges. At the stage when adherents link to a Campaign, use the passage arrangement to collect prompts usage for future boosting endeavors.

Instagram -- use the link on your Profile to connect with crusades where you're able to collect prospects, progress your eCommerce site, gain fans of your website, receive sections to get a giveaway, comprise records, and much more.

Pinterest -- Pinterest challenges display ways customers can use your items and advantages and progress infrequent supplies. You can redo what your audience sees at different events. For example, provide a lien briefly. You may likewise control permeability determined by the state that your group of viewers resides in and much more.

2. Heyo

Make Facebook struggles advanced for every gadget. Spare time with pre-made free Facebook formats. A simplified editorial supervisor gives you control. Drive devotion with sweepstakes, picture challenges, bunch deals, along with other Facebook page programs.

Drive greater devotion with Sweepstakes, Photo Contests, Group Deals, Hashtag Promotions and that is just the tip of this iceberg

Produce Conflicts improved for every gadget

Save Time together with pre-made formats which are worked to alter over

Drag And shed proofreader provides you complete control

Constructed Sharing highlights change your audience to a boosting power

Heyo provides Facebook conflicts which are Versatile compact [Free preliminary/$25/month]

3. Tab site

TabSite allows one to create and manage custom made Facebook webpages, applications, and conduct improvements. You can comprise different custom Facebook projects and give courses of action and Facebook challenges. Tab Site programs are not difficult to organize a pixel-ideal arrangement without programming or coding.

Facebook gadgets incorporate the capacity to direct sweepstakes, import blog passages, contain YouTube documents, incorporate thing slideshows, run pictures, and motion picture difficulties.

Free variant comprises one material tab, Two distinctively named sub-pages. Handle the habit of Facebook pages using an easy to use content manager, incorporate email arrangement coordination with Continuous Contact, MailChimp, and Delivera.

4. Facebook Timeline Contests

Run free challenges in your Facebook timetable. Prize lovers and increment devotion by conducting sweepstakes, evaluations, and picture challenges on your FB page.

Arbitrarily select victors in the lovers who Adored or commented on a post, pose inquiries at the point. Select your champs one of the feedback together with appropriate answers. Let your lovers remark photos and choose champs in the comments with the most enjoys.

Snap free tools from the Primary Menu: All these programs are 100% free, and also always will be. It's possible to run any obstacle, precisely the identical amount of occasions as you require, on any range of pages.

5. Woobox

Free alternative integrates six identifying programs, with no points of confinement on lovers or new pages: HTML Fangate, habit Facebook tabs for Twitter, Instagram, Pinterest, and YouTube. Choose a Winner device. Fans and brand webpages infinite. Paid programs include the usage of each one of the 19 programs, from Sweepstakes to Bargains to Photo Contests.

6. Simple Tab Creator

Simple Tab Creator includes a simple Port and also enables one to manage three webpages for nothing; many different destinations allow only one. Furthermore, it contains a 30-day unconditional guarantee. Straightforward Tab Creator is a program that abrupt spikes in demand for Facebook. It enables you to alter your Facebook Page by adding your material (content, movies, install YouTube files, and so on.). The program comprises a Welcome tab.

7. Pagemodo

Pagemodo enables you to manufacture your custom Facebook webpage as an invitation tab by shifting your substance. A completely free record allows you to appraise the highlights which follow Premium bundles. You're able to manage one Facebook enthusiast page, create one habit tab for this, utilize Cover Photo fashioner, find incredible substance with articles proposal devices, and calendar one Facebook and a single Twitter upgrade for every single day.

Chapter 4

————— ✒︎✒︎✒︎✒︎ —————

Facebook advertising

Ad campaigns on Facebook are a massive topic that takes years of marketing experience to perfect and understand in every detail. This book will give the readers an overview of why you need Facebook ads, how to set up the two most effective types of ad campaigns: "promote your page" and "boos post", how to specify a target audience for maximum campaign success and how to use Facebook Analytics to learn & improve future campaigns. I will also show you the details of an ad campaign I used to gain 5,000 likes for 15$; the campaign is perfectly repeatable and you will experience similar results when running it. I encourage you to run it when launching a new page in order to acquire your first 10,000 likes, hence achieve social proof for any new page visitor.

Overview of facebook ads

Over the past years facebook has directed a lot of effort towards building an effective advertising platform. In today's world, Facebook is seen as the most cost-effective and targeted framework to market a product or a service directly to the end customer. The great marketing success of Facebook is based on

3 key features: (1) Global Reach (2) Targeted Advertising (3) Instantaneous and Detailed Feedback.

1 – Global Reach: with facebook's 1.9 billion monthly active users, massive marketing campaigns can be launched to a truly global reach. However, one of facebook's great unique advantages is its ability to provide small-scale marketing campaigns for all budgets.

2 – Targeted Advertising: with society's increasing participation in social media, through every page you like and comment you place, Facebook gains more knowledge on your preferences, interests and activities. This data represents Facebook's strongest point in advertisement: the ability to target individual customers based on their social media activities. The ads targets can be narrowed down by age, nationality, language, interests, geographical location, and much more

3 – Instantaneous and Detailed Feedback: It has never been this simple and straightforward to analyze the success of a marketing campaign. Perhaps most useful of all, small ad campaigns can be launched to only reach a few thousand people (yes, that is small by facebook standards). By doing so, different ad strategies can be run in parallel and, using facebook analytics, the most responsive features of each ad strategy can be isolated before launching a large-scale ad

campaign. This quick and inexpensive feedback strategy was not available with older marketing approaches—such as magazine adverts.

Creating Ads

Before you can launch your first campaign, you need to have a verified billing method for your account (required to fund the marketing campaign). Enter the billing information as required in Manage Ads>Settings>Billing.

Now that your billing information is set, you can proceed to launch your first marketing campaign. To do this, you must select the "Create Ads" menu and navigate through the ad manager menu.

Boosting your post

Boosting your post can be very effective when releasing a particularly captivating and catchy post. This post is supposed to represent everything your page stands for in a positive and flattering manner. This technique is aimed at increasing user engagement, not page likes. However, you will gain likes for the post and if it is captivating enough, you can expect users to start tagging their friends and achieve a wider audience. In short, using this technique although you may gain few page likes, you will increase user engagement provided the audience you target finds your post very appealing.

To begin, create a first post that is captivating and eye-catching to your target audience as described above. Click the boos post button to begin the ad campaign. When you arrange for a delayed post publication time, the corresponding campaign will also be delayed.

Create a New Audience

Both of the above marketing campaigns require you to select an audience. For your first campaign you will have to create a new audience, for later campaigns you will be able to select/edit saved audiences or create new ones.

In this area, you can specify the demographics of the audience you would like to reach. The screen below shows how to create and specify a new audience for your first marketing campaign.

Pro Tip: If you are only looking to increase page likes, make sure you select the "Exclude people who like [your page name]", this prevents advertising your page to those who already like it.

Facebook provides a very helpful graphical representation of the audience details, breadth, characteristics and potential reach. Estimates for daily reach are calculated based on the campaign daily budget allocated (pricing is explained in the later section).

As you refine the audience requirements, the "potential reach" of your ad will change. This number represents the global facebook users that meet the characteristics of your audience.

If your potential reach is very large, then you can refine your audience further and ideally target more receptive customers (gauge points at "broad"). If your potential audience is too small for your campaign requirements, then your audience is too refined and you should proceed to widen your audience (gauge points at "specific"). Ideally, for your first campaigns you should maintain the gauge on the green area. It is worth mentioning that the more refined the audience, the higher the advertising costs.

Ad placement and pricing

In the next steps you will be required to select ad placement, budget, schedule and format. Facebook will walk you through these menus and most menu options are self-explanatory. However, I would like to point out a few lessons I have learned during past campaigns.

Placement – This option allows you to the location of your ad to the viewers. You can choose between different platforms and locations. I have experienced greatest marketing success when selecting facebook as a platform and the "Feeds" location (ads will be placed in the news feed section of your target customers).

Pricing – In this section you must specify budget of your campaign. Make sure you select "Automatic" for the Bid Amount option, as facebook will always deliver the cheapest bid available. This is preferential to the manual big pricing because, as your post engagement increases, the bid price will decrease also.

Test campaigns in parallel

When preparing any form of promotional content (radio ads, magazine ads, commercials...), it is common practice to prepare two or three versions, compare one another and pick the most responsive ad. In the past this was difficult to do: unbiased test candidates are gathered and they are exposed to the promotional content; their response is recorded and assessed.

Facebook ads make this process immensely faster, easier and more precise. Before launching a very large marketing campaign, you can set up small facebook ads of 10$ with all your different advertising strategies. Facebook can launch the ads immediately and within the next day UNBIASED, REAL-CUSTOMER responses are available.

This process is clearly fast and effecting; I ALWAYS recommend testing multiple advertising strategies in parallel over facebook before launching a large marketing campaign.

Chapter 5

─────── ❧❧ ───────

Using facebook audience insights to improve targeting

As you may already know, it is important to target the right audience with the right messages when creating and implementing your ads so that you will get the desired results as well as ample ROI. Better targeting simply means that you are investing in the ads to reach the audience that is likely to become customers. Your Facebook audience insight is your one-stop shop to knowing everything that is happening on your page. It gives you ample information on your target demographic. Pay attention to it and use it to figure out the kinds of messages you will send to which audience. The message, the tone, and the timing are great factors that determine how you will connect to your existing customers and even convert new ones.

Since you have already learned about the importance of Facebook Insights and their roles, we will go straight into learning how to use these insights to target our ads to the right audience.

Below is a step-by-step guide on how to improve on targeting with insights.

Select the audience you want insights for

On the audience insights dashboard, select the ad account you would like to get insights for (if you have more than one ad account) from the drop-down menu at the top right-hand side of the dashboard. You will now select whether you want to see insights for all of Facebook's audience or only those that are already connected to your page. If you have a custom audience set for your Facebook ad campaign already, you will also see an option for those audiences too so all you have to do is to select the ones you want information on.

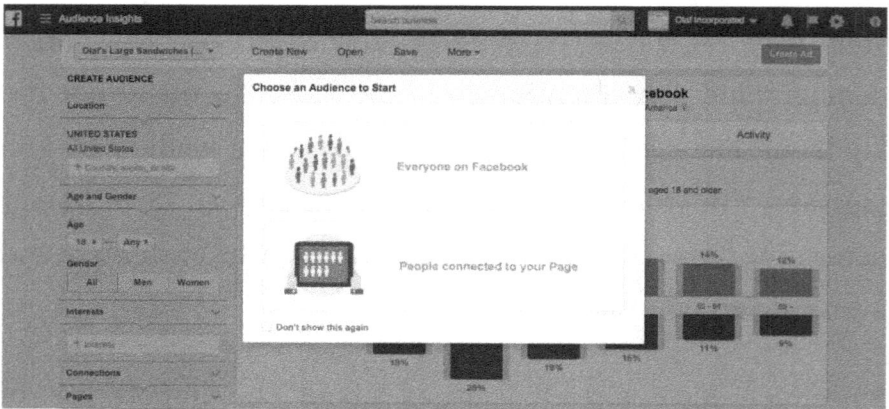

Since the purpose of this section is to learn about how best we can use Facebook audience insights to target ads, we are going to go with the first option, which is to get insights on 'Everyone on Facebook' and look at what we can gather from these insights to target our advertising strategy.

To choose an audience to analyze, click on 'Everyone on Facebook' if you are looking for ways to get information about potential customers that can be reached with ads. If you want to learn about your current customers in order to create contents that will suit them, click on people connected to your page. If you already have a custom audience like those that subscribed to your email newsletters, click on 'Custom Audience', to find out ways of connecting with them more on Facebook.

Like we said, this section will focus on ways to get new customers so we will stick to 'Everyone on Facebook' and look at ways to target Facebook ads strategies.

Build target audience demographics

At this point, you will use the information made available to you by Facebook to create a target audience for your ads. To do this, go to the Audience Insights Dashboard. Here, you will see all the characteristics available for you to choose from as well as those you might want to target on the left-hand side. On the right-hand side are graphs and charts that represent your audience, in relation to the overall audience of everyone that is using Facebook.

■ (New Audience)   People on Facebook
200M - 250M monthly active people ⓘ   Country: United States of America

Demographics   Page Likes   Location   Activity

Age and Gender
Self-reported information from people in their Facebook profiles. Information only available for people aged 18 and older.

■ 54% Women
54% All Facebook

16%   24%   19%   16%   14%   12%
18 - 24   25 - 34   35 - 44   45 - 54   55 - 64   65 -

■ 46% Men
46% All Facebook

18%   28%   19%   15%   11%   9%

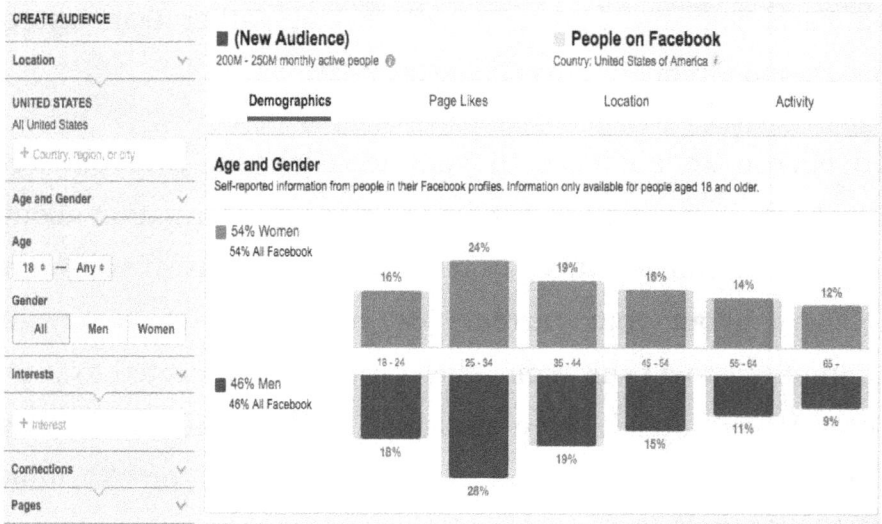

The graphs and percentages on the right-hand side of the screen are automatically updated whenever you make a selection to refine your audience. Below are other options and variables that are available on your Facebook Audience Insights that shape your ad targeting.

Location: The default location is set to the United States but this option may not be suitable for your business so you have to choose a country that is appropriate for your business.

If your business is a local business with a physical location, it is best for you to choose the city or state where your business is located. Online services give you the chance to include all countries in the world, depending on the kind of service you offer. Those that sell physical items, however, are advised to target those countries that they can ship to.

Age and Gender: Only those that are above 18 are available for targeting on Facebook Audience Insights so you will not be able to target those that are younger than that. In a case where you do not know the age that you want to target, it is advised that you leave this option at default for now.

Interests: When you click the 'Interests' option, a dropdown box will appear. By clicking on the dropdown options, you will be able to further refine your options. This is your chance to get as detailed as possible, using the information already at your disposal from your existing customers. If you look closely at the changes that occur in the graphs when you click, you will learn a lot more. As an example, when you click on the number of Facebook users from the U.S, the graph will show you that 45% of them are women while the remaining 46 % are men. Adding 'Food and Drinks' as an interest will, however, further change this data to 62% women and 38% men. Narrowing down this interest to 'Restaurants' will bring the percentage of women to 69% while that of men will reduce to 31%. If you proceed to narrow it down to 'Coffee Houses', the percentage of women will increase to 71% while that of men will reduce to 29%.

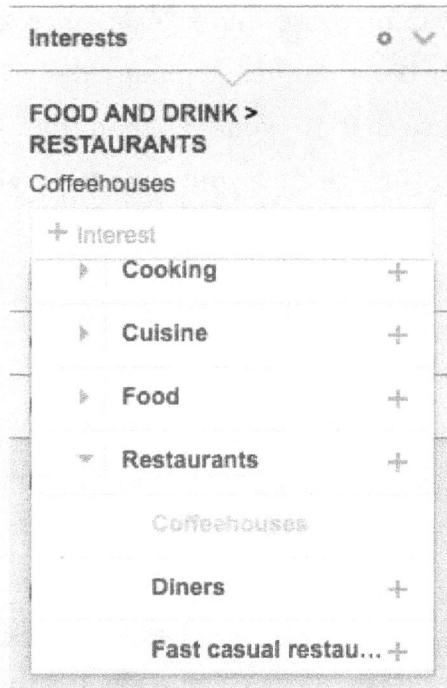

Interests ⚙ ⌄

FOOD AND DRINK >
RESTAURANTS
Coffeehouses

+ Interest

▸ Cooking +

▸ Cuisine +

▸ Food +

▾ Restaurants +

Coffeehouses

Diners +

Fast casual restau... +

Based on the interests highlighted above, let's say you are marketing a local coffeehouse instead of a chain, you will want to narrow down your interest by location. Let's take coffeehouse in Oregon, Portland as an example:

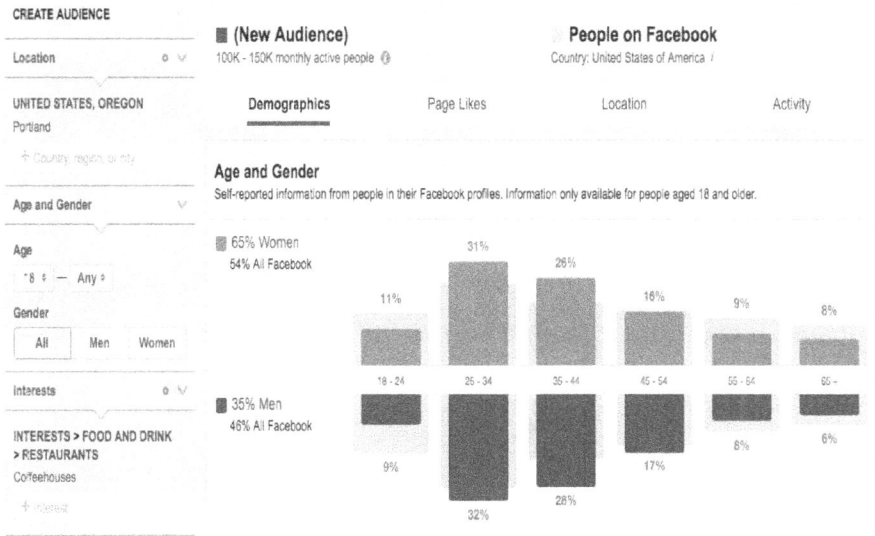

CREATE AUDIENCE

Location

UNITED STATES, OREGON
Portland

+ Country, region, or city

Age and Gender

Age
18 — Any

Gender
All   Men   Women

Interests

INTERESTS > FOOD AND DRINK
> RESTAURANTS
Coffeehouses

+ interest

(New Audience)
100K - 150K monthly active people

People on Facebook
Country: United States of America

Demographics   Page Likes   Location   Activity

Age and Gender
Self-reported information from people in their Facebook profiles. Information only available for people aged 18 and older.

65% Women
54% All Facebook

35% Men
46% All Facebook

18 - 24   25 - 34   35 - 44   45 - 54   55 - 64   65 -

The percentage of genders will change again. When you narrow down this option to Portland, you will see that the percentage of women will reduce to 65% as opposed to 71% nationwide. What this data means, therefore, is that someone marketing a coffeehouse in Portland on Facebook will have to focus his ads on women as they have a higher population of consumers in that area according to Facebook Audience Insight's data. This analysis only shows gender. There are other statistics on the graph which show data for age, education level, gender, relationship status, and job title. The Portland data, for example, shows that people between the ages of 25 to 34 are more interested in coffeehouses than other parts of the country.

44

Advanced: This option gives you the chance to narrow down your audience by different variables such as relationship status, job title, education level, cultural group, and office type. Here, in the drop-down box, you can select any option that suits your objective and even choose to target a certain class of people such as parents or parents of a certain age group. You can also target a group based on their activity like those that have just relocated or those that just started at a new job.

Still using the coffeehouse business as an example, if you wish to target parents, the audience nationwide will settle at 77% men and 23% women. When you enter the age and relationship variables, the graph changes as well. Let's say you want your ad to tell people that your coffeehouse is a good place for parents, from the ad, you will see that your target is concentrated in those Facebook users that aged 35 and above.

Once you have narrowed down your audience and are satisfied that you have what you need, click on 'Save' then give a relevant name to your audience. Bear in mind that detailed targeting reduces your audience to a small group but gives you a more responsive audience, therefore, increasing your ROI for Facebook ads. The best practice, however, is to get as detailed as you can be in every campaign but ensure that you test new audiences against existing ones so that you will know which of your campaigns has more conversion rates and which brings in more returns on investment.

Find out the things that you audience are already in love with

Now that you have set your demographics and gotten intrinsic knowledge of the variables that make up your target audience, click on the 'Page Likes' tab to discover the things that your target audience already likes on Facebook.

Top Categories: This is where you will learn about the overall interests of your target audience. For our coffeehouse example, it is not a surprise to know that the fans of this business are interested in beverages, food, as well as groceries. Surprisingly, we would find out that coffeehouse fans are interested in travel agencies, which means that they are open to travel.

This insight will help you try out new ideas in your general Facebook marketing strategy and in your ads too.

Page Likes: This section shows you which existing page or pages your audience is already connected with. These pages are ranked by Facebook by relevance and affinity.

According to Facebook, Affinity is the likeliness of your audience to like a particular page on Facebook compared to other people, while Relevance is described as those pages that will most likely appeal to your audience as a result of affinity, page, size, and the number of those in your audience that already like the page.

What you are expected to do here is to visit these pages with a motive of competition to know what these pages are already doing that inspires their success, then use these ideas to replicate this success of theirs.

It is also important for you to make a list of these pages so that you can return to the audience creation column to gather some more important data. Go to the 'Interests' dropdown, type in the name of the pages that you wrote down from Page Likes. Not all the pages will appear as interests but for those that do, you will be able to get demographic information about their audience. Complete a close study of the audience of your competition then use whatever information you are able to gather to narrow down your own targets. Remember, the narrower the targeting, the more ROI.

Here is what you should do after gathering all the information you need from your competitor:

Go to your audience by clicking 'Open' open a tab in the top navigation bar to revisit your existing audience, then effect changes, based on the things you have learned from your competition.

Once you have added the details, click on the 'More' tab in the top navigation.

Preserve the original information you have about your audience clicking on 'Save As' to create a modified version.

Now test run your new audience against the old one to see which brings in more returns on investment.

Remember that this information does not apply to an active ad campaign, which means that you cannot change the audience for a campaign that is already up and running.

Discover language, location and device details

Language and Location: For those whose businesses have a physical location, you already know the geographical location that you want to target. Those that are marketing online products and services, however, are expected to set their location as worldwide.

Now click on the location tab, here you will see the places that have most of your followers reside in and the language they speak. For example, if your business is selling Batman action figures, click on the right column to clear all the existing location selection then enter 'Batman action figures' as your interest. You will find out that the United States is the top market for this product with 52%. Tunisia, surprisingly, is the second largest market with 13% so if you already have Tunisia among your shipping options or you can ship to Tunisia, or you have a digital product that Tunisians might be interested in, you just found yourself a fresh market to explore.

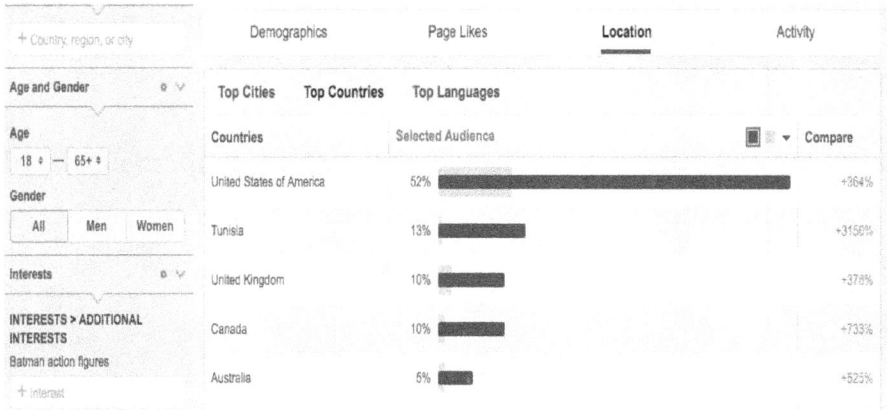

+ Country, region, or city	Demographics	Page Likes	Location	Activity

Age and Gender	Top Cities	Top Countries	Top Languages		
Age	Countries	Selected Audience			Compare
18 – 65+					
Gender	United States of America	52%			+364%
All Men Women	Tunisia	13%			+3150%
Interests	United Kingdom	10%			+378%
INTERESTS > ADDITIONAL INTERESTS	Canada	10%			+733%
Batman action figures	Australia	5%			+525%
+ Interest					

You will also want to take note of the language that is most common among your audience. For this example, 80% of people who are into Batman action figure are English speakers. 13% of the potential market for this product, however, are French speakers so it would be a good idea to create French ads which you may decide to show to only Facebook users who speak French.

Device: This information will be useful when you are designing your Facebook ad. As discussed in previous sections of this chapter, there are different specs of Facebook ads, suitable for different devices and platforms.

To see the devices your selected audience are using to access Facebook, click on the 'Activity' tab then go to the 'Location' tab, and then scroll down to 'Device Users' to see the devices your audience are using.

Among the fans of Batman action figures, we will find out that Android Users far outnumber other users as 82% of them use Android devices as their primary device to access Facebook.

Device Users   Primary Devices ▾

How the selected audience accessed Facebook in the last 30 days, based on user activity and environmental data.

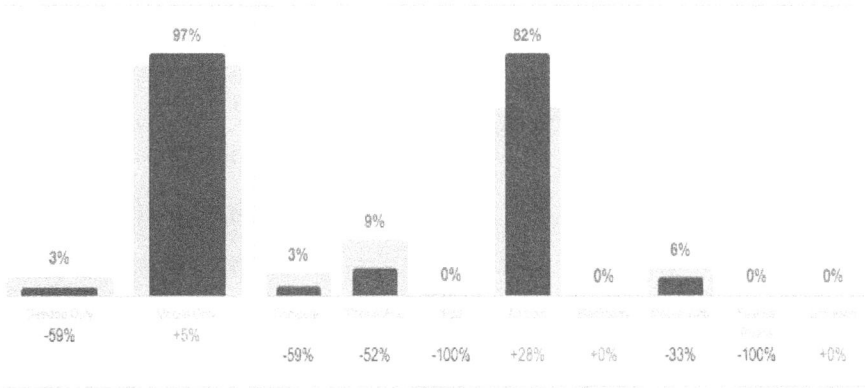

For the coffeehouse business in Portland, it will be discovered that only 33% of them use Android devices with 54% of the audience using iPhone or iPod as the primary device with which they access Facebook.

Device Users   Primary Devices ▾

How the selected audience accessed Facebook in the last 30 days, based on user activity and environmental data.

	Desktop Only	Mobile Only	Computer	iPhone/iPod	iPad	Android	Blackberry	Mobile Web	Feature Phone	Unknown
%	5% / 95%		5%	54% / 1%		33%	0%	7%	0%	0%
	-48%	+5%	-46%	+27%	-24%	-10%	+0%	-32%	+0%	+0%

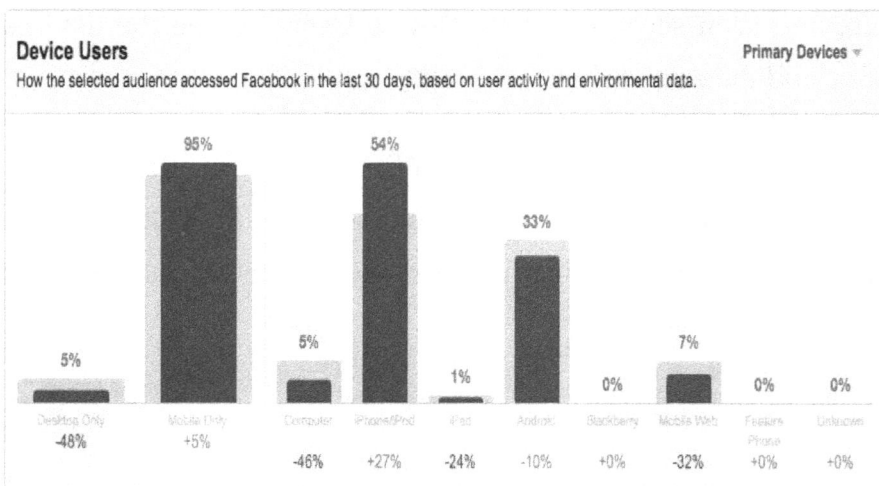

Target your audience with your Ad

If you have been able to gather up to one thousand people in your Insights as your audience, you will be able to use them to target your ad. To do this, click on 'Open' at the top bar then select the particular audience you wish to target with the ad. At the top right-hand corner, you will see the 'Create Ad' tab, click on it to place your ad targeted at the audience you have selected.

Create New   Open   Save   More ▾   Create Ad

CREATE AUDIENCE

Location ∨

UNITED STATES
All United States

+ Country, region, or city

Age and Gender ∨

■ **Coffeehouse parents**
10M - 15M monthly active people ⓘ

Demographics   Page Likes

People on Facebook
Country: United States of America ⓘ

Location   Activity

Age and Gender
Self-reported information from people in their Facebook profiles. Information only available for people aged 18 and older.

Once you click on the last option, the ad manager will help you spread the options you have already selected in the Audience Insights, into the targeting fields.

Make sure you keep close track of the performance of your ad campaign then compare it to the general Facebook returns on investment.

Do not be discouraged when you notice that the number of your ads conversions are dropping with your targeted ads. This is because you have adopted a strategy that narrows down your audience to a more specific audience. Remember, it is about the quality, not the quantity. The goal of this strategy is to increase your ROI with fewer conversions.

With proper testing and tracking, you will be able to find that sweet spot that brings in more ROI while attracting those conversions that you require to meet the goals of your social media campaign.

Chapter 6

─ ─ ─ ─ ─ ✤✤✤✤ ─ ─ ─ ─ ─

Tips to create high-quality content

General Tips

When it comes to marketing on social media sites, content is king. You need to churn out high-quality content that your target audience will find appealing, entertaining, or empowering.

Consider everything

There is only one way to determine if your efforts are working effectively, and that is completing an evaluation of all data. Some social networking platforms have built-in tools to help you do that. There are many options available for third-party analysis tools. Use them to see what gets the most feedback on the content you've shared or promoted, and, equally importantly, what does not get the required level of response. That way, you can find out where you are successful and where you need to improve.

Make sure you publish at the right time

It is important to post content that engages your audience by prompting them to like, comment, or share. When it comes to optimizing this, the timing of your posts is very important because that determines how many people will see the post. Most business to business companies tend to post during normal business hours, but even then, posting on certain days will produce a much better response than posting on others. Do your homework to find out when your target audience is likely to be online and plan to post messages while they're there.

Create your connections

One of the common mistakes that social networking marketers make is talking at the audience, not with them. Talk to your followers and interact with them by responding to comments and messages or liking their content. They want to know that you are human and not just some kind of computer that provides automatic answers. Ask them to share their thoughts and make sure you respond in good time to their comments. If they send you messages, contact them immediately. If you effectively ignore potential customers, they will be driven out.

Go visual

People are repelled by large blocks of text, but they pause and pay attention to the pictures. Photos, videos, and infographics contain information that is easier to recognize for people. Make sure your visual content is strong, engaging, and relevant to your business.

Make each of your selected platforms unique

Many tools allow you to share content across multiple platforms, and this can be helpful for important information. However, if you do this for each piece of content, all of your platforms will be the same. People following you on a platform are likely to follow you on all platforms, and they do not want to see identical content. This ensures that they only follow you on one platform. Make each of your accounts unique, and you will attract more people and gain even more followers and more potential customers.

Let people follow you

If someone subscribes to you on the social network, he wants to thank you. Offer bonuses for a subscription or a like such as a small discount on a product or a raffle. People need an incentive to join you, and providing perks for following you will keep them interested in continuing to follow you.

Remember to be personable but professional

While social networking can be a more relaxed way of marketing your business, you still need to maintain an atmosphere of professionalism. Yes, give out some personal information that will give your business a human face, such as birthday announcements of employee fun facts, but never express your personal views on things on your business page. When you start thinking about politics or talking about the latest celebrity tricks, you can easily start turning your followers away from you.

Social media manager

Not everyone can handle social networks well, and if you can't, it's better to have someone at the helm who can easily communicate, interact, publish, and share with others. In this way, you will be able to continue your business and take advantage of a successful marketing campaign.

If it does not work, let go

Not everything will work; no matter how much analysis you carry out or how many new team members you hire, there is bound to be a platform that is not right for your business. If nothing works and you get no results, drop it and go. There are better things to focus your time and energy on.

Build business relationships

If there are companies that belong to the same industry or the same niche as you, join them and follow them, but only if they are not direct competitors. You can connect clients, share subscribers, and get tips. You may wonder how much benefit you can derive from it. Interacting with other companies can attract their followers to your brand or business. It's a great way to network and increase your reach.

Fight trolls

The more successful you become, the more attention your social media accounts attract. With that fame inevitably come internet trolls. Trolls often get into fights with other followers and post hateful and upsetting comments. If you find your page contains trolls or people who only want to cause trouble, handle them professionally. Do not engage in a negative manner with them because this will reflect poorly on you. At the same time, don't allow them to post whatever they want because they may run off other followers.

Don't keep selling

Facebook is perceived as a domain where people engage in a kind of social activity, chat with their friends, view photos and videos of others, and relax. They want to engage in conversation and become part of the community, not be bombarded by "outsiders" who are trying to aggressively sell products.

There are certain hard sales tactics that you should avoid. These include the use of advertising slogans, sending multiple messages about a specific product or service, and providing redundant information about a product or service unrelated to a conversation. Your subscribers can unfollow you, but they can also do even worse: leave bad feedback about your business on your page. As a public page, these poor reviews can be seen by anyone who visits your page. Poor reviews will only hurt you.

Always have a clear goal

It is very important to have a clear goal in mind while using Facebook and a clearly defined strategy to achieve that goal. For example, a café can easily decide that its goal is to increase sales generated through Facebook by 10% within six months. The strategy could then include creating daily posts that use a coupon code to display unique specials or deals of the day so you can track a specific sale on Facebook. You can post a photo of the buyer with a cup of coffee at your café. You can also encourage users to post their photos (for example, in a coffee shop or with a small amount of coffee) to attract more attendees. Setting a goal as well as a strategy helps you to determine the direction and achieve the desired success.

Human side

In general, a Facebook user wants to communicate with another person and not engage in conversation with an impersonal company. Regardless of who is responsible for managing the Facebook page of a business or brand, that person should be able to write and develop content that communicates the "human" side of the business. Facebook gives you the chance to be more informal and lighthearted when interacting with customers. Do not make things sound too formal or hard.

Be regular

Unlike other media such as television, magazines, newspapers, etc., social networks allow you to include regular updates. Most Facebook users generally review their pages at least once a day, so you need to make sure your company publishes new content. Depending on your audiences' demographics, you can decide how often and when to post new content. Be regular, but don't go overboard.

Encouraging comments

You should encourage Facebook users to respond to your posts or comment on your posts about your business or its topic. When a user posts something, make sure that their message is answered within 24 hours. Refusing an answer can be seen as a lack of interest on your part. If you do not respond, you may not be tracked by users.

Use pictures and videos

One of the most attractive elements of Facebook is the fact that users can post photos and videos. Take advantage of this ability to keep your followers interested and engaged. As discussed in previously, there are multiple ways to do this. For example, a chain of clothing stores may post images of a new inventory as it arrives, or a personal trainer may post a training video with instructions on how to perform a particular exercise.

Try to be as interactive as possible and attract your audience by holding various contests, conducting polls, creating quotes, and so on. Facebook should be fun, so you should include the fun element in your marketing strategies.

The two most common reasons why a user visits a business page on Facebook are discounts and gifts. Competitions and games can make your site exciting. Customer surveys can be conducted via Facebook. If you want to do a survey, make the questions easy and make the survey short. Facebook facilitates short bursts of engagement, so try not to post long updates or surveys.

Develop relationships

It takes some time to build good relationships with other Facebook users, so you have to be patient. Try to get to know your followers. Take time to interact with them in the comments. You can like their comments or respond to them directly. Building relationships with your followers will make them more likely to continue a relationship with you.

Remember to use Facebook Insights

With Facebook Insights, you can better understand those who love your site and want to follow you. Once you know the characteristics of those who follow you, you can tailor your messages to their needs and their interests. For example, if a bookstore serves customers of all ages, but most subscribers are between 18 and 25 years old, the offers shared on Facebook should be designed according to that target audience of 18- to 25-year-olds. The offers in the store, however, should be more diverse.

Interaction

Make sure that you post actively on Facebook and engage in other ways. The more users come into contact with you, the more they will remember you. This can be achieved by posting content throughout the week. Use analytics to figure out when and how often to post, and don't be afraid to try different strategies. It can take time to figure out what best serves your audience. Once you find the sweet spot, you should see your engagement and follower count increase.

Tags are important

Tags allow you to identify who is in a certain post or picture. For example, in a picture of your employees, tagging each person will make it possible for followers to identify them and visit the employees' personal pages. Tagging someone in something will also make that content show up on their personal timeline. This increases the number of people who see your content. Don't overdo it though. Too many tags can be overwhelming.

Do not forget the commentators

This point cannot be stressed enough. Always remember to answer direct comments, opinions, and questions. Let your followers know that their opinions are important and that someone is paying attention to them. You may think it is best to ignore a critical comment or complaint, but remember that others can see your failure to respond. That doesn't reflect well on you.

Make sure your company profile is complete

You have enough room in your profile to give your subscribers a lot of information about you. It may seem tedious to fill in so many sections, but all of those sections contain information your followers want to know. The more detailed your profile, the better your audience will understand who you are and what you do. Remember that your Facebook page appears in Google search results and may be the first thing people come across when looking for your company. Don't leave them with unanswered questions after they visit your page. Make it as complete as possible.

Make sure your subscribers want to see your updates

The ultimate goal of a marketing plan is to get people to read your content. You want these people to cling to every word you write and strive to see what you will post next. You want them to check to see if you have published something recently. You can do this only with high quality, valuable, and relevant content.

Make it easier to share your content.

While the age of technology has allowed us to do as little as possible while still being productive, you need to work if you want your content to be engaging. You need to pack your content in a way that makes it easy to share and then give people the buttons they need to send content to a friend or other user on their social networking sites. Make it so easy for them that it's almost harder for them not to do it.

If you share something, comment on it

Do not just click the button that lets you share a post and leave it at that. Add a comment to let others know why you think content is worth sharing. This helps you build your own experience and reputation as an expert. This, in and of itself, increases the value of what you share.

Check your grammar and spelling

Texting lingo may be popular, but grammar and spelling are still important. You are a professional business, and the worst thing you can do is to publish content that is poorly written and contains mistakes. Review your work, then review it again. Make sure it meets professional standards before hitting send.

Learn the rules of the platform

Look at the recommendations for each platform and make sure you know what is acceptable and not acceptable in terms of behavior and content. Common sense should determine the nature of the content. You must review the platform's terms of service before publishing. Some platforms, especially Facebook, are constantly changing their rules for conducting competitions, and their violation may result in removed content, suspensions, or total exclusion from the platform. This is not what you want for your business.

Strategies for Facebook Pages

When it comes to promoting and using your page on Facebook, it's best to use page-only strategies to increase your appeal. This means that you will be posting exclusive offers on your Facebook page rather than publishing them elsewhere.

Below are some Facebook strategies that you can use.

Product

It's a good idea to start with the goods. This includes offering exclusive products that are not available in the store. For example, you can offer a full product that can only be purchased through your Facebook page or website, but not in a store. You can also offer an individual product that is exclusively available online. For example, you may suggest customizing the product by changing the color scheme or encrypting a message. You can also suggest a product in a color scheme or pattern that differs from the one available in the store. You must make this clear by making relevant announcements and telling your customers that they are exclusively online. You can also ask people in your store to like it online to get your "page" noticed.

Deals

You can make exclusive online deals. You can offer programs like "buy 1, get 1 for free" or include a bonus gift or a surprise coupon. Such offers will certainly attract interest and increase the value of your site. Again, it is important to promote this so that people know about the offer. You can send emails with details and inform others about the offers you have made to your online audience. You can also promote it in your store or distribute flyers to people telling them to visit your Facebook page for special information.

Awards

You can reward people who bring likes. This works well because people are being asked to get more and more people to like your site. The reward should be attractive enough to arouse the interest of your audience. You can offer coupons, free goods, or specially designed goods. Make these deals specific to Facebook users. You can place an ad on both the page and your other social networks telling them to visit your page to be eligible. You can also mention this on your website and inform people who visit your store.

Discount coupons

You can offer your customers discount vouchers and special coupons or codes. These vouchers give you a discount on the goods and services you offer in your store. You can only use these coupons on the Facebook page. Again, you must announce this on all your social networks, such as Twitter and Instagram, to let people know about what is happening.

Competitions

Competitions are a fun way to get people to visit your site and encourage them to interact with you. You can announce the contest on your Facebook page. The competition may be associated with products or services you offer. It could be something like asking your followers to create a slogan, come up with a phrase, or post product photos. Make sure the prize is desirable enough to entice people to actually participate in the competition. Set a short time limit for the competition, such as a week, to encourage immediate engagement and quickly increase followers.

Events

You can also announce upcoming company events on the pages. These can be events where people meet and get to know each other better. Such events also help you get to know your audience better because you can interact with them in person. Providing free refreshments or some other free gift is a great way to encourage attendance.

Events can help you a lot if done correctly. All you have to do is create an interesting event, invite as many people as you can, and spread the information on your page. Try to use the event to promote your company and your product. This has the advantage where you do not have to spend a lot of money on sponsorship events organized by other people. Many people sponsor local events to gain recognition for names. You can use Facebook to get name recognition without spending a lot of money on events. Events can spread beyond just your target audience if you make them public and invite many people. First, determine the type of event and when your target audience is most likely to be able. Start inviting people immediately to help spread the word as fast as possible. Give ample notice before the event. Announcing it with too short notice is a great way to host an event that no one attends.

Chapter 7

------ ༄ ༅ ------

Facebook sales

On the off possibility that you have never tried Facebook promotions (or on the off possibility that you have tried and fizzled), you may be thinking about how to conduct a victorious battle, which will make more leads and bargains. In this chapter, we will show you the four phases to create Facebook promotions, which convert.

Facebook is perhaps the best place to find qualified prospects, due to over 2.38 billion energetic month clients and indoors and outside focusing on highlights. Regardless, similarly with any promoting a campaign, how well your Facebook advertising work depends upon if you've got a successful system.

Without the Right methodology (realizing The way to enhance Facebook advertising), these publicizing bucks go down the station along with your latent capacity drives cruise straight forth.

This way, before we get in the piece by bit process of how to produce a Facebook advertising that affects over, we ought to speak somewhat concerning the overall system.

Facebook Ads Not Working? Here is Why.

A fantastic many Men and Women envision that Facebook Marketing works like any other type of marketing: you have an item or some help, you place an ad, and you also make deals.

Regardless, that's not so much that the way Facebook advertisements do the job.

Facebook is a social platform. When your prospective customers are on Facebook, would they state they're looking for things to buy?

Most probably not.

They are on Facebook enjoying an entertaining video of the company's feline drinking water from the company's water glass as it had been poured just for them. Or on the flip side, sharing a statement about how nobody in their town understands how to push.

What they are not doing is looking for Advertisements. What is more, on the off possibility they chance to see one that's

"Hello, I am a marketing, and I am quite sales," they are probably ignoring it.

All is not lost, however. You should Be deliberate regarding your promotions and everything you are marketing. What is more, you need to understand the way to progress Facebook promotions to break through into the individuals who matter to you. We are going to let you know the ideal way to do this within this manual.

How about we start, will we?

The Best way to Run Facebook Ads, Step-by-step

Instead of leaping directly in and Asking a bargain instantly, you may set your position and bonus together with prospective customers by providing something significant for them for nothing: an exceptionally concentrated on the direct magnet.

This methodology enables your goal Customers to become more familiar with you as you receive the chance to collect their email address to use to advertise to them in the future.

Our favorite method to do this is to create An advertisement which guides visitors to a greeting card page having an option to your guide magnet, and improving your promotions for website modifications.

Try not to worry if that is not overly clear yet. We are going to take you through the whole process, bit by bit.

Presently, we ought to enter the Four phases To creating Facebook advertising.

Phase 1. Select Your Marketing Objective

Have you ever at any stage seen a hockey or Soccer game when neither among those groups is scoring? The group of audiences could not care less, and also the bands only seem to be edgy.

With no sensible objective, your Advertisement crusades are somewhat like this.

That's the motive Facebook causes one to Decide on a marketing objective before you can perform anything else at the Facebook Advertising Manager.

You can navigate three different destinations:

Mindfulness

By choosing the awareness goal, you will have the choice to create either indicate mindfulness advertising or arrive at promotions.

Here is the boosting that You Need to pull In prospective customers and start to create prospects. It's called the top of the station (TOFU) showcasing.

Thought

For your Consideration objective, you are Trying to drive dedication. Facebook allows you to do this at a few Distinct ways:

• Website, Program, or Messenger visitors

• Engagement Through your webpage, articles, opinions, enjoys and provides

• Program Shop and Google Play shop presents

• Video sees

• Lead Era

• Messages

The idea stage is the location you are drawing and instructing your planned interest group on your picture and items. These are called the center of the pipe (MOFU) marketing.

Change

The conversion goal spotlights on getting people to make a move. With these ads, Facebook enables you to decide on a goal of transformations, shop visits, or record bargains.

At this stage of showcasing, it is tied in with getting your planned interest group to create a guarantee to buy. Concerning our marketing station subject, we predict this foundation of this pipe (BOFU) promoting.

Each stage of marketing is essential, And you'll need them sooner or later. Be as it may, you can not just toss a mindfulness advertising out to a possible client who is trying to select one of you along with a contender.

After all, not around the off chance that you want them to select you personally, at any speed.

The advertising material needs to coordinate The showcasing phase. Along with the entirety of the must coordinate an essential piece of any marketing campaign: your planned interest group.

Phase 2. Create a Custom Audience

When you have chosen your target, it is a perfect opportunity to select who you are focusing.on

You could just set your Advertisement before a massive number of people. Really. Facebook advertisement audiences can be colossal:

That is right, That's a potential advantage of 210 million people.

Sounds incredible, is not that so? More People, more money?

One moment.

Except if those folks are the Opportune people, your kin, your advertising will not change over.

To correctly focus on your Promotions, you are going to need to make a personalized set of audiences that's satisfactorily huge, yet at precisely the same time quite sure.

That's the place custom audiences become an integral element.

You will see that the default set of Audiences in your new advertising is everyone in the USA between the ages of 18-65. That's the matter that gave us the possible creature reach of 210 million.

Start entering the data info you Believe About your planned interest group. That is precisely what it'd look like at the event that we concentrated on everyone in Florida between the ages of 25-40 who communicates in Spanish:

The next section, Thorough Targeting, Is essential. There is where we get to concentrate on our best client using practices and interests genuinely.

By Way of Example, suppose our best Customers Are people that are aficionados of the Miami Marlins baseball team. Considering that the Marlins have a Facebook fan page, we could target people who"like" this webpage.

Just type in"Miami Marlins" To the Interest area and snap the ideal results to add it.

That is precisely what resembles after we have Comprised fanatics of the Miami Marlins.

You can likewise recall general pursuits By clicking for Browse or receive suggestions determined by the interests you have only included by clicking Tips.

Regardless, focusing on specific enthusiast pages Is an increasingly precise approach to find people to target, and that means you will generally show signs of progress results in that manner.

A quick tip: Do not target Multiple Intrigue bunch for every single group of audiences. Blending vested parties makes it difficult to research your results afterward. On the off probability, you will need to concentrate on another fansite, create a different set of audiences for every single unrivaled run each ad to a unique audience in turn.

Because You've characterized your collection of Audiences, hit on the Save This Audience button at the bottom of the audience section.

A discourse box will spring up and ask Which you give your new set of audiences a title.

Give it a title that will Help You with Remembering that you recalled for this particular fragment. Now click Save.

You've spared your audience, and you can use it for another ad you earn.

You can generally create custom audiences by Launch the menu at the point tapping Audiences beneath the Assets section:

Phase 3. Keep Setting Your FB Advertisement

After sparing your Customized set of Audiences, you are going to need to decide where to display your advertising from the Placements section.

We propose staying with programmed situations.

In the last, you Want to set up your fiscal Calendar and limit. Now, click Continue.

Stage 4. Plan Your FB Advertisement

Now it is the perfect opportunity for The enjoyable and advanced part, in which you receive the chance to draw guests along with your narrative.

Facebook provides you eight different Configurations to use, and each brings its attributes, yet for now, it is possible to create a single, single-picture advertisement merely.

Now, add the images that you Will Need to utilize. It is possible to transfer your photos or use free stock photos.

At long last, you'll include the features and Replicate to your advertising:

When you have your promotions were appearing the Way where you want, then click the green Confirm button at the lower right corner.

By then, your audience will probably proceed to Facebook for audit, and you are finished! You're going to be informed once they have been confirmed, and so is live.

Step-by-step directions to Maximize Facebook Advertising to Skyrocket Your Favorite

You will see that earning Facebook Advertisements is not that confused. Just 4 phases.

Making the ad material Can be dull, but putting the advertising itself is only going to take you two or three moments.

Now, however, we get the opportunity to advance! That's to make sure that our ads are calling them perfect people and playing out the way we want them to better.

Here are how to update Facebook advertisements to find the maximum value for the money.

1. Create a Facebook Business Manager Account

Facebook Business Manager goes about as a Centre for one to bargain with every single Facebook tool which you utilize for your industry.

You can incorporate different ad Pages and records, include occupation-based customer records, and monitor advertising implementation over the entirety of your advertising accounts.

To make your record, proceed to business.facebook.com and click Create Account.

Once Making Your Organization Manager Accounts, include your existing advertising accounts by heading to the Company Settings:

Then click Advertisement Accounts beneath the Accounts Section on the lefthand menu:

From here, it is possible to view a rundown of your Current advertising accounts. To incorporate a different one, tick the blue Add button.

Pick the Best Way to Add your new Advertising Account and complete your arrangement.

You can pursue an identical process to include Facebook Pages for your Company Manager accounts.

2. Publish the Facebook Pixel

The Facebook Pixel is a bit of code that You add on your website. This code permits you to monitor and measure guests to your website, at the point enhance and build crowds for your advertising crusades.

Together with the Facebook Pixel introduced, you will have the choice to see information regarding your website's guests around the Pixel dash to show signs of progress comprehension of how they use your website.

3. Portion Your Audience... But Not Too Much

In email showcasing, portioning your group Of audiences is the best to exercise, span. Be as it may, Facebook promotions are fantastic little brutes.

Facebook Ads are all about touchpoints and learning. On the off chance, your group of audiences is too restricted, with too few touchpoints, you are disclosing to Facebook, which you should not bother using it to get the hang of whatever.

At the stage when You've Got a limited Group of audiences you're displaying to Facebook Ads, you don't require spending improvement. Instead, you want your promotions seemed to any particular number of people, in any instance. Besides, this can push your advertising expenses.

Pick what amount of people you Want To arrive at each day and play with your fragments till you are in that array.

One frequently disregards approach to Goal Facebook customers is via their life events. What number of different ways may eCommerce organizations be keen about somebody's significant life events?

With everything that we put on Facebook -- from fresh openings to graduations to birthdays -- you will find boundless approaches to produce custom made audiences from using this parameter alone!

4. Use Multiple Facebook Ad Formats

Using the Right organization to your Advertising is equally as important as the advertising replicate and symbolism.

Here are the 8 Facebook advertising designs. You can use and marginally about each one. Even though we went with simple single-picture advertising with this educational exercise, you will need to exploit each of these advertisement layouts and that which they bring to the table.

Photograph Ads:

Photograph promotions are eloquent and Easy To create by dispersing a post with an image and then fostering it with an ad.

These promotions operate to induce people To your website and bring matters to light from your items.

Video Ads:

Video ads are extraordinary at Catch's consideration ancient. While creating video articles, direct with the most potent and magical substance that'll attract your audience immediately.

You can use non-metallic imaginatively with movie promotions to curiosity watchers. For flexible recordings, the phone itself provides a feature casing; however, you can also mess with square yields, piled documents, vertical video, as well as 3D surrounding impacts.

Video promotions can help you with conveying the desired data instantly. Truth be told because folks will generally fly through material so fast, it is essential to trap watchers and receive the crucial aim of your message crosswise over in the absolute beginning point of your movie, clearly and with influence.

Tips to Boost Your Business Sales

The one goal that every business wants though, is to boost sales. In order to do that, you need Facebook on your side. You need Facebook to be able to engage with your audience, to give them incentives to want to buy your products. Ultimately, the most effective way to boost sales is through Facebook. With that said, these tips will come in handy to help you effectively increase your sales volume and keep your business booming:

Attention Grabbing Content: Your audience needs to be interested in your content. For that to happen, your content needs to be something that grabs their attention. You are marketing your products through your website, but you need to conquer the "selling" aspect of it with finesse. Your audience doesn't want to just deal with hard selling all the time. They want you to build a connection and a rapport with them. The bond should be strong enough to get them to engage with your content. Sometimes, attention-grabbing content isn't enough if they don't feel that connection with you. To make your content stand out enough to drive sales, you should remember to include visuals, either questions or facts, be inspiring and always include a strong call to action. If all you're doing is focusing on the selling act, it is only a matter of time before your engagement will die off completely.

Don't Hold Back from Showing Off Your Products: You believed in your products enough to start a business based on selling them. So don't hold back on showing them off on your social media account either. On Facebook is where the power of suggestion is at its strongest. Using images to ignite passion, excitement, and even awaken the senses can dramatically drive your sales in ways conventional marketing methods couldn't. Create content that is going to appeal to your target audience, list down all the details that are going to get them excited and fired up, and of course, don't forget to accompany all of that with a visual that is so captivating they simply have to stop and take a second look at your ads. That is how you give your sales a boost.

Give Your Content a Boost Too: If you want to give your sales a boost, you need to first give your content a boost. Facebook has a feature called Boos Post, and it's about time every marketer started taking advantage of it. Why? Because it is effective, it's simple and easy to use, and more importantly, it gets results. It is also easy for marketers to measure the effectiveness of the results they get from that boosted content. Boosted posts really get your content out there in front of the audiences who matter. You can target your existing followers, their friends, and you could even target demographics specifically depending on your preference based on age, gender, and past activity.

Make Contacting You a Breeze: You've put in all that hard work to get your content seen by as many audiences as possible. Now, what you need to do is make it easy for them to reach out to you. In the old days with conventional marketing, you could reach the company through the phone number which was included on every radio, TV, and print ad that was distributed. For customers, being able to contact you is a necessity. The advertising mediums may have changed over time, but this necessity remains the same. On Facebook, your customers should be able to contact you through either Facebook Messenger, or through a phone number which must be clearly listed on your profile. With Messenger, you want to ensure that your messages feature on your profile is turned on. This allows your audience to be able to easily send you a quick message on any of their devices and ask any pertinent questions they may have. People are not keen anymore on email addresses, they prefer to reach out to you directly through an instant message on Messenger, or ring up your company if they need to speak to you directly. Needless to say, a phone number is also a must-have on your Facebook profile. No exceptions.

Run Sales Offers on Your Profile: What better way to increase sales than to give audiences an offer they simply cannot pass up? Running offers on Facebook can easily be done through your page's Publisher section, all you need to do is post the relevant details of the offer and you're set. A limited-time offer that is worth their while will make it hard for your audiences to resist taking some action. That action will ultimately lead to a sale and there you go! A boost in sales.

Using Carousel Ads: Carousel Ads are popular for a reason. They are interactive. They are intriguing. They get results. These ads allow your audience to scroll through your products and see either multiple products or multiple aspects of the same product, with a simple swipe. What's great about this ad platform is that it allows you to show groups of your products which work well together. It lets you tell a story which reminds your audience why they should be purchasing this product and how it is going to enrich their lives. Carousel Ads allow you to demonstrate a much wider range of your products, thereby giving your audiences even more reasons to click through and see what you've got to offer. If they like your products enough, you've got a sale on your hands right there.

Using Video Ads: Among one of the most powerful ad forms on Facebook is the video ads. Not only does Facebook's algorithm work to make video content a bigger priority over visuals, but statistics have shown time and time again that video content gets more engagement than any other ad form. Not only is your ad more likely to make its way into your audience's news feed thanks to the algorithm, but what they are seeing is your most engaging content format. Facebook's statistics reveal that audiences are a lot more likely to stop and pause their scrolling when faced with video content. Plus, showing how your products are working (showing them in action) is a great method of convincing them even more why they need these products in their life.

Bonus Tips to Get More Likes on Facebook

Because more likes equal more prospective customers, this then, in turn, leads to more sales. Therefore, part of your marketing strategy to boost sales should also include boosting the number of "Likes" you have on your business page. Use the following strategies (if you haven't already) to get your page out there in front of even more prospective audiences:

- Invite everyone you know to like your page. Literally everyone. Family, friends, long lost relatives, colleagues, ex-colleagues. Everyone you can think of. The more people you invite, the better.

- Do you have a list of prospects? Send them a quick and friendly email reminding them that you're on Facebook and why they should connect with you.

- On your website or blog, embed a social plugin for Facebook to remind anyone who visits your website to connect with you on Facebook. Offer them an incentive to like your page, like a discount voucher for their first purchase.

- Join or participate in Facebook groups where audiences are likely to have an interest in your products or services. Regularly post content on the group about your products which will help to drive and increase traffic to both your Facebook main page and your website.

- Keep track of the emails that you acquire from customers, they can be a big help in your newsletter marketing. Each newsletter should remind them to connect to your Facebook page for even more exciting offers and reveals.

- Entice audiences to like your Facebook page by offering them a one-time discount code which they can use for their next purchase if they connect with you on Facebook.

- Engage with your followers on Facebook often so that your updates regularly appear on their newsfeed. Just because they like your profile, it doesn't automatically mean new content gets displayed on their news feed. Facebook's algorithm works to determine which audience see your page updates, and this algorithm is based on how closely you engage with your audience.

Bonus Tips to Boost Engagement on Facebook

Boosting engagement is also one way of boosting your sales figures. The more engaged and riveted your audience is by your content, the more likely they will be to buy from you. Having Likes on your Facebook page alone is not nearly enough to keep your business booming. You've got to make sure that they're engaged too. Engaged means that they are paying attention to your content, noticing what you're putting out there. If you've got their attention, you may just be able to persuade them to take that final step towards making a purchase. Looking for ways to increase engagement? The following strategies will help:

- Frequently engage your audience in polls to get them to answer questions. Make the topics or questions interesting enough for them to want to participate.

- Third party survey tools are great for acquiring more in-depth information. You might need to offer your audience an incentive for participating in the survey though. Some might do it more willingly. Survey Monkey is a good third-party survey tool to consider.

- Link your Facebook to your Twitter profile, it's another channel for engaging with your audience.

- Update your content frequently. Whenever there's something new on your website, update that onto your Facebook page too.

- Never neglect your Facebook comments and always make an effort to respond to your audience in a timely manner. Even if the comment is less than favorable.

- If your business has a YouTube account, don't forget to post your YouTube content on your Facebook page too. Cross-promoting across social media platforms keeps your content interesting and engaging.

- Host frequent competitions on Facebook. Nothing gets your audience more excited than a chance to potentially win something.

- Post behind the scenes photos or photos of events that show other aspects of your brand - the more human aspect of it. Audiences like to see more than just what you're selling; they want to get to know the people behind the brand.

Chapter 8

———— ❧❧❧ ————

Facebook Business Manager

A company's Facebook Marketing campaign may demand that it should have more than one ad account or pages. Also, you may need to keep track of the ads of separate clients and possibly give reports on them. A company may also employ the services of more than one person to manage their Facebook page. If you are faced with all this, it is important that you use Facebook Marketing to manage all of this from one place.

Facebook describes this tool as one which is used to "manage ad accounts, pages, and people who work on them--all in one place." It is a tool that helps you to create, monitor, publish, and give reports on different assets that relate to your business. This includes your pages and advertisements. It allows you to give either partial or full access to different employees, and give them different roles to perform within the platform. This tool gives room for a division of labor in the virtual world while staying organized and focused by creating, monitoring, and publishing ads, pages and anything that concerns your business on Facebook. This is an important tool for any business that wishes to establish itself as a big name in the Facebook market. With this, you can tap into an array of possibilities that are made available by the platform. For example, if your brand produces internet services, you may want to have different pages for different purposes like installation, customer services, and self-care. The role of Facebook Business Manager is that it helps you to manage these pages at one login so you only have to switch between tabs to access any of the pages. Therefore, you do not need to have multiple logins in order to access the pages. You will also be able to manage the ads for different pages from one place. This tool will let you access other platforms like Instagram, as well as your products catalog. You can track your efforts by getting detailed reports and visualizations, which will show you how well your ads are doing.

Creating a Facebook Manager Account

It does not matter if you have already created a Facebook page or you have a personal profile, the first step to take if you wish to use Facebook Manager is to create a Facebook Manager account. To do this, you will have to log on to business.facebook.com. Once you are there, you will see the screen below so you have to click on the blue 'Create Account' icon on the top left-hand corner of the screen.

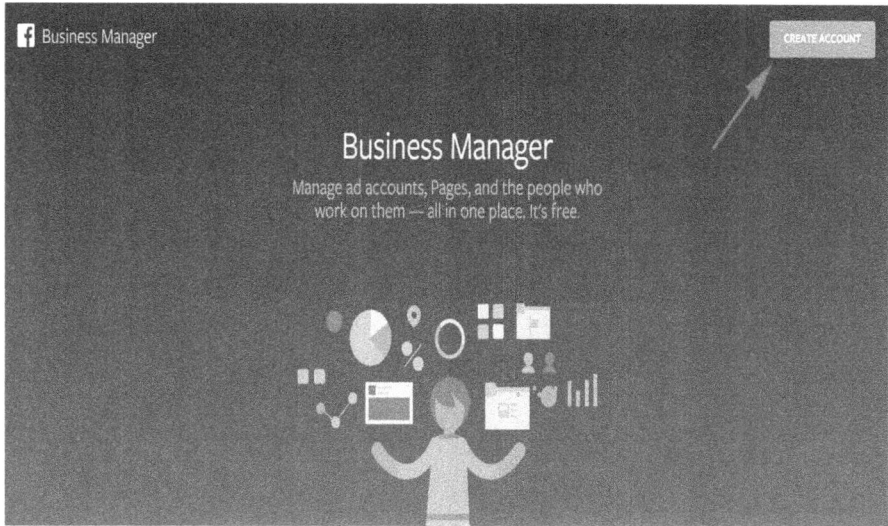

Next, you will be asked to fill in the name of your business in the pop-up as seen below. Enter the name that is unique to your business in the pop-up box, then click continue.

Create Your Business Manager Account

X

With a Business Manager account, you can assign roles and permissions to people, and add the Pages, ad accounts and more connected to your business on Facebook. To get started, add the name of your business.

Your business name

Olaf Incorporated

Your business name will be shown to all employees, and can't contain special characters.

Continue

Step 1 of 2

You will be requested to enter your email afterward, your name, and the email address. After that, click 'Finish'.

×

Create Your Business Profile

Add the name and email you want to use for Business Manager. Nothing from your personal Facebook profile will be shown to people in your Business Manager account.

Your name

Olaf Sandwichmaker

Your business email

olaf@olafsolafsolafs.com

We'll send notifications about your business to this email.

Finish

Step 2 of 2

This is just the first step to begin your journey with the Facebook Business page. The next step is to:

Add your Facebook Business Pages

This step gives you two choices: you can either create a new Facebook page or add existing pages. For someone that manages pages for other people, you can request that the owner of the page grant you access to it. It is important that you request to be given access to your client's page instead of adding it directly to the Business Manager because adding the page directly will give the owner of the page limited access to his page. This may cause distrust between you and your client. We would, however, like to assume that you are managing your own pages, so here is a step-by-step guide on how to add pages to your business manager.

First, on the Business Manager dashboard, you will see the 'Add Page' icon. Click on it. A pop-up screen will appear, and on this screen, click on 'Add Page' again.

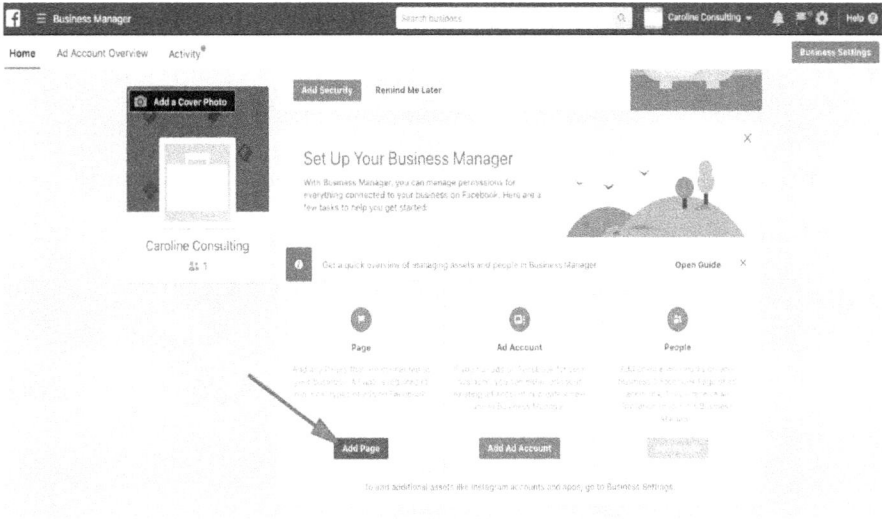

Add Pages to Business Manager

Add a Page you own

Add Facebook Pages that you manage to your Business Manager account.

Add Page

Add someone else's Page

Request permission to add a Facebook Page to your Business Manager account.

Request Access

Create a new Page

If your business doesn't have a Facebook Page, you'll need to create one. A Page is required to run most types of ads on Facebook.

Create Page

On the next page, you will see a search bar, the next thing to do is to type in your business name to the search bar. If you already have a page for your business, the business name will pop up immediately. Click on 'Add Page'. If you already have administrator access to the page, your request will be granted in a very short time. If you see a green check-mark, then you have successfully added your page. Follow the same steps to add the other pages that are associated with your business if you have more than one.

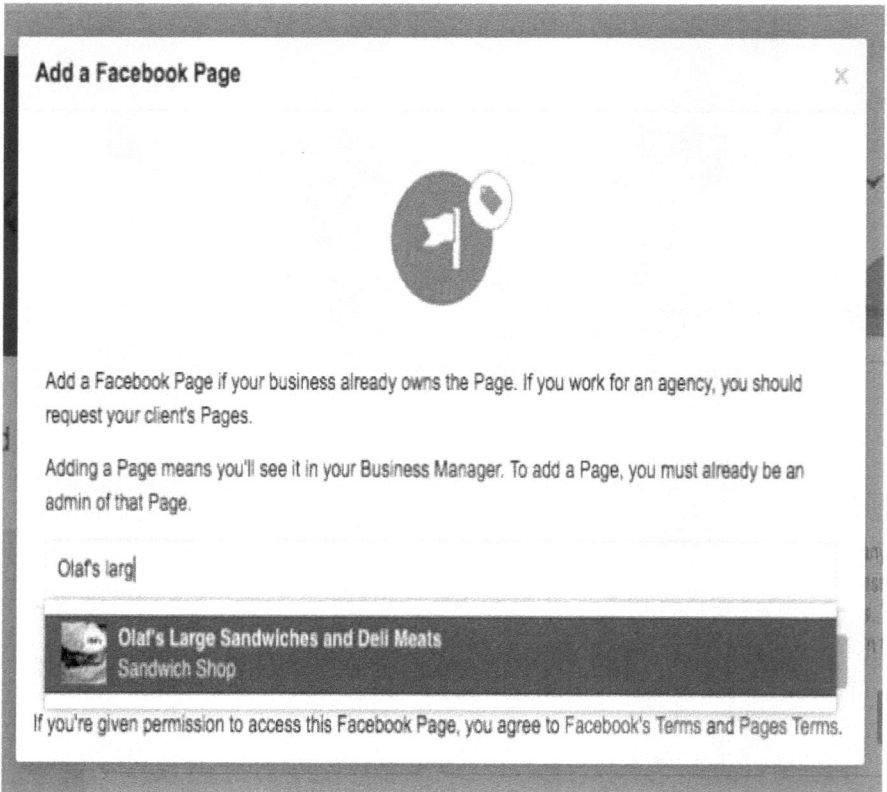

Add a Facebook Page ✕

Add a Facebook Page if your business already owns the Page. If you work for an agency, you should request your client's Pages.

Adding a Page means you'll see it in your Business Manager. To add a Page, you must already be an admin of that Page.

Olaf's larg

Olaf's Large Sandwiches and Deli Meats
Sandwich Shop

If you're given permission to access this Facebook Page, you agree to Facebook's Terms and Pages Terms.

Add Facebook Ad account(s)

Before you delve into this, it is important to note that once you add an ad account, you will no longer be able to remove it, so if you are adding an account, make sure you have permission to access it, especially if it is a client's page. In this case, you are expected to click on 'Request Access', instead of adding account. In cases where you are already using Facebook ads, you can add existing accounts by clicking on the 'Add Ad Account' icon on the Business Manager Dashboard. The 'Add Ad Account' prompt will appear again on a new pop-up screen - click on it again. You will then be requested to enter your ad account ID, this can be found in Ads Manager.

In cases where you do not already have a Facebook ad account, here is how to create one: when you click on the 'Add Ad Account' icon on the Facebook Manager dashboard. Click on the 'Create Account' icon on the page then enter your account details.

Create New Ad Account   ✕

Ad account name Olaf's Large Sandwiches
Advertising on behalf of Olaf Incorporated ▾
Time zone (GMT-07:00) America/Los Ang... ▾
Currency USD — US Dollars ▾
Payment method No payment methods available

Cancel   **Create Ad Account**

By creating an ad account, you agree, on behalf of Olaf Incorporated as its authorized representative to Facebook's Terms including the payment terms for the selected payment method.

Facebook Business Manager can add one ad account at the start. Later, you will be allowed to add up to four more ad accounts when you start spending money on your business. You are, however, not allowed to have more than five ad accounts on your Facebook Business Manager.

Add people to help you manage assets

Once you have added your pages and ad accounts to your business manager, it is time to get people to work with you to help you manage your assets. You see, it can be quite tasking to keep track of your Facebook Marketing campaign, so Facebook Business Manager allows you to add a whole team to work with you on it. For this to come to life, you'll have to set up your team on your Business Manager account.

On the Dashboard, you will see the 'Business Settings' icon at the top of the page (Gear Icon). Click on it and it will show you the 'People and Assets' tab. Click on people on the left side. A list of people that have access to the page will be displayed. Because you are the only one that currently has access to the page, it is only your name that will be displayed, so you have to add more people to work with you. To add people, click on the 'Add' icon. Once done, you will get a pop-up box. When you see it, enter the business email address of the people you wish to add. These may be members of your staff, freelancers, or business partners. As you are entering their business email address, you are allowed to decide the privileges that you grant to them. The choice of whether they are coming on board as just employees or admins is up to you and you will have to decide that as you are adding them to the account. Once you are done, click on the 'Add People' icon at the bottom right corner of the page.

After adding the people to your page, you will have to decide which of the pages you want each person to work on. The next step will show you how to do this. The role of the page admin is to manage everything that concerns the page, which includes assigning new roles to other members of the page. The Page Moderator create ads and branded content for your page. They will send messages, respond to comments, delete messages and comments, as well as view your page insights. The role of the page analyst is managing branded content settings and also viewing insights. The page editor has almost the same power as the page moderator. They will publish content on the page too. The page advertiser will create ads and perform all the other roles of the page analyst. To assign pages and roles, choose the name of the person then select the pages you want them to work on and choose a role for them. You may also choose the default role then click on the pages you want them to work on. Once you are done assigning roles to different people, click 'Next'.

The ad account admin has the responsibility of managing every aspect of the brand's campaigns which includes editing the billing details and giving specific roles to other members of the group. The ad account analyst, on the other hand, can only monitor the performance of the ad, while the ad account advertiser edits and creates new ads. To assign ad accounts and roles, click on the name of the member then select the ad account and choose a role. You can also choose a default role then click on all the ad accounts you want them to have access to and work on. Once you are done, click next. A screen will pop-up, asking you to assign people to catalogs. Ignore this screen by clicking 'Skip'. This will give you a notice, telling you how many people you have added and the roles you assigned to them.

Now, everyone you have added to the team will receive notices so you have to wait for them to accept your request to be a part of your Facebook Business Manager team. They will receive an automated email with information about the role you've given them as well as a link for them to get started. You may, however, want to inform them personally of the access you have granted them so that they will expect the email. On your dashboard, you will see a list of those that have not accepted your request so you can withdraw the invitation from those who have not responded. In case of a person leaving your company or switching to another role, you can revoke the permissions you gave to them. To do this, click on the dashboard of your business manager at the top left-hand corner and click on the gear icon (Business Settings), here, you'll see the 'Peoples and Assets' tab, click on 'People', this will show you a list of those that have been granted access, click on the name of the person you want to remove, then click 'Remove'.

You are now done adding people to your Facebook Business Manager so now, you can move on to connecting with your business partners. If you are just getting started with Facebook advertising, this step is not for you but you can return to it later.

To connect with business partners or ad agencies, go to Business Settings from your Dashboard, then click on the 'People and Assets' tab. Select either your Facebook Page or your ad account then on the left-hand corner, click on 'Partners'. Click on 'Assign Partners' then click on the role you wish to assign to each partner. Repeat the same steps you followed to manage ad accounts. You will be provided with a link - copy and paste this link and send it to your partner or agency to invite them to your Facebook Business Manager Account, then click 'Close'.

Add an Instagram account

Remember, you can add your other social media accounts to manage them from your Facebook Business Manager. To this effect, you may want to connect to your Instagram account, here is how: from the Dashboard, go to the 'Business Settings' section at the top right-hand corner then click on 'People and Assets'. Click on 'Instagram Accounts' then click 'Next'. This step will display a pop-up box, here, enter your Instagram account's login details and click 'Next'. Also, you will have to add ad accounts that you want to link to your Instagram account. To do this, you will select the ad account that you want to use with your Instagram account when you are advertising on the platform. People who have access to this ad account will be able to use the Instagram account. A pop-up telling you that you have added your Instagram account successfully will show up, click done and you are set.

Facebook Business Manager dashboard

Now that you have set up your assets and your Facebook Business Manager is running fine, it will now serve as the central point (Dashboard) for all the marketing and advertising activities that you will perform on Facebook. From here, you will be able to view your page, update it, view and insights, begin new ad campaigns, and so on. When you want to see all the functions you can perform through the Business Manager, click on the Facebook Business Manager link at the top left-hand side of your Dashboard. From here, you will see everything categorized into five different categories: Measure & Report, Assets, Plan, Create & Manage, and Settings.

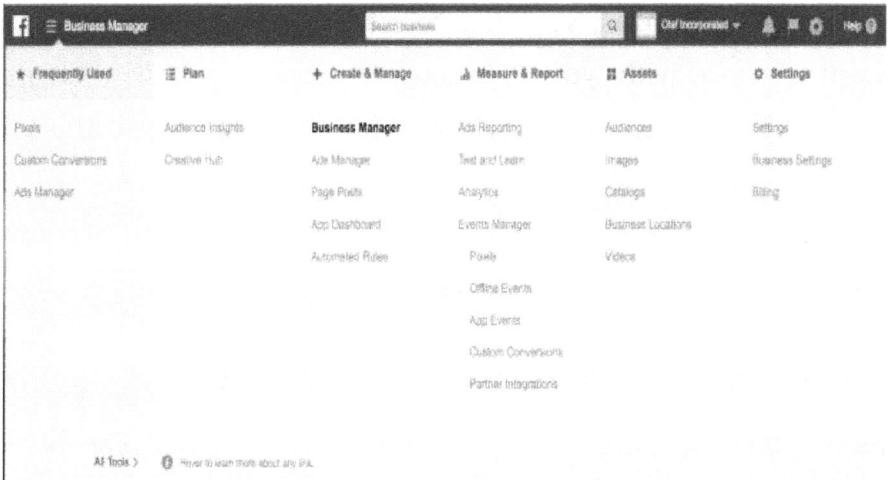

Since you already know about Assets and Settings, we will now go to the 'Create and Manage' section which is the fun part of this journey and it is here that you will create your first ad, but to get the most out of this platform, you will first have to set up Facebook Pixels.

Chapter 9

— — — — — ❧❧❧❧ — — — —

Psychology behind Ads

Setting up a Facebook Ad

Now that you understand the tools to use when creating a Facebook ad, it's time to examine how to actually create the ad.

Step one: Setting goals

Before you can start churning out ads, there is one step you cannot afford to skip: determining the goals for your Facebook ads.

Here are some examples of potential goals you can set for yourself:

- Increasing the traffic to your website via Facebook ads

- Increasing your reach

- Improving the engagement rate of your Facebook page

- Increasing awareness about your brand

- Increasing purchases of a certain product

Step two: Facebook Ads Manager

Any ad campaign you want to run on Facebook must be supported by Facebook Ads Manager. You can access it from your Facebook account by selecting the "Manage Ads" option from the drop-down menu. Once you enter the Ads Manager, you can go through the different tools discussed in the previous section. To start creating your ad, you need to click on the green button located on the top right-hand corner of your Ads Manager page.

Step three: Selecting your objective

Now that you have opened the Ads Manager and are ready to create a Facebook ad, you must establish your marketing objective. You will find 15 options displayed on the pop-up window on your screen. The three main categories you need to set marketing objectives for are awareness, conversion, and consideration. Go through the different options available and select those that are in sync with the marketing goals you established in the first step.

The different objectives available under the category of "Consideration" are collecting leads, getting video views, increasing the number of downloads of your app, increasing the attendance for any event, and directing the traffic to a landing page.

The different objectives under the "Conversion" category include increasing the rate of conversion on your website, encouraging users to claim any offers, promoting a specific product or catalog, increasing your rate of engagement for your app, and increasing the number of visitors to your physical store.

Once you select your marketing objectives, the next step is to name your marketing campaign.

Sep four: Budget and audience

There are two things you must do during the step: define your target audience and establish the ad budget. Customizing your target audience is critical. Regardless of how wonderful your ad campaign is, it will not generate the results you expect if it is not directed toward your target audience. You can customize your target audience according to different demographics such as location, age, gender, languages, interests, behaviors, and connections.

Once you select your target audience, you must concentrate on establishing the ad budget. When you are setting the ad budget, you must keep in mind that the amount you set represents the maximum limit you want to spend on the ad. The budget you want to set can be a lifetime budget or a daily budget. The daily budget refers to the average cost you will incur on the ad per day. The lifetime budget refers to the maximum amount of money you will spend during the lifetime of the ad.

Step five: Creating the ad

This is where the fun begins. You can select the images or the video, the header, the text, and the location for the displaying your Facebook ad. The text you want to include in the ad must not exceed 90 characters and will appear in the form of a quick message above the images or video in the ad.

There are two options you can use while creating ads on Facebook. The first option is to use an existing post, and the second option is to create a new option. You must consider which of these options meets your requirements before you decide to choose.

For certain ads, as with boosting posts, you can create the ad by using an existing post which was already published on your Facebook page. If you want to do this, you must click on the "Use Existing Post" option from the dashboard available on Facebook Ads Manager.

The other option you can go with is to create a new advertisement from scratch. Before you can start working on the creative elements, you must decide the format of the Facebook ad. There are five formats you can use for creating

Facebook ads, and they are a carousel, single image, canvas, single video, and slideshow. A carousel ad includes two or more images or videos the viewer can scroll through. A single image ad is, as the name suggests, an ad based on one image, and you can create six variations of an ad using a single image. If you want the ad to include just one video, then the ad format you must opt for is a single video ad. A canvas format enables you to tell a story through an amalgamation of images and videos. The slideshow format helps loop video ads using up to 10 images.

The objective that you established in step three will determine the different ad formats available to you.

Once you have chosen an ad format, you must add content to the ad. This is a critical step and whether your ad will stand out or not depends on the content you include. If you want your ad to be successful, you must include appealing and enticing images, videos, or text, or a combination of all these three things. There are certain specifications given by Facebook for the images or videos you want to include in the ads.

The image specs recommended by Facebook are as follows: the image ratio must be 1.91: 1 and the image size must be 1200 X 628 pixels. To improve the effectiveness of the ad, you must avoid using images with text overlay on them. Facebook recommends that the videos you use for ads be in .MOV or .MP4 files format with a resolution of at least 720 pixels. The file size must not exceed 4 GB, the ideal video ratio must be 16:9, it must be at least one second long, and the maximum duration of the Facebook ad cannot exceed 240 minutes. Sound and subtitles are recommended but optional.

Step six: Selecting the ad placement

The ad placement refers to where you want the ad to be shown. Your ads can appear in the desktop News Feed, in the Facebook app News Feed, and the right-hand column. You also have the option of the ad appearing on Instagram. Facebook will recommend that you opt for the default placements based on the objective of your ad. When you select this option, Facebook's algorithm will automatically optimize the placement of the ads to generate the best results. However, you do have the option of selecting the placement based on what you want.

Step seven: Placing the order

Now, your ad is ready, and you must click on the "Place Order" option. Once the ad is submitted, Facebook will review it before it goes live. You will also receive a confirmation, usually an email, about the ad. Remember to make sure your ad meets Facebook's requirements as discussed.

Optimizing the Ad Budget

Now that you are aware of how to create an ad, you must also understand how to budget the ad. Are you struggling to decide how to structure your marketing budget for producing Facebook ads? Well, you will learn everything about optimizing the Facebook Ads budget in this section. Simply put, it all boils down to basic mathematics, and it isn't complicated. Once you carefully go through the information in this section, you will be able to establish a clear Facebook ad budget. Here is a quick overview of the different steps included:

• Establishing your campaign goals,

• Taking the time to work backward,

• Calculating your ideal size of the audience,

• Estimating the target impression count,

• Estimating your CPM,

• Calculating the cost per ad set and

• Combining all your ad sets to establish your overall ad campaign budget.

The first step is to state your goals. This step is essential when trying to set up a budget for your ads. When your goals are tangible, you can easily determine the costs involved in attaining those goals. The goals for your ad campaigns can be increasing the following areas: your product sales for a given period, the number of leads produced, the engagement rate on posts, RSVPs for events, user responses to a specific offer, video views, and the number of new followers acquired during the campaign. These are merely examples of the goals, and you can go through step one in the previous section to determine what goals to set.

To make things easier for the sake of explanation, we will consider a hypothetical situation throughout the next steps to understand how you can calculate the budget for a Facebook Ads campaign.

Now, you need to start working backward. This means you must start at the bottom and make your way up the conversion sequence.

Let us assume that you want your ad campaign to generate 300 product sales. Ask yourself, what comes before you close a sale? You will need to generate leads. If the rate of conversion is around 30%, then you will need to generate at least 1,000 leads to attain your goal of 300 sales. When it comes to Facebook leads, it essentially refers to your list of email subscribers. To produce leads, you must include the link to a specific landing page in your ad that will encourage the users to sign up for your email list. There are different ways in which you can generate leads (email subscription list), like offering a free eBook or an analytical report in exchange for a user's email address. However, your work doesn't end here. Essentially, you will need to work backward until you arrive at the top of your Facebook marketing funnel.

Here is a simple way to go about working this process: Relevant Facebook users > Followers > Leads > Customers. This is the path of how customers can be obtained.

As you start working backward, you will find that you may end up with a couple of different ad campaigns. You can use the "Page Like" campaign for converting your target Facebook users into the followers of your page. To convert followers into leads, you can use a list-building ad campaign. To convert your leads into customers, you need a website conversion campaign. That's three different campaigns to achieve the one goal of generating 300 sales.

After this, you must calculate the size of your ideal audience. In the previous step, we assumed that the goal of your ad campaign was to generate 300 sales. According to the rate of conversion of 30%, you need about 1,000 leads. So, what must the size of your target audience be on Facebook to generate 1,000 leads? There are various variables involved here. Consider the following: How many users will view your ads? How many of your targeted Facebook users will be active on

Facebook daily? What if your targeted users don't view the ad event after the Facebook ad is live?

Since you have no control over the number of times Facebook will display your ad to your targeted audience, what will be an ideal ad frequency to attain your goal? This is where you must set some limits and estimations. Some questions you must answer in this regard are: What is the duration of your ad campaign? How likely will your targeted audience be on Facebook during your ad campaign? How likely is it for Facebook to display your ad to your targeted audience?

So, do you plan on running the ad campaign for a week, two weeks, a month, or maybe six months? It is essential that you don't consider the entire duration of your overall marketing campaign. Instead, you must concentrate on how long you want to run this specific (ad) aspect of the campaign. Once you know the duration of the ad, you need to figure out whether your leads will be active on Facebook at least once during the length of the ad campaign. To determine the activity of your target audience on Facebook, you can monitor the data you gather from Facebook Analytics or even the Facebook pixel. The final question you must answer is whether or not Facebook will display the ad to your target audience while they are online. The higher the likelihood of your target audience viewing your ad, the lower your ad budget will be.

So, to go ahead with the previous illustration, let us assume that the ad campaign is being run for three months, the chances of the target audience being online during the length of the campaign is about 99%, and the likelihood of Facebook displaying the ads to your target audience while they are active online is 100%. So, if these are the numbers, will you be able to generate 1,000 leads? The answer is that you very well might be able to given the fact that you are running the campaign for three months. If you use basic math, then you must be gaining at least 10 more leads to cover the 1% loss in views. It means 1,000 leads divided by 99% gives you 1,010 leads. Usually, for a shorter campaign, you will need more leads.

Now, you will need to calculate the target impression count. To do this, you must use the ad frequency. This refers to the average ad frequency within the length of your campaign. You can optimize the ad campaign for post engagement, the CPC, impressions, and unique daily reach. When you select the option of unique daily reach, it allows you to limit the ad frequency to 1. So, to estimate your budget, you must estimate the average frequency.

To continue the example, let us assume that for a 3-month long ad campaign, you must aim for an ad frequency between 10 and 15 users per lead. So, for an audience size to generate 1,000 leads, and with the estimation of ad frequency between 10-15 for three months, you will have to aim to achieve an overall impression count of anywhere between 10,000 and 15,000 leads (multiply the number of leads you want to generate with the ad frequency).

The next step is to estimate the CPM, CPI, or the cost per impression. You need to figure out how much the ad impressions will cost you. CPMs usually differ according to the industry you belong to and your objectives. For instance, if you aim to run a campaign for website conversions, then a $10 CPM is a good starting point. To calculate the total cost of your ad budget, you must multiply the total impressions you want with the average cost of impression and divide it by 1,000.

So, (total impressions X CPM)/ 1,000 = total cost.

The final step is to calculate the cost per ad set. Now you have to follow the formula mentioned above. Using the formula, your cost per ad set will be: (1,000 impressions X $10)/1,000 = $100. It essentially means you need about $100 to convert 1,000 leads into 300 potential sales over three months.

Chapter 10

— — — — — ❧❦❧ — — — —

The way to promote your company and earn money on Facebook

Irrespective of whether You're promoting, selling, or posting on Facebook, you need to understand how to gain on Facebook with your endeavors.

Everybody utilizes Facebook. Alright, slight embellishment. However, with over two billion customers across the world, recalling in surplus of 214 million to the United States alone, it's hugely, boundless.

It is mad news, culture, societal cooperation, and the sky is the limit from there. Be as it may, it is not merely a path that you remain in touch with older secondary college companies, share your intriguing pooch photos or article recordings from the seashore trip.

Additionally, whatever company or market you're in, chances are you can arrive in a fragment of the group of audiences on Facebook.

Facebook is also a Lucrative ground-breaking stage. There are various methods you may benefit from on Facebook. How about we explore different ways that you can use Facebook to showcase, promote, and progress your company - or gain as an afterthought.

1. The Facebook Marketplace

This is perhaps the most straightforward approach to gain on Facebook. Fundamentally, Facebook allows one to sell items within an essential sector of the website. A lot of towns, urban locations, and networks have put up purchase/sell webpages, or you may look by geographical area, item title, or course. That way, buyers can quickly observe a broad range of choices in the surrounding territory.

You can post new or utilized items to Market everything from PCs to cellular phones to vehicles to furniture. It resembles Craigslist on steroids. Here are a couple of tips with regards to selling to the Facebook Marketplace:

• Make Sure to include clear images of what you are selling.

• Supply subtlety like version number, condition (be simple), etc.

• Make Sure you're selling it at the right price. Assess what the same or relative things are available for from additional

Marketplace venders or about distinct locales such as eBay or Craigslist.

• Maintain As a leading priority, there's some market with prospective buyers, and several will try to low-ball you. On the off probability, you don't think it is a sensible value; you are under no commitment to take the offer.

Odds are you are not likely to make a Full-time small business buying or selling items on Facebook; nevertheless, this is a quick technique to produce some extra money. In the event, you're as of today selling items on eBay or Craigslist, that is just another street that you get more folks and increase your possible group of audiences of buyers.

2. Facebook as a Traffic Driver

The Unbelievable thing about Facebook is that its calculations examine where you go online, what you click on on the site, what records you see, and so on. Now it attracts a larger quantity of these sorts of gifts on your account. Facebook is also, of course, a way to connect similar individuals, institutions, and associations.

You may exploit this to gain on Facebook. You will do it by merely providing to folks straightforwardly on the platform equally as using the Marketplace yet quite compelling people to tap joins in your FB page, which takes them to an online business page, presentation page, or alternative website related to your internet business.

These are often called two-advance promoting. You are doing whatever it takes to not make a bargain on Facebook (on the reasons that people, for the most part, are not there to buy); instead, you are trying to stand out enough to be detected and intrigue and get them from Facebook clicking over to your website.

There you can sell them things or ask to connect your email list (we will disperse that indoors and outside in the subsequent segment). This Facebook traffic is qualified--all these are people intrigued by your product provides. At the stage when you conduct promotions on Facebook that you can concentrate by socioeconomics, interested, as well as those who have only communicated excitement for your product, organization, and manufacturer, so the visitors are qualified.

To encourage your visitors, you Need to Present regularly on your Facebook page. You may post efforts to market something, thing dispatches, and other associated items to your small business. Active copy and persuasive offers can find a lot of traffic. Whatever the situation, you should also have useful substance in your page, which brings in the chance -- which is what will keep them returning. You can post things like business, news, and funny stories. Pictures and records are essential nowadays, folks want to see them. What's more, they do not have to be professionally delivered.

On the off possibility that you have a site, you Should similarly present a link on every new post on your Facebook page. Same with almost any new YouTube records or another material that you post somewhere else online. It is tied in with driving, yet many visitors as can reasonably be anticipated. You might even think about paying for ads to have folks see your free material and come back to your website too. Along these lines, you'll be able to build a retargeting audience and conduct promotions to them in the future.

The idea would be to incorporate substance. That makes people enjoy your FB page. Therefore it seems in their news station and they ship it to companions too.

3. Using Facebook to Generate Leads

These go straight alongside #2. Nonetheless, we Liked to focus on this type of gain on Facebook about the grounds that it is durable, regardless of the fact it is a larger volume of a consistent approach to gain wages.

All of the Facebook customers, you will find out possible leads for your small business. Not every individual, of course, only people that are keen on your things. Interestingly, Facebook makes it easy to find these folks... and also for them to detect you. Once again, you want a Facebook page for your industry.

You will incorporate invaluable substance to connect with the customers. And then, you will also integrate hyperlinks to your website or a demonstration page asking them to connect to a rundown to acquire a bulletin or upgrades as unique provides. You must offer them some inspiration for sign upward, very similar to a free digital publication or rare report identified along with your specialty.

Together with Facebook, you can similarly incorporate an email pick in arrangement straightforwardly on your Facebook page.

You need to go out to buff pages or Facebook bunches in a similar business or specialization and begin submitting --this systems management can carry more visitors to your webpage or straightforwardly to your website or greeting site.

When these folks are in your email, Reveal, you can keep on sending them provides as precious material just like a bulletin. This is an outstanding technique to heat them from buying from you. What is more, it is possible to provide them progressively more expensive items after a while since they buy the lower price items first and then are ready for higher ticket items.

Another system that's working admirably is to links articles that go to articles pieces or website entries on your website. You are only running promotions to good excellent material you have made. When the property to your substance, there it's possible to provide a material overhaul by the way for getting on your email listing. These can be a less instantaneous technique; however, it will make your ads more informed.

4. Facebook Ads

The famous axiom goes, "you require To undergo money to gain." That's undoubtedly the case with conducting paid ads onFacebook. You have seen these promotions, they are the small flags on the right side of the webpage, in the same way, the supported articles that appear officially in the information station.

After again, treats that chase after you on The internet, tail one to Facebook. Together with the aim that promotions that appear are something you might be enthusiastic about, and you are bound to click as well as buy the merchandise. At the stage when you are a host, that's fantastic news on the grounds your promotions are facing the eyeballs of these ideal people.

One note of alarm. Like any internet Based publicizing, Facebook promotions could be costly, and it is very straightforward to experience a fantastic deal of money free of coming in the event you don't have the foggiest notion what you are doing.

Before you use this strategy to gain on Facebook, you need to have each one of your frameworks set up, you need to have been doing business for a limited while, and you should have some cash available for later because there'll be some experimentation before you find advertisement copy and an offer which works. You ought to likewise have following good setup so that you understand precisely which promotions are working and which ones aren't; this way, you are not wasting cash on ads that don't function and will siphon more money into the promotions which are working.

Boosting articles is the least complicated strategy to perform a Facebook advertising; once you find a lift article that works admirably, you need to use Facebook's additional developed marketing choices to progress those articles that improve well.

5. Carrying Clients For Your Bricks-and-Mortar Business

Clients expect each company they collaborate with to have a Facebook page. These integrate organizations with bodily places like stores, retail locations, cafés, and the sky are the limit from there. So you must have a Facebook page which clearly shows your home, what your situation is all about, what things or administrations you provide, etc.

You can also incorporate upgrades on Deals and markdown provides or exceptional occasions. As an example, you can post about the week per week celebration time in your eatery. What is more, on the off chance that a person posts a question or comment -- be sure to respond intelligently. Receive a discussion moving along with your fans.

The objective here would be to have folks Enjoy your page so that your new articles are in their newsfeed. Now when they visit an incredible deal they enjoy, they come into a real place. You have to keep your place of business high in mind with your chances so that they come to see you.

Honestly, this system may be working. On the off probability, you get a physical company, nevertheless it worth referencing here. You also need to encourage the entirety of your customers to enjoy your webpage and also have them tail you on Facebook for information, specials, coupons, and upgrades. An underlying hint at the register advocating people to tail you on Facebook could work, or you might even encourage people to tail you by providing something.

Another Substantial notice: you can just run Paid promotions into a company page, not your profile.

6. Sell Affiliate Products

Partner boosting is possibly the speediest approaches to start working together on the internet. What's more, interestingly, Facebook is a fantastic procedure to enter this type of experience. It makes it natural.

The basic model works this way:

1. You pursue a spouse program. You can find handfuls out there; nevertheless, an excellent place to start is ClickBank, CJ Affiliate, and Amazon.

2. You advance items out of these destinations on a Facebook page based on a distinct hot specialization.

3. Whenever Someone taps on the link and buys the product, you receive a commission -- for the most part from 5% to 25 percent.

Likewise, as with any method to gain on Facebook, it is essential to post regularly and draws with your audience. These make trust and makes nearly certain people will buy. Furthermore, be sure to stick to these amounts so that you understand which crusades are working and which ones are certainly not.

Some Methods of Making Money on Facebook--Pick 1

There Are Many methods to benefit From investing energy and effort on Facebook. It is among the most elastic phases for profiting on the net. Try one or even some of those methods to determine which works best for you personally. Fantastic luck.

TEN WAYS YOU CAN MAKE MONEY WITH FACEBOOK

Facebook is the most significant net based life Arrange on Earth. Irrespective of whether you have an indisputable company or you have something to market, everyone can gain with Facebook.

If you're using Facebook to message boards and take examinations, look at some of those tips, encourage your wages or begin a side hustle.

Who Can Earn Cash with Facebook?

Everyone can gain with Facebook! Like Anything during everyday life, you ought to be continuous and never cancel in case your conflict does not function the first run throughout.

For the more substantial part of those Recommendations, the character of your Facebook profile is going to be the best way of establishing the first link. There are tons of people on Facebook who promise that the entire world rather than complete. You'd like to not be among those individuals as your likelihood of earning money will be lean.

Make sure that your Facebook profile makes it look As though you are a real individual. Place a picture of your small business badge on your profile image or disperse photograph area.

Likewise, Make Certain You record the Ideal city You reside in so people do not believe your post in an unsuitable gathering. At long last, integrate contact information and a website port on the off probability that you maintain a local or internet company.

Contingent upon the way you're planning to gain with Facebook, you need to consider making another listing similar. Along those lines, you can keep your personal and company action isolated. On the off probability, you have to keep everything under a single document; that's okay too in the event you need you are a single vendor trying a Craigslist optional.

What Can You Promote Facebook?

Virtually anything can be marketed on Facebook. The considerable majority use Facebook to sell their trade-in vehicles, used items, carefully constructed things, electronic publications, and also to sell their end of this week's whole lot deal.

A Few things you can not sell on Facebook comprise:

- Alcohol

- Illicit Medications

- Tobacco

- Firearms

- Animals

- Actual Cash gaming things

- Particular Social insurance things

Overall, you can sell anything on Facebook, which is possible to buy in a nearby shop without demonstrating an image identification or an expert's alternative.

Directions to Earn Cash with Facebook

If your profile is complete, you are Now ready to start profiting. By and large, you may sell items or administrations you efficiently maintain. Be as it may, we will also incorporate a few different proposals too.

1. Write a Facebook Post

In case you need to provide To your present Facebook companions, you can write a post. From the"What is in the forefront of your ideas?" Field, begin writing what you want to market. You may likewise incorporate a picture of this thing too. Posts only offer along with your companions. Nevertheless, they sometimes observed by other people you do not have the foggiest idea if your company shares this article.

Maybe you have seen your companion Circles selling vehicles, property, and distinct possessions instead of experiencing the issue of supplying into an outsider. In case you have never sold anything on Facebook, you can use their gifts, for example, on the version of your article.

Follow Up On Facebook Messenger

When a company or amassing component Communicates intrigue, proceed with the dialogue on Facebook Messenger. This personal conversation telling the government enables you to stay in touch with previous clients and possible customers that didn't make a bargain the initial run through. In the event you're continually switching utilized things, you can recall these folks and send them a message once you last detect something they needed initially been.

2. Combine Local Purchase and Sell Groups

If you're trying to market locally, there is a good chance you won't provide to a company. That's the reason you need to combine your local buy and market events. Facebook makes it rather straightforward to market as you can ordinarily produce the post in 1 gathering, and you've got the option to select various parties before the article goes live.

For Example, suppose You Have to market your vehicle. Your local city or state has, on any occasion, two identifying buy and market bunches that admit used auto postings. Although you make one article, it seems in various parties, and you receive the chance to arrive in more Facebook people.

Possibly the most well-known parties are Carport deals and automobiles. To quickly find the parties in your general area, click on the"Buy and Compare Groups" from the Explore menu. You may similarly search for bunch titles to channel throughout the numerous options too.

Each gathering has varied selling approaches, so make sure you read the collecting rules before you post. Additionally, the amassing arbitrators can erase your article or dissuade you from the collecting.

Produce Your Group

On the possibility that there's not a local gathering for those things you want to market, you need to mull over start your audience seriously.

3. Economy on Facebook Marketplace

Don't forget to market on Facebook Marketplace too. The Marketplace is a free-for-all part where you can buy, sell, or swap almost anything in your area. Regardless of how it is not as unique as local buy and market events, everybody approaches the Facebook Marketplace so that they can undoubtedly exude your article to their companions and possibly locate that outstanding something they have been looking at.

4. Procure Refer-a-Friend Bonuses

Can you use an Internet help that you enjoy and want to impart to other men and women? Verbal suggestions are among the most productive kinds of promotion. Organizations understand one or another why they provide allude a-companion benefit as soon as your companions connect by web-based social websites.

One organization that provides internet-based Life allude a-companion benefits is Rakuten. Maybe you of now rely on them to acquire money back on virtually every online purchase! It is possible to send email welcomes or snap the internet life share fastens on your document to talk about your referral port. In case your companion joins through your referral link, you'll win a cash reward!

The more organizations that you utilize that provide referral benefits the more you could understand. Pause for a minute or two and assess if you may acquire some extra money by discussing your loved programs and websites via online media.

5. Participate in Contests

A Couple of associations and internet journals operate Challenges, and you're able to obtain passages by sharing your link on Facebook or after their FB page. You may also join giveaways and challenge parties to find the most up to open doors too.

A Substantial number of those challenges Are free. Hence the primary departure necessity is the time. Each giveaway is exceptional; however, you might find the chance to win Amazon gift vouchers, kitchen apparatus, or a different lawn barbecue collection.

6. Make Facebook Ads

With this recommendation, you may initially need to generate a Facebook Page to your small business or site. Contemplate the different pages, "Facebook for Business." Making a Page is free and only takes a few minutes, and any company or website is qualified. On the off probability that you want a visual version, check out the Well Kept Wallet Facebook webpage to acquire an idea of what the Page could resemble.

When your webpage is created, you can impart gifts in your Page adherents, just like you may write articles on your path of events. Facebook Pages would be the online social media likeness using a mailing display; you can always send messages to your steadfast supporters. For example, frozen yogurt parlors may disperse a week per week article referencing the sort of this week.

Be as it may, do not forget that you can make money presenting promotions on Facebook on contact folks that now do not chase your Page.

Suggestions to Produce Facebook Ads

While Page articles can help you with profiting, you need to use compensated Facebook promotions to get in touch with another group of audiences. You may create your advertisements or use help like Flourish Using Facebook Ads to earn skillful ads that may draw more taps the initial run through.

As you create posts in your Page, you may have the decision to tap the gloomy"Lift Article" button. In the aftermath of drawing on the grab, you'll be brought to the advertisement manufacturer apparatus. Although there are a more significant number of highlights compared to what is referenced under, you will find three pieces of equipment you should Provide careful consideration to:

• Goal (Do you have to connect with your group of audiences or create deals?)

• Audience (Target a specific set of audiences or not?))

• Budget (Just how much could you say you'll spend, and how long do you want the struggle to continue?)

An immense benefit of Facebook Advertisements is that you're able to concentrate on a specific set of audiences determined by where they live, age, gender, and pursuits. Or on the flip side, it's possible also to promote your fans and their partners on the off probability that you select too. You may also screen the people who came to and even the number of dedication. Following the crusade finishes, you can contrast the number of devotion with the total conflict cost to figure out your expenditure per-click (CPC) amount.

In case you have at any stage publicized someplace else for company, you understand that marketing could be expensive in a hurry. Advertising on Facebook usually is small for paid ads because it is possible to select your planned interest group for only a few dollars contrasted with thousands or hundreds of dollars for every crusade.

Running Facebook promotions is a learning Process determined by experimentation. As a consequence of the ease requirements, do not hesitate to try a couple of small crusades that only expense $10 to $15 per with different target audiences to discover what works best for you.

7. Put funds into Facebook

This is another suggestion that anyone can use to gain with Facebook. What's more, you do not have to produce Facebook accounts! Even though you might find this funny, Facebook is traded on an open marketplace business on the Nasdaq Index.

Facebook's stock ticker picture is FB; also, it has been with any financier on your IRA or assessable money market fund. You should seriously consider buying Facebook inventory with Stockpile for all these three reasons:

• Every exchange is simply 99 pennies versus the company typical of $4.95.

8. Host a Fundraiser

While you won't benefit from this suggestion, you can, in any situation, assist fund-raise for a single reason or non-benefit. Crowdfunding is getting a well-known approach to help others with cash related needs, which take good care of the tabs with no external assistance.

You Can Create a gathering pledges webpage for Among the causes under:

• Personal crisis

• Crisis help

• Health and therapeutic

• Instruction

• International

• Faith

• Sports

There are a whole lot of nobles goals that Facebook people group people are pleased to assist. The principal issue is they don't have the foggiest notion where to search. Luckily, this part helps address this matter.

9. Proceed after a Position

Facebook also has its unique action board to help you with getting a different line of work. Nearby organizations will encourage open circumstances in the "Employments" tab. You are going to see full time and meager maintenance positions for several ventures within this page; therefore, look down and have a gander at all of the possibilities.

Notwithstanding the Facebook Jobs button, there are various parties that rundown online job leads too. You can combine different parties to fasten position leads and get pieces of information on the application process and perform understanding from additional amassing people.

10. Become a Social Media Manager

If you're online life-wise, you can get paid to manage corporate web-based social media accounts. As a web-based life distant helper, your duties may contain:

• Scheduling Web-based life articles

• stinks To opinions and linking with devotees

• Creating Web-based existence designs

• Tracking Advertisement crusade dimensions

• Construction, The group of audiences size

There is a decent possibility that you'll have to manage internet based life accounts on distinct phases aside from Facebook. Along these lines, it is inclined as a wise notion. In any event, you should be more comfortable with the more extensive steps like Instagram, Pinterest, and Twitter additionally.

If You're Facebook excited, this is a perfect opportunity to telecommute and create low care pay with flexible hours.

Chapter 11

───── ❧❦❧ ─────

How to build a solid twitter following the right way

The Basics

No matter how much amazing content you produce, it's going to be challenging to create an engaged Twitter community without a solid growth strategy in place. Sure, some people will follow your account for your content, but you'll be able to get followers much more rapidly if you give some love first.

Reciprocity is the practice of exchanging things with others for mutual benefit. In the case of Twitter, it means following people (the RIGHT people) with the hope that they will follow you back.

Following People

There are a number of ways you can do this, but if you're just getting started, I recommend starting off slow. I didn't grow my account from zero to 18K overnight. I started by manually following 25 people per day, growing to 50 and then, after a month, 100 people per day.

Eventually I discovered Social Quant and passed off the task of following and unfollowing, which was the best thing I could have done, since my growth increased exponentially and my followers will still highly targeted.

Either way, whether you use a tool to grow your community or do so manually, you definitely want to start slowly to stay off Twitter's radar to avoid the potential risk of ending up in "Twitter jail." Besides, you can only follow 10% more Twitter accounts than those following you.

If you rapidly follow hundreds of accounts, you won't be able to accumulate followers as fast as you're following other people. You can grow your account without those limits up until you hit the 2K mark. At that point, you need to have at least 1819 accounts following you or you'll have to unfollow in order to follow more.

Unfollowing People

If you're growing your account manually, you'll need a strategy for unfollowing. Just make sure that you aren't churning your followers - rapidly following and unfollowing. Make sure you follow people for at least a week to give them ample opportunity to follow you back. Remember, not everybody logs in to Twitter every day, but that doesn't mean they aren't a great potential connection. Don't miss out on these connections by unfollowing too quickly.

Engaging for Success

One thing you definitely don't want is to be one of those accounts that just broadcasts and never actually engages. Trust me, that WON'T build any relationships. After all, social media is supposed to be sociable! Sure, large businesses can get away with just spewing out content with marginal success, but the best are the ones that engage with their audience. Look at Zappos, for a great example. They are famous for their awesome content and unparalleled customer service.

Respond to @Mentions

Check your account daily - at the very least - to see if anyone is reaching out to you. In fact, I recommend using a tool like Mention or Brand24 to monitor what's being said about you online so you get notified and can rapidly engage. If nothing else, at least use a free Hootsuite or TweetDeck account and set up a stream to monitor your Twitter mentions.

Respond to Direct Messages

Yes, a lot of what you're going to get in your inbox is spam. But check it just to be on the safe side. You never know who has been lurking and is finally deciding to reach out and engage. You don't want a great opportunity to pass you by because you aren't checking your messages.

Remember Your Manners

If someone is tweeting or retweeting your content, thank them! But don't just stop there - use it as an opportunity to start a conversation and get to know them better. Take a moment to look at their bio and ask an open-ended question. Or ask how things are going in their business or how their week is going. Remember, social media is all about making connections and Twitter is one of the best networks to cold connect with strangers and quickly build a relationship.

Jump into Conversations

Perform keyword searches to find out what conversations are happening on Twitter around topics in your niche. When you find them, jump on in! What would be considered intrusive or inappropriate on Facebook is completely acceptable on Twitter.

Engage with people. Answer questions to show you're an authority figure. Be helpful. Provide value. Trust me. All of those things will help you to win new followers. Not just regular followers, either, but followers who appreciate you and what you have to offer. Raving fans.

Join Twitter Chats

By joining these chats and engaging with others in the chat, you'll get the chance to meet others in your niche. You'll learn valuable information, demonstrate your knowledge of the industry, and shine a spotlight on your Twitter account, getting more followers.

The Follow-Back Strategy That Works Like Magic

Did you know that 25-30% of the people you follow will follow you back? It means that for every 100 people you follow, 25-30 of them will return the "favor." Awesome, right?

It's one of the most effective ways to build your following quickly. However, there's a problem with this approach: Even though this technique can give you results very fast, you can attract a lot of garbage if you're not careful about who you follow. Some users will follow back absolutely anyone - some even have automation set up to follow back everyone. So, again, be mindful of who you're following if you want to grow a targeted following for your account.

So how do you find these quality, targeted accounts to follow? Leverage Twitter's Advanced Search to find the right people to follow and, you'll attract followers who are actually interested in whatever you're promoting.

Here's how:

Step 1: Head over to Twitter.com/search-advanced

Step 2: Fill out the fields strategically

For instance, if you want to find people who follow competing brands and/or have shared their content, you can use the section "To these accounts" and find people who have recently mentioned one of those brands.

Let's say you run a Link Building Software and one of your competitors is Ahrefs. In this case, you should add "@ahrefs" in that section.

Then, Twitter would show you all the tweets that are mentioning Ahrefs. This is super useful. Why? Because if people are following Ahrefs or sharing their content you know two things:

1. They follow brands in your industry

2. They share content related to your industry

The bottom line? They are very likely to follow you back and give you the opportunity to build a relationship with them.

There are infinite ways to find relevant people using the Twitter's Advanced Search, and I couldn't cover all of them in this post. However, Zapier has published an article where they guide you step-by-step through the different functionality of this tool.

Step 3: Start following the people you find

Now that you know how to find relevant people, it's time to start following them.

I highly recommend that you follow at least 100 people every day so you can grow fast enough. About 25-30 out of those 100 will follow you back, and since you're focusing on follow highly-targeted people, I'm confident you could even increase that number.

Chapter 12

— — — — — 𝒶𝒶𝒢𝒢 — — — —

Twitter marketing basics

With the increase in the access and use of social media tools, Twitter has become one of the most powerful social networking tools. On Twitter, one is able to find all kinds of the latest information on typically any topic. This has become a beneficial tool for many companies and businesses, as they can be easily accessed, and they can also access people easily.

Twitter marketing basically helps different brands reach hundreds of millions of people through a free social media platform. However, this only works best when the content being shared out, and if it is fantastic enough to attract more followers or customers.

Right here's an agenda of everything your service needs to do to hop on (or back on) Twitter and begin seeing incredible results.

Select an Appropriate Username

Your username (@username) is your Twitter picture. If you connect the record with your association, try using your company name or a selection of it. Twitter enables up to 15 personalities for usernames.

Make a Brand-driven Account

Your account consists of a biography, photo, and cover photos. It needs to define the account of your business in a single look, so choose visual parts that ideal address you.

Type a sensible, quick biography, a delineation of your association in 150 personalities or less-- that portrays your image, points, and organizations, and that settles an organization with your site or a factor of access. Your business' logo design can fill in as the picture.

Transform right into an Excellent Listener

Pay attention first and also tweet later is a far better than ordinary stating for utilizing Twitter in an advancing setup. Usage Twitter pressed demand or gadgets like HootSuite or Sprout Social to seek tweets that fuse your organization name, points, and companies. In like manner, search for your challengers and also others in your industry, to see what they are tweeting.

Interact and React

Reply to tweets about your organisation, paying little regard to whether they are specific or unfavorable, and also do all things thought about swiftly (inside 1 day). You can such as and retweet favorable messages, give thanks to individuals that identify you, and address crucial tweets in a consistent, conscious way.

Tweet Frequently

In light of its short-term nature, a tweet you post presently is neglected rapidly, which recommends you can publish completely extra frequently than while utilizing various other casual networks. While there is no charm number for just how regularly you ought to tweet, when constantly is an average location to begin. You would certainly then have the capacity to test apparent revealing regularities on see what works best. Twitter's within assessment phase and also pariah tools.

Utilize Tweets that Captivate with Couple Of Words

Notwithstanding the way that Twitter has a 140-character restriction, it's a keen concept to relinquish some space-- 15-20 personalities or close-- for other people, who want to retweet your message or include material.

Constantly Provide Praise to others when Retweeting

Coming another person's tweet to your lovers is a fair technique to fabricate social resources and develop legitimacy. This preparation can lead to various people retweeting your material. Similarly, see others in your tweets by including their @usernames. Prized possession tweets that contain important, tweaked substance can create unselfishness.

Make a Web Content Arrangement

Make a substance date-book and logbook a couple of relentless tweets throughout a few days or weeks. Reserve particular days for specific type of tweets.

For example:

Monday-- include unique headways

Tuesday-- go out of sight of your company with photos or narrates

Wednesday-- Share suggestions with others

Thursday-- limelight drifting sector subjects

Friday-- base on consumers and agents

Not most of the material you use should be novel. Curating web content from pariah sources can fill out too.

Chapter 13

─ ─ ─ ─ ─ ⚬⚬⚬⚬ ─ ─ ─ ─ ─

Rules for twitter marketing

Just like any other social media network, Twitter has a few rules that would need one to abide while marketing. These are always helpful in keeping every user in check on the right and helpful content to share, that would be beneficial to everyone. There is a need to know the right and proper etiquette to save and keep your business or brand from damaging their online reputation.

- Authenticity

The tip on this is always to add value to your content. Your audiences will always appreciate it more if they know that you take time to go through your content before sharing it with them. Also, they are most likely to respond better when they get to interact with the real you in the media platform, as it creates a form of trust.

Always start a great challenging conversation and actively participate, do some follow up to your best followers to keep conversations going. In case you retweet any content or share links from other people, view the content, and ensure it is authentic and true. This saves you from sharing fake content, which might end up compromising your brand.

- Safety

Is your handle a safe space for users to interact and have great conversations? As much as it is a social media platform, many people and brands have used their handles the wrong way, which has got their accounts reported and closed down. Your users should know that their interaction in conversations is safe, and they should not worry about anything getting personal.

- Privacy (private info and non-consensual nudity)

You have to give a right to privacy to your followers, as some always want to stay anonymous, especially when they do direct messaging. In such a case, stay true to your word and keep their concerns private, and this will definitely nurture more trust and greater referrals.

Also, posting nudes on your platform only creates a negative reputation for your brand or company. In most cases, users would be offended and report the account for closure. That is why it is advisable to keep things clean and not compromise anything.

- Useful content

What type of content do you want your target market to access? Is it beneficial to your company or brand? Sticking to the right content always helps in keeping followers more interested. It also sets you apart from the rest of your competitors. Having random content on your platform can be quite confusing to those people who interact with whatever you are marketing, as it would take more time for them to access that which then need quickly.

Stick to sharing information that is valuable to your followers, and also retweet or share links that would still be beneficial to your brand in general. When followers find your content very useful, they will always come back for more and will keep referring other people to your handle, which means more exposure.

- Avoid blanket follow-backs

You can have 5,000 Twitter followers, but does that mean you have to follow all of them back? No. You have to filter out your followers and know whom to follow and who not to. This is because you would not want to follow someone with a negative reputation. Some people will check who you follow to know the kind of brand you are.

It will be ideal to follow like-minded people so that you can benefit or learn from them — also, people who are more likely to push followers your way.

Chapter 14

— — — — — ❧❦❧ — — — — —

Why use twitter for marketing

One rule for marketing is to get people where they are, and that would be on Twitter. It has a lot of active monthly users on a daily basis, and it is a great platform for any kind of business marketing. Those who have made good use of the platform in the past have got immense gains.

1. Affordability: There are some businesses that are not well abled financially, and Twitter makes it easier for them to reach a wide variety of client base. Twitter does not require one to pay to open an account and maintain it, so it barely needs one to have much money to do their marketing. It mostly depends on one being proactive enough to ensure they reach the right audience and are able to sell their ideas/products.

What one needs at most is the Internet, and a device to use can be a computer or mobile. With mobile phones, one can be flexible enough and do marketing at any given place. It would not need an individual to have an office set up as everything is virtual. Twitter also offers some free marketing tools which a beginner can use and start paying for more as they grow their brand.

2. Instant communication and feedback: As a marketer, Twitter allows you to send out messages immediately at any given place. This can be in cases where one comes across information or updates that would be beneficial to their followers or would work best against one's competitors. One is able to make quick updates that would work to their advantage.

The amazing thing about Twitter marketing is that one can get the feedback they need instantly. They would be able to know if whatever they are selling has good receivership on not. An example would be, a client uses a product, and they give feedback directly on the Twitter handle. If it is a review, it is instant, and if possible, many other people will be able to see it. Followers can also do direct messaging, which gets to you the owner instantly.

3. One can keep up with the latest trends: While on Twitter, it is very easy for one to know what is trending and how to use it as leverage for their benefit. Most trending topics will have hashtags, and an individual is able to know how to use such to gain mileage. An example, if one uses a certain trending hashtag, they are bound to attract more

following depending on the kind of content they will constantly share.

Also, depending on the kind of services being marketed, knowing what is trending will help one know what to do to move with the trends. Most Twitter users go with mass

4. Easy user or client engagement: Unlike so many other ways of marketing, on Twitter, one is able to engage their users much more easily. This is because the messaging is instant, and any time one gets feedback, they can respond immediately. Also, a marketer can start conversations in which they can actively engage their followers to know what they think of either their product or service.

From such active conversations, it is helpful as one knows areas they need to improve on and any big or small differences they need to make in order to penetrate the market. Also, by involving followers actively, one is able to know their needs and things they are more interested in, hence using that as leverage to meeting the user's needs.

Many customers appreciate great client relations, and when they are actively engaged in a matter that directly affects or involves them, they are bound to give positive reviews. They are also likely to refer other people to you when they know they have a great customer relationship with you as a business owner.

5. Target marketing: With Twitter, it is much easier to know the needs and likes of one's followers. This can be found out with simple, quick surveys or by tracking the feedback one gets from the content they share. Because the responses are always instant, one is able to know what to focus on and the people to target.

These mostly vary from one group to another, as it comes with preference and even age groups. Knowing how people interact on Twitter and the things that excite them, one will always be able to know what market to target. This makes it easier as you are able to tailor-make the content for the right market or audience.

3.3 How to Succeed at Twitter Marketing

Create a strategy first, so it can help you see the bigger picture and know the right places to focus on when marketing. The use of a strategy is also for you to attract new followers and leads and also improve brand recognition. Simple steps to follow when creating a strategy:

- Research about your audience

- Create unique content that is tailor-made for them

- Organize and schedule when you will be posting the content to gain maximum effect

- Analyze the impact and results over a period of time to know where you would need to change or improve.

1. Customize and perfect your profile

When a new follower gets to your profile, you need them to immediately know what it entails and what expectations they should be having. This means you should customize your profile with your logo, brand colors, and anything that you identify with as a business.

- Handle: What is your username? Is it catchy, or would it leave someone guessing? Always include your brand or company's name on the handle to make it easy for your followers to find you with one quick search.

- Header: This is the background image on every Twitter handle. Is your unique enough to attract new people to follow you? One can use a unique image or its logo for these sections. Most brands go the extra mile to brand an image with their details to make it easier for them being identified.

- Bio: Your bio needs to be catchy and provide a brief synopsis of what the whole handle entails in about 160 characters. This is where most brands share their mission statements, objective, vision, etc. It is helpful for this to be simple and with enough detail to capture someone's attention, without them having to go through your whole Twitter handle.

- Other media platform URLs: At the bottom of one's profile, it is great to add links that lead to your other sites. This helps in directing traffic to your other media platforms for effective wider reach.

2. Create exciting content

Knowing what captures your followers' attention can be hard at times, but it is worth it to know what spikes their curiosity. Do not create plain text content all the time, as it can get quite boring. There are so many ways to make your content a little bit more exciting than the average ones being created by everyone.

- Visual tweets (gifs, videos, photos) – Combining these with text is always exciting. Most people are attracted to visual elements as compared to text, so finding a great balance with this will definitely get you a great response.

- Use hashtags – Be in the know of what hashtags are trending and make sure you use them in the right way. This will always put you out there any time someone searches that hashtag; your handle or profile will also come up. You can also decide to create your own hashtags depending on the content you are sharing.

- Get personal – Once in a while, share something about you as a person, which makes your followers feel like you are just as human as they are.

3. Host Twitter chats to engage followers

One can schedule Twitter chats to engage followers and discuss certain topics. This always creates a sense of community, and the audience always feels like their opinion is highly valued.

These chats can be at certain times of the week or month, especially when one is sure of getting high traffic on the handle. It simply means one is able to keep the audience looking forward to the conversations. It is advisable to make the topics to be less controversial so that that discussion can be sane and liberal. Having controversial topics might only lead to online fights, which is a compromise on followers.

When one has mastered what works best and has the conversations going, it ends up promoting interaction, which gets more and more people talking about your brand. It also creates a more personal relationship with the audience, where they are more likely to lead more people to your Twitter handle.

4. Link to your other online platforms

Another effective way for marketing would be to link your Twitter handle to your other online platforms. This is Facebook, YouTube, or even a website. This makes it easier for your followers to reach out and get more detailed content or information when they need some clarity. It also boosts traffic on your other platforms.

5. Know your audience and target them

This is one of the best areas to focus on, especially when marketing. If you do not know your audience, you will most likely not know what they need. Engaging them online and asking the hard questions or doing surveys is the only way to best know the people you are serving.

Once you know them and what works best, you are able to know what to share with them easily. You can achieve this by:

- Tweet at the right time: Knowing when to share content online is mandatory, as so many users also have day jobs and would not be fully engaged during the day. Depending on what you are offering, know when most of your audience is online, then use the time to your advantage. Tweeting at the right time will always get you the right traffic on your handle.

Listen broadly: As a marketer, you do not want to look like you know all the answers. Engage the audience and listen broadly, so you can be able to know where to improve from their perspective. They would know more than you do as they are the consumers of your content.

Chapter 15

−−−−− ✌☙✎✌ −−−−−

Benefits of more twitter followers

Just like any other social media platform, Twitter has a whole lot of benefits that you can take advantage of. In a nutshell, the platform:

Increases brand awareness: The higher the number of followers one has on the Twitter account, the easier it gets to get their brand known. This mostly happens when your tweets are retweeted and even shared on different online platforms. It will help it to be distributed faster and over a widespread market. The more a brand gets exposed to the masses, the faster and easier people get to follow it and identify with it.

Increase web traffic: The more people your content attracts, the more it will be accessed, which in the end, increases web traffic. The more traffic your handles attract; the high leads it will generate. This means you will attract more new followers.

Effective marketing: The fastest and easiest way most brand owners use to market themselves is through Twitter. This is always helpful when one has many followers, as they will most likely retweet and share with their connections. This will lead more people to the handle, and hence, they will be more interested in gaining more knowledge on the product or service.

Increase sales: Great sales always make or break a company. With many Twitter followers, it is easier to make sales as the audience can be easily reached, and it is also easier to attract new clients. Always treat Twitter fans as future prospects, as you would not know when they would need your product or services. Also, since they interact with other fans on other platforms, they are a great referral base for your business.

Cost-effectiveness: Twitter is free, and people also post their content for free. Once you have enough followers, it is basically you marketing to your audience without incurring any charges. This is because your market is just a click away. The only time this can be different would be in cases where one does pay for ads. This means that a company will incur no cost to get their brand out there. It takes skill and time to be able to attract enough followers, but one has a good base, the benefits start coming in.

Increased communication: Imagine if you were to send out emails to all you 10,000+ Twitter followers? Wouldn't that be hectic? Twitter makes it so much easier to send out messages or share an update at any time, any place, and be sure that everyone will be able to see it. It is an easy communication channel that is free and easily accessible. One is able to keep the audience constantly updated even as they go by their day to day activities. Also, the audience has an easier time getting in touch with you by simply sending a message or engaging you on a post. In the end, this saves everyone time and money, but still manage to get the message home.

Chapter 16

---- ❧❧❧❧ ----

How to get enough followers

- Have an inviting profile

The way your profile looks at first impression is what will attract on make followers be interested in what you have to offer. Always ensure that your profile is very simple but inviting. It should also be detailed enough so that one can know enough about your brand without having to go read so many pages of information about you.

- Post useful content

The kind of content you share should be interesting enough to have your followers comment and also want to retweet. Retweeting is the best way to attract other followers to your profile, and if you don't have great content, this will not be possible.

Followers will always yearn for content that is beneficial to them, or at least that which is exciting. Once a marketer achieves this, they will attract a great following.

- Tweet frequently

How often you tweet also determines how much you attract numbers. A dormant Twitter handle will never gain many followers. The Twitter fan base is like a flame that has to be constantly fanned. The more you tweet, the more likely you are to get traffic on your profile.

This is an area one needs to consider as they work on a social media strategy. Have a clear breakdown of the right topics to feature on, and also have the timings you want to tweet constantly.

You can have a content-sharing schedule to share automated updates that you need to send out at any given time, even when you are not online. This way, your audience is constantly taken care of, and there are no chances of them losing interest or contact with your profile.

- Partner with influencers

Another great option would be to partner with other people to get you more followers. Most influencers have a huge following, and command authority in their field of expertise, or better still, in content creation. The majority know what works best for social media marketing and would be better placed to give advice when one needs to grow their following.

When partnering with influencers, one has to share the content they would like to send out, and the influences will use their handle to market you. This means that all their followers will see the content, and if interested, they will, in turn, follow you. This mostly works well if the influencer has a big following and is listened to.

One also needs to be careful when choosing whichever influencer they would want to work with. Some have negative reviews or are known to have explicit content, which would not be beneficial to your brand. This is why you would need to choose someone whose values align with your brand.

- Create Twitter campaigns

Social media marketing campaigns are currently a big thing and are always an easy way to reach a wide audience. It also helps to drive sales and increase your website traffic. These campaigns are helpful if they will help you raise your brand awareness, so it is vital that you have in mind what the campaign should be about, and it's objective:

- Know who your competition is: This is helpful in knowing how to leverage against your competitors.

- Know what you will use to catch the attention of your audience

- Choose the type of content you want to share

- Share and promote it, using the right type of unique hashtags

- Analyze your results: This comes at the end of the campaign, and it helps you to know how many more followers you have got after the campaign. It will also help to know whether to do more campaigns in the future or not.

- Use unique hashtags

Using hashtags is a great way to direct people to your profile in order to expand your influence. Most users go by what hashtags are trending, and you would want to take advantage of that to get more users. You can also create your own hashtags and push them out to trend.

- Use hashtags that are unique to your business

- Create relevant and memorable hashtags that the consumers can relate to.

- Analyze your account to know which previous hashtags have worked best and re-use them in the future.

- Ensure content is shareable

The more your content is shared and retweeted, the wider the audience. Always ensure that the content you share can be retweeted so that you can get other people who are not your followers to be able to see what you are all about. When your followers share your content, they will have other people they know gain interest and end up following you.

Chapter 17

---- ❧❧❧ ----

The science of tweeting better

First, let's discuss the need for brands to advertise on Twitter. Twitter is a social media platform that makes it easier for people to come in contact with friends, celebrities and brands. It offers a direct contact between people and their favorite brands. Hence, it is smart of brands to utilize this connection to influence their customers.

Twitter users follow an average of 6 brands on Twitter. Since a majority of people spend a lot of time on Twitter, it makes sense for a brand to invest on promoting their products on Twitter.

The potential buyers on Twitter are ready to attack any link they find attractive. So, if you perfect your Tweeting skills, you could potentially attract a swarm of customers. Studies show that a large number of people admitted that a product they bought online was something they saw on Twitter.

The three major areas that you should focus on to capture the attention of customers is:

- Writing great tweets

- Perfect timing

- Testing and measuring

Let's have a look about each of these aspects individually.

Chapter 18

————— ❧❧❧❦ —————

Writing great tweets

Conversations

You should use Twitter as a mode of communicating with your customers. This also includes having conversations with them like you would over the phone. The customer needs to feel a bond with your brand. This will make them more inclined to buy your products and vouch for you to other friends.

Here are some tips that you can use to improve your conversations:

• Talk with the people not at them. Reply to each of your customers personally and address both the negative and positive feedback that they mention. Never neglect the negatives. This will look like you don't care. Since Twitter functions in a real time scenario, make sure that you reply as soon as possible.

• Think about your content. Think about whether your content is catchy enough for the average Twitter user. Will they retweet the tweet? To ensure that they share it with their followers, you need to captivate. Use humor and interesting content to draw the Twitter users.

• Differentiate between tone and voice. You should ensure that your voice of communication should never change throughout any Twitter exchange. However, your tone needs to vary depending on the situation. Your tone should always be professional. If a follower had a bad experience with your brand, you need to assume an understanding tone. If you opt for a defensive, this will only further anger the follower and you will surely lose a customer. Your tone of voice decides whether you win over a customer or lose them.

• Keep your tweets professional yet casual. Be professional without sounding formal. You need to engage them in a conversation not conduct a meeting. Avoid speaking in business terms as much as possible.

Viral expressions

The center of any tweet is your content; the content that you want to convey to the Twitter users. The power of Twitter, however, lies in the form of its amplification of tweets, that is, its retweets. It is statistically shown that most of a brand's spread comes from retweets. So if you need to expand your connections, you need to work on words and phrases that help catch the idea of potential buys and cause them to retweet your tweets. Let's have a look at some of the important words and phrases that need to be included in a Tweet:

- Use a lot of superlatives such as "the best", "mind blowing", "amazing" and "outstanding" and so on.

- Words that ask the customers to do something like make or look or see.

- Use 'How-to' phrases to explain processes or techniques.

- Use visual words such as photos or videos signify that there is some important multimedia content.

- Refer to the audience as much as possible. Use phrases such as, "do you see", "make you", "tell you" or "when you". If you directly talk to the customer, they are more likely to pay attention to the content and retweet it.

Most popular tweets will have similar kinds of words. They will all address the audience and will have a lot of imperative words. It was found that tweets that specifically ask the users to retweet were 12 times more likely to be retweeted than ones that did not ask. Hence, do not hesitate to ask your audience to retweet. Using the shortened form of retweet, RT results in nearly a 10-fold increase in number of tweets. Tweets such as "Retweet if you think this dog is cute", are most likely going to get retweeted by almost anyone who see the tweets.

It was also found that tweets that have a large number of verbs and adverbs are most clicked on tweets when compared to those that have more adjectives or nouns. So, it is considered a general rule that action words result in a more persuasive and stronger tweet.

Formatting

Different types can have different outcomes. You can modify your tweet in order to change your target audience or the outcome of the audience. These marketing outcomes can be achieved by changing the format of your tweets. For example, if you want a direct response from the target audience, then you should simplify your tweets. The simpler the tweets are, the most likely it is that users will reply.

Start your tweet with a compelling offer or goodies or an attraction and then convey to the audience a sense of urgency. Then, include a link to your brand's website along with a call for action. Finally, do not use @mentions or hashtags if you want people to pay attention to your tweets. The focus of such a tweet is to get the average Twitter user to click on the link of your brand's website.

If you are sharing blogs on Twitter, it is found that people prefer a "sentence case" where every letter in the title of the blog post is capitalized rather than all capitals or all lowercase.

The use of formatting can attract people because it signifies that there is something special in your tweet that could possibly be retweeted.

Hashtags

There are some requirements for a good hashtag:

• The hashtag should short. A long hashtag is just annoying and meaningless.

• It should be recognizable. Only if people recognize the hashtag will they even follow or search for it.

• The hashtag should be easy to follow.

• If you are going to use an existing hashtag, make sure that it actually has some relevance to your tweet and that your tweet adds more information or content to the existing hashtag.

The number of hashtags you use in your tweet also matters. If you use two hashtags or even one, it will increase the value of the tweet while those without hashtags are not given as much attention. However, using a large number of hashtags is also detrimental. If you use more than 2 hashtags, your following could drop because of clogging of your tweet. Choose your hashtags carefully. Use the most relevant and popular hashtags in your tweet.

Length of the tweet

While there may be no way to find out the exact number of characters that make a tweet perfect, the closest number could possibly 100.An exact number of 100 characters was found to be the sweet spot for a tweet. There was also an increase in number of tweets in the range between 71 and 100. If you can keep your word count down to a bare minimum. It you can keep your tweet short, you can include a lot more links. If you add photos and videos instead of written content, you are saving on both space and the content will be interesting to the audience. In Twitter, the key is to have a lot of content but use it wisely. For example, use pictures or videos to link to the content rather than post it all. Mention all the rewards or quizzes to get a glimpse at the exclusive content.

Given below are some special promotions found on Twitter:

Amplify to unlock: This concept allows followers access to exclusive content or special products by retweeting the tweet to a specific number of people.

Exclusive to Twitter: Give out offers that are exclusive just to Twitter, so that your followers will not be exposed to such offers elsewhere on the internet. Use coupons to reward the customers. If you have a ground store, then give customers a specific coupon or code that they can use at the counter to avail a discount or gift. If it is an online sale, then give them a discount code that the customer can use at the time of checkout.

Generation Cards: These cards allow your customers to express their interest in your brand. When a customer expands a Tweet that contains the card, they will see your offer. Then, if the customer clicks again they can share their contact information. Note that this information is shared over a secure server.

Chapter 19

–––––– ❧❦❧ ––––––

Finding the perfect time

Every target audience is different. The reach also varies depending on kind of brand that you are selling. It is best to test different days of the week and even times of the day in order to see what day and time works the best for you.

If your brand needs the direct connection to the customers, then the weekends, Saturday and Sunday would be the ideal choice of days to post tweets. It is on these days that people are free enough to spend large amounts of time on Twitter. Since most customers will be working people, the weekend is when they will all be on holiday and free to check Twitter.

A study found on that the engagement with brand tweets is higher on weekends when compared to weekdays. Sports, fashion, books and entertainment see a large increase in audience on weekends.

The good thing is, you don't need to lose your vacation just to keep your customers happy. There are various solutions such as Buffer that allow you to schedule your tweets so that they post it at the time you want it to be posted. However, you should keep an eye on the replies and response to the post. You should keep your sufficiently free enough to respond to people and have a normal conversation.

People working with business-to-business brands should probably stick to weekdays or start small on weekends. This is because most businesses are off on weekends so there will be nobody to check your tweets because they are on weekend vacation. During the week, they are at work and will check the tweets.

Daytime and afternoon was predicted to be the ideal times to post tweets. Between 8am and 7pm, there is a much greater activity on tweets than later in the night. This is because most activities occur during daytime. Afternoon and early evening seem to be the preferred timings in the entire daytime. The highest number of retweets has been around 5pm. The tweets at noon and 6pm tend to be popular for their click through rate. Another study showed that the best time for click tweets is from 1pm to 3pm. Even though some studies might produce conflicting data, it is evident that afternoon and early evening is the best time for you to tweet about your brand.

Chapter 20

————— ⊷⊶⊷⊶ —————

How to earn with twitter

As we all know, Twitter is one of the powerful tools of social media used for marketing.

Introduction

Twitter business-model is a micro-blogging platform that is very popular in the whole world. This makes the 9th in all social networks in the world. It is credited for its reliability in communicating most current and breaking news.

Twitter-Business-Model

This is similar to other network models. With Twitter, you are required to develop a profile for users to post status tweets. As a registered user, you can tweet, but if you are not registered, you cannot post; instead, you just read. Posts are made on different platforms ranging from short messages on phones to website media or apps content.

Followers of tweets do follow other people's contents on their accounts. Posts may be in the forms of photos, videos, and other links to their contents or tweets.

Lately, Twitter has shifted its attention to content developers and videos and is escaping mere text tweeting.

This is the beginning of Twitter money-making schemes. The content makers are paid by tweeter in a ratio of 1:7, where the content and video makers earn 70% as Twitter takes up the rest amount.

This is much better as compared with YouTube, which shares the amount with content makers at a ratio of 1:5.

Each and every network has got its own specifications plus the lowest possible number of followers. Whichever way, the higher the number of followers, the greater the pay-per-click as the content writer.

I addition to that, the more you are known in a given position, the higher the chances of being picked upon by relative advertisers who aim at the masses in your followers and the kind of audience that you have.

There are three key things or factors that affect the rate at which you will make money on Twitter. They are branding, a number of followers, and the influence that you have on the network. They play great roles in determining your Twitter paycheck.

Most of Twitter advertisers and others, who use Twitter for money, ever use the third party platforms for advertising on

Twitter. You can tweet for your own benefit or for the benefit of other companies or individuals.

Twitter is fun in itself as a way of refreshing and can also be used to make income from it. In the next section, we will be looking at possible ways and means of making money through the use of Twitter. Just follow closely and keenly to learn much out of this publication. I hope you will enjoy it and retweet the book!

It doesn't mean that without a blog, you can't make money via Twitter. There are very many other different ways that you can apply to make money on the network without necessarily selling your own services and products.

Twitter is so powerful by itself other than acting as a medium for marketing other sites. You could come up with a Twitter account revolving around a position that is profitable, thus generating income online.

It could be education or any other area that is profitable and ensure that you bequeath followers around that area who have an interest in the niche. After that, you need to tweet some links associated with the position that leads to captivating information around the web and not necessarily your own content.

The question that you need to ask yourself is how money is finally made on Twitter. The answer is quite easy, and we are going to exploit some of the ways you apply in order to earn that money.

i.   Through Sponsored-Tweets

This is an ad service for Twitter that is well known, which enables you to place prices on the tweeted ads. You have a list of ads to choose from and more, especially the most updated ones. You need to have not less than fifty followers with one hundred tweets and an account that has been existence for not less than sixty days in order to register for this service.

ii.   Use of 'Mylikes'

This is a general ad podium that is applicable to Twitter, YouTube, blog, and Tumblr. Ads are selected from hundreds of thousands of advertisers. You need to allocate the time when the advert from an account shall be tweeted. You can make at least 0.42 U. S Dollars per single click to be paid on a weekly basis.

iii.   Use of Ad.ly

This is yet another service for ads which allows adverts to be sent out through your tweets. The difference here is that payment is not made per click; instead, you are supposed to develop a list of your interests for advertisers to choose from for their own campaigns.

You will agree on the possible number of tweets scheduled from your account then the payment is made in lump sums.

iv.   Use of Rev Twt

This is a Twitter oriented service for advertising, which like the first one, is paid on a per-click basis. When you have many followers, you will gain a good reputation hence great access to high paying campaigns. Payment is made through PayPal accounts as soon as you hit twenty dollars as your earning.

v.   Use of Twittad

This is yet another most sponsored Twitter platform on the tweet networks. In this platform, you are allowed to place your own costs per click. The challenge, however, is waiting until advertisers agree with your bid terms.

You as well need to spot a position where advertisers match-their-products appropriately with you. Payment is made through a PayPal account after it reaches $30.00 earnings.

The Twitter platform is being widely used in many areas like politics, sports, and movies, among others. These are the most current updates after Instagram. There are very constructive discussions, you will learn about new brands in the city as well as celebrity controversies.

vi.   Sell of Products and Services

It is easy to reach millions of people on Twitter through your Twitter handle. You need to frame your advert in a way that will attract masses to read your tweets and retweet them. Include links to a sample of your products or services that you wish to sell. Branding is a key aspect while advertising products because there are millions of services and products being sold across the world.

vii.   How to Advertise on Twitter

•   Identify Your Right Audience

You need to choose the right audience based on the services and or products that you need to promote. The second thing is the aspect of the geographical location, target gender, the device, and competitor users.

•   Voice out your message to the right people who need to hear about the promotion

•   Plan, budget, and only account for what works for you. You only need to make payment when the users retweet your posts, like, respond, or even click on the promotion tweet. You have captured the concept, and off you go.

Viii.   Work for Bukasa.com

This is a well-established and renowned website that deals with content publishing. Writers are hired to develop appealing content to their website, invite as many followers to the web site and inline, and advertise your services and or products within their columns.

For your article to fetch you much money is entirely dependent on its capacity to attract many ad-clicks. That can only occur if your content is of good quality and attractive, thus invites many clicks.

More traffic can be amassed through the sharing of articles on other social platforms like Twitter, Instagram, Facebook, among others.

ix.   Come Up with Your Own Twitter-Related-Service

You have an audience on Twitter; therefore, you understand what they use during their free moments. Use this as an advantage to come up with a product or service that you feel they will go for it.

For instance, many Twitter users will want to engage an application that could create automatic hashtags basing on popularity. It doesn't matter whether such issues exist, what you are up to be to find a product that your audience will admire you for.

On the other hand, you can use other websites to encourage members to develop their Twitter presence. It is possible to help others to come up with followers for a small fee.

x.   Go for Leads

Twitter provides a very creative search engine for many, which can be used for searching for potential clientele emphasizing on their bios and their tweet preferences. For example, assume you trade-in pool tables. It is so easy to discover leads by merely searching such terms as "Anyone interested in pool tables." Afterward, you can go individual by advertising or promoting your product. Be creative by introducing coupon codes to those who may have that interest.

xi.   Try Out a Twitter Contest

When people hear of a prize-winning game or activity, many will flood there. This can be done if you established a relationship with some potential companies or individuals who would want publicity for their products.

Create terms and conditions for payment as you launch in for the Twitter contest. You may agree to be paid a sum of money on every sale made for the company. Contests can be made a more creative way to your followers. They could be your judges, source them for information related to the products, or maybe let them retweet or favorite anything.

xii.   Use of YouTube

You can make videos as tutorials for a certain category of followers who would wish to have videos rather than text and images only. You can monetize your content by use of AdSense on YouTube, which in return, can fetch you lots of money simply because of your YouTube knowledge and expertise.

xiii.   Twittad

Twittad is another platform that you can make money on Twitter. It is among the largest and most effective advertising Twitter platforms. You can monetize content on Twittad by choosing who to promote through approvals. Ads and sponsors can be approved or disqualified based on your interests.

As soon as you chose a specific campaign to promote, the Twittad administrator takes up the mandate to inspect your Twitter activity to ascertain your qualification for the campaign. You can only ask to be paid as soon as your account hits thirty dollars.

xiv.   Twtbuck

This is yet another Twitter money-making platform that is widely used. The uniqueness of Twitter is the fact that its ads have got key words that merge with the tweets.

There is a tweeter publisher able to evaluate their worth by use of the tweet-worthy calculator provided by Twitter. This will indicate the total amount one can get for a single ad publication.

Earning with Amazon

Making money on Amazon comes through advertisements. There are various individuals, companies, or teams that hold promotions on Amazon. You can take part in the promotion to earn money. By tweeting and retweeting their messages, you increase the flow of followers and favorites hence making money.

Others win Amazon vouchers simply by liking and following the trends and customer surveys. Whenever a survey is being conducted on Amazon, people or companies whatsoever are invited to support hence earning some money.

The second way of earning through Amazon is by getting additional contact, which can act as your promoters and followers to whatever event or promotions you will be having. That is a credit to you.

Making Money through Video Posting

Most people are making millions of money through YouTube videos across the globe. A YouTube session, on average, is about 40-minutes. Everyone has an equal opportunity to make money on the YouTube channel. There are ways of making much money for yourself using YouTube, as we are going to explore below.

Acquire a 30-day YouTube Planner

Suppose you are making content to last for one hour, viewers may want to get to know what it is all about. We need to understand that YouTube isn't for film-makers only. Every other person can create captivating, educative content to post on YouTube channel.

YouTube, being a free and entertaining channel, will empower the users through strengthening their brands and as such, provide an avenue for them to have access to multitudes of audiences. It can literally build a strong foundation for its subscribers that other companies Using YouTube can make payments in order to advertise their services and products.

There are points to note before launching your YouTube channel for profit-making. It is prudent to have a rough estimate of the profits expected from the channel. Ask yourself first if your channel is merely for your own product promotion or for monetary purposes.

There are two possible ways that you can make money in this instance. It is through advertisements and ad platforms. If you are an advertiser, you will have to pay YouTube for Bumpers, Preroll as well as TrueView ads, which make your videos available to viewers and prospective buyers.

Secondly, if you use YouTube as an ad platform, then the videos that you publish should be watched frequently so as to host other people's content as paid YouTube partners.

When tweeting content, you will want to introduce links to these videos on YouTube channels for your viewers or followers to view. Followers have the opportunity to view the content on YouTube and may much time watching they may download to watch in their free time.

Earning on Twitter through Affiliations

Twitter, as a social media website, provides its users with a public stage for news sharing and posting short messages of approximately 140-characters. Trending events and breaking-news usually catch on extremely on Twitter by far, even before it reaches other social media platforms.

This is one of the reasons that make savvy-marketing-affiliate to make cash via retweeting or creating content that trends and such information.

We will be looking at some of the ways that affiliate marketers make money on Twitter.

1.   Establish Trending Topics

The first thing is to identify trending topics then make some posts by use of those hashtags. You must use quality clickbait messages besides your links. The messages that you tweet must remain in line with the trending topic for plausibility. There is a great need for creativity in this context.

2.   Run Contest and promotional Offers

You are required to run offers as well as contests on Twitter. That is to say; you need to have some incentives to give to people who like and or retweet your posts. To do this, you need to incorporate polls in your tweets and provide the answers through the affiliate links attached.

For instance, post a question of not more than 140-characters and supply the answers on the affiliate link with one as the correct answer.

3. Use Open-Ended Questions in your posted Conversations

You need to post conversations with open-ended questions to your crowds about interesting and funny things. Make other people's conversations a priority to you by observing news feeds. On Twitter, there are massive topics that trend, including breaking news. Ensure that Twitter helps you to remain ahead of the game through tracking and other analytical tools.

4. Self-Promoted-Ad-Service

This is done based on the kind of affiliate-links that you are involved in. In this regard, you will be able to budget for your ads and then identify your demographics. Afterward, Twitter comes into showcase the identified content to your followers.

By doing all these, you need to consider Twitter advertisement policy. For you to be safe and make more money on Twitter, ensure that you comply with the set rules and policies that govern your paid advertisement on Twitter.

In a Nutshell

•   Identify your followers. You need to find out the kind of followers for your tweets and ensure that whatever you put on your profile captivates them

•   After that, you need to acquire followers. Make as many followers as possible based on the level of exposure that you would have acquired so far from Twitter.

•   Post captivating content for your followers to read. Ensure that you do that regularly make your followers active and ever online.

•   Remain engaged to your followers. Retweet their tweets, post questions for review and remember to go back to the answers supplies to your questions

•   Apply images, trending topics, memes as well as polls that come with Twitter to keep engaged with your supporters and begin chats

•   Twitter does not need hard-sell because it is meant for socialites. You do not need to be so pushy over sales issues, which may make it discouraging to your fans.

•   Be careful to take advantage of promotions and contests on top of other marketing platforms to speed up relations as you gain mileage to your affiliate content.

• Avoid being rowdy, shooting unnecessary arguments on Twitter. It is normal to have differences in opinions over controversial issues, but you do not need to let your followers get involved in the issue for that will spoil your reputation.

Twitter versus YouTube

Twitter and YouTube work hand in hand to ensure that advertisements and promotions are conducted holistically. Some can earn money on YouTube through tweeter links. How?

i.   Become a YouTube Advertiser

You have to populate your own literature on your YouTube channel and establish links from Twitter to the YouTube channel. On YouTube, more ads are viewed by interested partners to your literature as co pared with other advertising media such as radio or televisions.

There are long adverts and short adverts. The longer ones are called pre-roll adverts, whereas the shorter ones are referred to as bumpers. Preroll adverts come at the beginning of the video and can only be stopped before the expiry of five seconds else they will have to run to completion. They can take up to 30 seconds.

On the other hand, bumpers are those short adverts which last for not more than six seconds and usually appear shortly before the beginning of your selected video.

ii.   Be an ad Platform

On YouTube, there are two phases: the client-side and the host side. If you have been paying for your advertisements, you now graduate to an ad host where clients will be hosting their adverts on your YouTube platform as you make your money.

What you need to do is to market your YouTube channel to potential users through Twitter. You tell them about your service as you place links at the beginning of your tweets.

Many followers can be obtained through the captivating content which you post on your Twitter handle. Proper Twitter marketing will lead you to have many clients worldwide.

Being an affiliate to several brands is one way of earning a lot of money. But this cannot be compared with being a YouTube affiliate. When a company makes sales that are off the link that you posted, you stand as a loser. It is as opposed to if you were a YouTube advertiser.

In order to join many affiliate companies or networks, you need to establish links to their various sites, for instance: Amazon's affiliate-program or the click-Bank to sign up for an account.

Point to note is that every program has got a unique percentage of payment based on sales as your commission; furthermore, your success is relative to your YouTube channel popularity.

Travel-play outs and travel-bloggers and some travel affiliate plans which enable you to create earnings from travel tickets, tours and travels, hotels, and restaurants, among other associated travel services. In this case, the percentage of your commission depends on the sales by volume made based on the service you chose.

When you are a video streamer, the video itself should prompt you to view it and review and even recommend it to others and not the messages or adverts accompanying the video.

Use of Ad.ly as a Money-Making Tool

This is one of Twitter's best tools or platforms for advertisement. By using ad.ly, you can monetize important content that you create on Twitter. You get paid by ad.ly for the literature or information in the form of ads of specific brands that you pass on to your followers.

They will do an email requesting you for an offer if you have then, you will respond by either approving or dismissing them. If you approve, they automatically tweet the ad through your account at the required time. You are only requested to approve the ad, and the rest is left for them to do.

Use of RvTwt for Money Generation

This advertising platform is deemed the largest on the Twitter network, among other advertising tools, as opposed to ad.ly, where you are paid for updating Facebook status as well as wall posts.

This network is free for all, but it may not be conducive for all. If you do not have a strong network of followers, you may end up earning peanuts on RevTwt. The main advantage of this platform over others is that it is free; hence, anybody can try it out.

Chapter 21

————— ❧❦❧❦❧ —————

Twitter tips and strategies

Twitter is an extraordinary platform for bloggers as it can give a fast and effective approach to get their substance out and in the Twitter surges of their focused on intrigue gatherings and group of onlookers.

So here are some basic Twitter tips and strategies to give a toolbox to reference today and tomorrow for bloggers, organizations and real brands.

1.   Twitter Marketing Tips and Tactics

Introduction checks since it makes the initial introduction. Anything that may raise warnings ought to be evaded no matter what. For example, on the off chance that you pick a username that is related with marketing products you will right away harm your validity. Truly, some usernames have the ability. You can significantly build the level of trust just by acting naturally on the grounds that your personality will be predictable. Marking yourself on Twitter is fundamental on the off chance that you need to achieve the largest amounts and offer the most extreme measure of products. Another alternative is to setup distinctive client represents each of your products so you can focus on your messages and marketing much more. Keep in mind, when you market to a gathering you need it to be as important as could be allowed and you can't keep things pertinent by marketing to at least two specialties that are grouped together.

2.   Secure Twitter followers

You can begin following individuals with high impact and expansive Twitter followings that are inside your objective market either utilizing Klout or Twitter Grader as aides. Amount is essential on Twitter quite recently like a vast email database and don't give anybody a chance to reveal to you any unique. As your Twitter following ends up noticeably significant then the way you draw in with your gathering of people should change as its absolutely impossible that you can connect as personally with everybody in your follower base.

3.   Draw in and Develop Twitter Followers inside your Niche

There are devices, for example, Tweepi.com which makes it simple to follow followers of persuasive bloggers on Twitter. Twellow.com likewise gives an apparatus that empowers you to discover capable Twitter follower records in your specific specialty or vertical market. The quality piece of the Twitter condition is guaranteeing that you have followers that are occupied with your industry specialty. In the event that you needed to procure followers that were occupied with Facebook for instance you could do no superior to anything following some of Mari Smith's followers (otherwise called the Pied Piper of Facebook) utilizing a device like Tweepi.

4.   Offer the Content of Influential Tweeps

Sharing other blogger's substance on Twitter can enable you to pick up their consideration. You can tell them that you have tweeted their post or substance by including your Twitter name eg @Jeffbullas. This sharing considers some portion of engagement and association that gets saw and on the off chance that you request a retweet of your connection or post by that individual later on then you may find that they will enable you to out.

5.   Automate the Tweeting of Other Content in Your Category

As you find different bloggers and compelling tweeters in your specialty you may need share that substance that you now trust and increase the value of your followers by tweeting their substance. This can be robotized utilizing Twitterfeed.com.

Accomplishment on Twitter goes to the individuals who offer value to others, those are the general population you catch wind of profiting there. The implicit Twitter run is basic, form an association with your base of followers, enable them, to move them, engage them, at that point pitch to them. That is the manner by which you manufacture trust, by helping individuals, and they will help you by obtaining your put stock in products. Marketing with twitter will furnish you with deals however steadiness and guille are required in the event that you wish to succeed.

6.   Keep Away from Spammers

Since Twitter is such an awesome specialized instrument, it's regularly utilized by spammers. Spammers may really make an offer all over yet they need to always make new records and get new IP addresses; you, then again, don't need to all that and will profit. There are a wide range of traps that individuals utilize that are truly harming them; for instance, some utilization auto responders to consequently tweet, however this is clumsy in light of the fact that the discussion can go toward any path and the tweets won't bode well. Follow the rules in this article, and separate yourself from the horde of marketers who are stuck in one spot getting no place quick. Utilizing spam strategies will get you prohibited from Twitter.

7.   Know precisely what to tweet.

Utilizing Twitter marketing for your online business does not imply that you can simply tweet everything that you need to state. You must be extremely watchful with regards to tweeting. Tweet just intriguing stuffs and those that are associated with the sort of business that you have. You need to ensure that your Twitter page is beneficial to be followed by posting just applicable topics. This will enable you to effectively catch the consideration of online clients.

8.   Run a Competition on Twitter

Twitter competitions can be extremely effective. Out of appreciation for its tenth birthday celebration, London-based do-it-without anyone else's help Web website manufacturer, Moonfruit ran a Twitter rivalry based rivalry and gave away 11 Macbook Pro computers and 10 iPod Touches. Competitors needed to tweet utilizing the hashtag #moonfruit. (Hashtags group Twitter reactions.)

The Results

Movement to Moonfruit's Web webpage went up 300%.

Deals went up 20%, more than paying off the $15,000 investment.

The Moonfruit Web webpage climbed onto the principal Google page "with the expectation of complimentary website manufacturer" after initially being in fourth position on Google search comes about.

9.   Utilize Twitter as Your Focus Group

Twitter can be an incredible listening post and gives advertise feedback progressively and it is free. Organizations pay research offices huge totals of money to request their clients conclusions. There were 3.37 million notices of Starbucks

(SBUX – news – individuals) on Twitter through early May 2009 that furnished Starbucks with an abundance of information on how clients see them.

10.   Tweet Something Controversial

It was in certainty part of an incorporated social media and conventional marketing strategy to inspire individuals to break with their present bank and to make buzz about their new focused estimating over a scope of their managing an account products that they were putting forth to the market .

Chapter 22

Hashtags

We're assuming that if you're reading this book about Twitter, you at least know what a hashtag is. However, we won't assume, and don't want you to assume either, that you know the purpose of them or how to use them properly.

As mentioned above, the early followers of my (Sarah's) author account were mostly writers. To find them, I used writing-related hashtags. There is a wonderful community of writers on Twitter you can connect with for empathy and encouragement. Don't expect them to buy your book, though! They're trying to promote their own books. I'd love to help them, too, by buying and reading/reviewing their books, but I simply don't have time right now, so I understand that they probably don't either.

I now know that I need to gain followers who are readers, and fans of the type of book that I write: people in my market. So I've started using a lot of reader hashtags, like #ReadingCommunity, #readers, #reading, #BookLovers, #BookWorm, etc. etc. We've provided a long list below with more. And make sure to be genre-specific with your hashtags. Since I write books about werewolves, I use #werewolf,

#werewolves, #shapeshifters, #FantasyBooks, #Twilight, #TeenWolf, and others like that. You can even get creative and throw in other random/fun words that go along with your genre, like #howl for my books.

Purpose

Hashtags are a way of categorizing your social media content, which makes you more discoverable. There are millions of users of the major social platforms. Inevitably, a lot of content gets lost. Computer algorithms curate the content we see, meaning a lot of it gets potentially overlooked.

This discoverability has a number of underlying purposes:

1.Share your work.

By making a social media post linking to some of your work, and applying a hashtag, you categorize the post. For example, if you linked to your latest young adult dystopian novel as #ya #dystopian, it would help people interested in this genre to discover it.

2.Join an event.

Many events in the writer community have hashtags to go along with them. For example, #PitMad has its own hashtag, and there are many others associated with different writer challenges. By using these hashtags as an author, you gain a sense of participation and can see what others in the challenge are up to.

3.Get connected.

Many users of Twitter follow specific hashtags. They are then presented with a feed of all the content that is relevant. By applying relevant and popular hashtags, you can connect with people who are interested in the same areas of writing as you are, which is how you find your market.

Overall, hashtags are all about sharing and connecting. They help you put yourself and your work out there to kindred spirits who might otherwise never encounter it.

How to use hashtags
With the amount of marketing options available, you should be sure that you're getting the biggest "bang for your buck." Even though using hashtags is free, it's still an investment of your time and energy. Remember, you have limited time and need to prioritize.

Like anything in the world of author marketing, there is a right and a wrong way to use hashtags. If you're interested in adding hashtags to your Twitter marketing, but aren't sure of the best way, here are some of the best practices for authors using hashtags:

1.Don't spam.

Sometimes, you see people stack endless hashtags in a single post, and it's a little cringey. It comes across as desperate and attention-seeking. The key to using hashtags is to restrain yourself! Select a few relevant hashtags for each post. If you need guidance on the right number, get a feel by following different authors you admire and seeing how they do it.

2.Use humor.

There is an art form to humorous hashtags. If you have a comedic side to your personality, don't be afraid to show it. A well-placed sarcastic or ironic hashtag can put a smile on the face of your followers.

3.Provide value.

Don't be the author who shamelessly uses social media and its hashtags for endless self-promotion. Try to provide value with your content. Inform or entertain your followers. Ironically, this is likely to lead to better outcomes in terms of promoting your work!

4.Utilize tools.

Consider using tools, such as HootSuite. They help you to manage your social media presence in an efficient and effective way, and they can stop you from falling into the trap of undisciplined and excessive scrolling through various apps!

You will get a better feel for hashtags as you use them. If you're already an active Twitter or Instagram user, hashtags might already be second nature to you. If they're not, don't worry. Just don't go down the hashtag rabbit hole and get stuck in the trap of finding the best hashtags. Remember, prioritize!

And Just So You Don't Go Down the Rabbit Hole

Our hive queen and assistant extraordinaire, Ali, has already done some hashtag research for writers, and we've included a list of a few that you can start off with. Just don't go overboard and use them all at the same time.

1.Genre-Specific Hashtags

- #SciFi (100 tweets per hour)

- #Fantasy (104 tweets per hour)

- #Romance (133 tweets per hour)

- #Horror (121 tweets per hour)

- #Love (1188 tweets per hour)

- #UrbanFantasy (84 tweets per hour)

2.Writing Process

- #AmEditing (25 tweets per hour)

- #Writing (200 tweets per hour)

- #AmWriting (267 tweets per hour)

- #Creativity (46 tweets per hour)

- #Editing (21 tweets per hour)

- #WordCount (120 tweets per hour)

- #WriteChat (30 tweets per hour)

- #WriteGoal (<100 daily use)

- #WritingPrompt (150 tweets per day)

3.Self-Publishing & Marketing

- #AskAgent (250 tweets in current archive)

- #AskAuthor (<100 daily use)

- #AskEditor (<100 daily use)

- #BookMarketing (190 tweets daily)

- #Publishing (700 tweets in current archive)

- #SelfPub (~100 tweets)

- #PubTip (510 tweets in current archive)

- #MSWL = "manuscript wish list"

4.Creative Ideas

- #WIP = "Work In Progress"

- #1K1H = "Write 1000 Words in 1 Hour"

- #WritingPrompt (150 tweets per day)

- #StoryStarter (daily use, often comedic)

- #WordAThon (daily use)

- #Creativity (60 tweets in the last hour)

5.Connect with Readers

- #MustRead (70 tweets in the last hour)

- #BookGiveaway (daily use, mixture of authors running giveaways and fans saying thanks)

- #FollowFriday (spikes in popularity on Fridays)

- #Novelines (to quote your own work)

- #FreeBook

- #FridayReads

- #TeaserTues

- #Bookish

- #Shelfie

- #ReadMore

6.Connect with Writers

- #AmWriting

- #WriteTip

- #WritersLife

- #WritersLifeChat

- #5amwritersclub

- #WritingCommunity

- #ASMSG (Authors Social Media Support Group)

- #RWA (Romance Writers of America)

- #ACFW (American Christian Fiction Writers)

- #SCBWI (Society of Children's Books Writers and Illustrators)

- #BookMarketingChat

- #TheWritersZen

- #StoryCrafter

Chapter 23

------- ❧❦❧ -------

Tweet effectively

Have you ever sat in a room, with lots of people around you, chattering about different topics? That's exactly what Twitter is like, a cocktail party. All those different conversations can make it hard to focus. At a real-life cocktail party, you can huddle in a corner with one or two people for a minute, then scoot across the room. On Twitter, you can do much the same. Learning the ropes of effective tweeting will enhance the conversations you join in on, and at the same time, give you the knowledge you need to block the distractions you're not interested in.

What to know about tweeting

Twitter can be a fabulous tool, but successfully using this tool is another story. While the learning curve for Twitter isn't steep, it can seem daunting. To get the knack of effective tweeting, you've got to consider:

- Conversing vs. broadcasting.

- How to effectively communicate.

- Twitter-specific jargon and techniques.

- Twitter etiquette.

Broadcasting vs. conversing

Have you thought about the differences between "broadcasting" and "conversing"? You can't broadcast with a telephone, and you can't converse with a megaphone. Knowing the difference is key to your success on Twitter.

Remember that room filled with chatting people? If you stood in the middle of that room and shouted a message that everyone else could hear, that's broadcasting. By contrast, conversing directs your message toward one conversation, and only those folks involved.

Broadcasting

When you're logged into Twitter, you see the question "What are you doing?" above a text box. If you type in your tweet with no preceding characters, and then click "update," you're broadcasting. If you have no followers, you can be assured that nobody is listening—unless someone stumbles across your words in a search.

If you've attracted followers, your broadcasted tweet will go to all of them. Broadcasting is a great way to put a message out there. But you can't broadcast all the time, if you want people to pay attention. Here are some guidelines for when to broadcast:

• When you have something worthwhile to broadcast. This could include things like a contest you're holding, an announcement, or alerting followers to information in your niche.

• When you focus on the specific topic that speaks to your brand. If you're establishing yourself as an expert in a subject, then many of your followers will be following you because of your knowledge.

• When you want to drive traffic elsewhere. Maybe you want people to visit your blog, Facebook page or Web site, or perhaps to a video you've posted to YouTube. Go ahead, shout about it. But make it good.

Conversing

Holding a conversation in Twitter is just as easy as broadcasting, but there's one difference you can see: "@". Remember that text box on your Twitter home page? The one that asks you what you are doing? Instead of typing in your tweet straight, you'll precede it with: "@username."

This focuses your tweet toward that specific person. You're either entering into a conversation that person has started or is involved in, or you're starting a new conversation. Other people can read it, but they know you're talking to @username.

The distinction between broadcasting and conversing is important, even if you're on Twitter mainly for business. In most cases, you want to balance your broadcasts with conversations, so you're viewed as someone both with interesting information to share, and as someone involved and interested in the Twitter community. That's not to say you can't be successful by primarily broadcasting messages. If the type of information you're broadcasting is informative, interesting, and engaging, then you'll do much better than a spammer who repeats the same promotional material time after time.

Before you broadcast a message, ask yourself: "Will this tweet give something of value to my followers, or am I only pimping myself, my company, or my product?" If your followers can glean value from your message, then go ahead and broadcast it. But remember, if you get repetitive and tiresome, your followers will lose interest and leave.

Tweet with impact

Communicating on Twitter is a skill you must develop and polish. Here are some tips on tweeting with maximum impact:

• 	Don't be vague. Every tweet you write should have a focus. Use that limit of 140 characters to sharpen your mind and message. Being too vague creates confusion, especially within a series of replies. When replying to another tweet, in addition to using the "@" symbol, include a reminder of the tweet you're responding to.

• Keywords are good. Pack your tweets with keywords, and you needn't worry about being vague. Your followers will get your point, and new followers will easily find you. Win, win.

• Be interesting. Sounds obvious, but requires effort. Even mundane tweets can be spiced up with a little thought. And you needn't be clever, humorous, witty, and unique—you just need to look that way.

• Share information. Instead of just answering the "What are you doing?" question, think of more questions:

What are you thinking?

What do you want to do?

What is the funniest/scariest/coolest thing you've seen/read/heard lately?

What has you excited (or any other emotion) right now?

What are you most looking forward to?

What was the best thing about your day?

What's your biggest pain in the butt?

Mix it up. Have fun.

• Be interactive. Take the time to interact with other tweeters, even just a few times a week. Remember, it's not all about you, you, you. What people really care about is them. So make it about them sometimes.

When you deliver great content combined while interacting with the Twitter community, you'll find your Twittering gets plenty of results.

Understanding Twitter's secret codes

Every club has its own lingo. Here's a quick guide to what you need to know for Twitter:

• Reply (@): To direct a conversation toward a specific user, or to continue an existing conversation with a specific user, you start your tweet with "@username." The Web-based interface, as well as nearly every Twitter application, has a reply icon you can click to automatically add the prefix. Without the prefix, you're broadcasting, which doesn't work all that well if you're trying to continue a conversation with a specific Twitterer.

• Direct Message (DM). The letters "DM" refer to a "direct message." Basically, a DM is a private message that only the sender and recipient can see. To send a direct message to another user, you'll use the prefix "d" followed by the receiver's username. If a subject isn't meant for public consumption, or if you and the other person have sent several replies back and forth, moving to direct messages make sense.

• Retweet (RT): A retweet is simply repeating a tweet already sent. You can retweet anyone you like, or even yourself (sparingly, please). When retweeting, it's good form to leave the original tweeter's username and exact words intact. The great thing about retweeting is it allows you and others to share knowledge, and creates more exposure for both the original tweeter and the person retweeting. You can retweet a message simply by copying and pasting it, adding "RT @username." Many Twitter tools have a "retweet" button, making it quicker and easier.

• Hashtag (#): Hashtags allow any user to create a categorization of tweets that then can be found through a search function. To create a hashtag, use the prefix "#" before the keyword term for which you want to create a category. Then folks can contribute their own tweets to the same hashtag. Later, people can use the "#keyword" in search functions to find all tweets associated with it. To learn more about hashtags: http://twitter.pbworks.com/Hashtags.

Twitter etiquette. Really?

Although Emily Post hasn't published a Twitter guide, there are several unwritten rules. Stuff that's good to know:

1.	Twitter is a conversation. Ask questions, contribute interesting information, and have fun.

2.   Don't be creepy. Don't be too familiar with folks you don't know.

3.   It's quality, not quantity. A few good tweets go a long way.

4.   Use good grammar when you can. Sure, lots of folks substitute 4 for for and 2 for to. But people can only stomach so many shortcuts. If you can't say it in 140 characters, rethink your tweet.

5.   Be discreet. If you wouldn't say something to someone's face, don't say it on Twitter.

6.   When someone follows you, follow them. If later you find they're not supplying valuable information, you can unfollow them.

7.   Don't be slanderous, rude, or cruel. It's unattractive, and you could get yourself in trouble, too.

Chapter 24

------- ❧❦❧ -------

Twitter marketing

Twitter is a pretty powerful platform for marketing, and a lot of inbound and content marketing is supported with the help of Twitter. People like to share that sort of stuff with others, which makes Twitter ideal for marketing. But Twitter or no Twitter, marketing is hard. Good marketing requires a lot of effort. To generate solid leads and build up your brand with Twitter, you need to do much more than just fill out your bio and send Tweets every once in a while. You have to take pains to grow your audience and turn Twitter into an actual lead generation tool.

Just talking about an occasional product release and upcoming events isn't enough. You have to really connect with your audience and engage them in meaningful dialog. That's how you will harness the full power of Twitter marketing. You will definitely unlock new opportunities for your business if you learn to use Twitter like a pro.

What makes twitter different?

Every social media platform has a different core experience, and that's why your approach to each one of them should be different too. You can't use the same marketing strategy on Twitter that you're using on Facebook or Pinterest. You will have to understand how Twitter works and how you can take advantage of its landscape to help you sell your product or service.

Here are some of the most popular ways most businesses use Twitter:

- Sharing useful content and information

- Interacting with customers

- Driving promotional activities by engaging people

- Branding and networking

- Reputation management

- Grievance addressal

Most of these activities deal with interaction. If you don't interact with your customers, you won't be able to propagate and expand your brand. Unlike Instagram or Pinterest, you can't just sit and broadcast your content. As we continue to learn more about Twitter marketing, keep in mind that interaction is the most important thing about Twitter.

Once you have set up your profile right and followed some influencers, it's time to jump into action and take some concrete steps to execute your marketing strategies.

Twitter chats: the growing market

When Twitter first came about, people kept asking how to get more followers for years. But now, it's evident that just having followers is useless. Having active followers is much more important. So the question you should be asking yourself is this: How do I get more active followers? And the answer to that is Twitter chats. Slowly but steadily, marketers are realizing the power of chats in the pursuit of gaining active followers.

Twitter chats are effective because only those people engage in chats that are active on the network. People who use Twitter chat use it to actually interact with people and not just share and consume content. When you interact with such people, they will respond to your tweets, retweet your content, and even amplify your messages.

You can easily look for and find chats in your niche. Content marketing, social media and business are some of the hot topics that have a lot of active chats around them. You can also use Google to search for chats that may interest you. If you can't find any chat for your industry, you can simply start your own! The most important thing after joining a chat is to be more than a spectator. So interact with people and add value to the conversation to get yourself noticed. Think of better and more creative ways to share your thoughts, like images and beautiful graphics instead of plain text. Canva can help you create great graphics for Twitter in just minutes.

Respond to other people chatting in the conversation, and make sure you use the @mention to let them know you've replied to them. It's a great way to build connections on Twitter and get people to follow you. Another thing you can do is create lists for the chats you take part in. Add people you interact with to each chat-specific list, and then start going through their tweets, responding and retweeting the content you like. It's important that you don't let the connections fade away once the chat is over. Keep them alive!

Plan ahead

Think about any important upcoming events or festivals, and create special Tweets for those occasions. It is important that you do so because your customers like it. For example, before Halloween, you should start tweeting about Halloween related things, things that tie it to your industry in a way beneficial to you. It goes for things like Christmas and Thanksgiving. Always plan ahead for holidays and special events so you can take advantage of the hashtags that could be trending at that time.

You can, and probably should, use a tool to help you remember and plan for upcoming events. Get ready with a campaign for any event at least two weeks before it begins. Twitter has its own native tool for this very purpose, called the

OwnTheMoment planner. It gives you details on upcoming events and even ideas for potential tweets. How sweet is that?

As the day of the event starts getting closer, start tweeting about it with your already prepared tweets and make sure to use the trending hashtags. It will help you reach more people and engage in real-time marketing. People will be engaging with you more and you will create a momentum for your brand.

Make tweets conversational

Most brands tweet in a very one-dimensional and bland manner, and consequently, they fail to engage their audience. Don't fall in the trap of sending of broadcast-like tweets all the time, because it won't do your business any good. Headlines, inspirational quotes and funny statements are cool, but not all the time. They should invite people to talk to you, not discourage them. Gary Vaynerchuk is one guy you should learn from if you want to know what conversational tweets look like. Ramit Sethi is another great example, and you will find that most of his tweets are actually replies to other people, not broadcasts. This is how successful Twitter marketers build their audience.

So make sure you execute a smooth and efficient marketing strategy by actually interacting with people. Take a marketing approach similar to these guys and concentrate on conversation, not broadcasting. Here are some tips to help you:

• Every once in a while, tweet out questions that you'd like your followers to answer.

• Make sure at least one-third of your tweets are replies to other people.

• When sharing links, don't just add a generic headline to them all the time. Try adding a short insight or quote or even a sentence from the original post you're sharing. This attracts attention and sparks conversation.

• When sharing your own blog posts, infographics or other similar content, try to make it interesting. Instead of tweeting something in the format of "Title, <link>", try talking directly to your audience. Use something like "Hey, what do you guys think of this new article? Title, <link>"

Being conversational leads to more engagement with your tweets, and thus, helps in reaching more people.

Create a tweeting strategy/schedule

If you regularly do your research and keep careful watch on your analytics, you should know what times are most suitable for what types of tweets. You should maintain a tweeting schedule for this very purpose, so that you can engage people in the right kind of tweets at the right time. Make a detailed plan of what you're going to tweet at what time.

This should be a part of your content strategy on the whole, especially if you tend to publish content across multiple platforms. For a marketer, one channel is not enough. So you need to use multiple channels. Most successful ones have a blog, a podcast, a YouTube channel, email campaigns, and more. Guest blogging and media coverage is another great way to get exposure, so you should have a sound tweeting strategy in place. It will help you keep your tweets varied and interesting, and will also make sure you don't miss out anything. Whenever something new is published, you will share it for sure.

Another problem you will avoid with this strategy is only tweeting once about your posts. It's a common practice among people, but it gets worse on Twitter. And because of Twitter's poor signal-to-noise ratio, the probability of many people seeing your tweet is very low. So you have to tweet about your content multiple times. Some management tools have inbuilt options to deal with this problem, like Sprout Social. It will help you choose the most optimal times to share things with the help of its ViralPost feature. It's very quick and easy to use, and it will definitely help you boost engagement on your posts.

Set goals and milestones

This is one of those crucial tips that often gets lost or glossed over in a host of marketing advice online. Without measurable goals and key performance indicators, your marketing strategy is incomplete. It is extremely important for you to have attainable goals and objectives for your marketing strategy. If you don't, you will keep making the same mistakes without learning from them. Small businesses often fall in this trap and then wonder what's not working right for them. Don't be one of them.

You won't believe that more than 40% of businesses have no idea whether their social media efforts are effective or not. This is because most of them don't keep track of their activities or decide concrete goals for their strategy. Instead, they just keep publishing content in the hopes of a miracle. Great content is important, sure. But what's more important is how it's served to people and tracking how they respond to it. The "publish and pray" approach is absolute rubbish and you must stay away from it at all times. Take time to create some objectives and goals for your Twitter marketing strategy.

Start with simpler goals like these:

• Improve brand reputation and build an engaged following

• Respond to customer grievances in a speedy manner

• Generate leads

- Generate more traffic for your website

- Connect with influencers and bloggers

Once you've done that successfully, you can move on to more concrete objectives, like:

- Maintain a steady response rate of at least 90%

- Respond to all tweets in under 15 minutes

- Increase retweets by 10%

- Generate a minimum of 15 leads per week

- Increase referral traffic by at least 20%

Remember to always keep a deadline for all your goals. Without a set deadline, you'll just keep dillydallying. So make sure you keep weekly, monthly, or quarterly deadlines, whatever works for you. Use Google Analytics and social media management tools to track your progress.

Following these tips will definitely help you reach your goals and go beyond them. Remember to engage others and stay conversational.

Chapter 25

------- ❧❧❧ -------

How to identify influencers for your targeted market

You can't build real influence unless you are a part of an influential community. If you are a celebrity in real life, you are already a part of such a community.

But if you are an average Joe and want to build your influence on Twitter from the ground up, it will be very difficult to accomplish if you are alone.

You definitely need to attract the attention of the industry thought leaders and influencers.

The good news - it's not an impossible thing to do. And when you successfully engage Twitter influencers, you can get a lot of exposure for your brand, more new followers, and traffic to the website of your choice.

How do you know that the person is a real influencer rather than just an average Twitter user?

The obvious step would be to look at the number of followers, but follower count doesn't tell the whole story.

Some people buy fake followers just to inflate the numbers, though it's a horrible idea. They are not only useless, but actually quite harmful. You can't formulate any solid Twitter marketing strategy if a significant percentage of your accounts are fake. Plus, it's very easy for people to find out if your followers are fake, so it's a bad move reputation-wise too.

A big following by itself is not a sufficient parameter for identifying influential networkers. Influence is also measured by the quality and quantity of responses triggered as a result of calls to actions executed by an influencer.

You need to find Twitter users whose tweets are frequently re-tweeted, have impressive reach and whose opinion matters.

Twitter Directories

As you remember, I recommended you register your Twitter account with different Twitter directories. Guess what, millions upon millions of others use this method, and it's an easy way to find influencers for any topic.

Brainstorm the list of keywords that are most important for your industry, see who shows up on the first page, and use them as seed influencers. By "seed" I mean that you can build an initial list of influencers this way, and then use those accounts to find other candidates.

Twitter Lists

The first step to finding other influencers is to research public Twitter lists created by seed influencers. Most influencers have different lists – look for lists containing your main keyword, plus a variation of the words "gurus, masters, professionals, Top", etc.

After you've found the right list, copy its members, and see the lists created by them, etc.

Topsy

Topsy can be used not only to find the most popular content for your keywords, but also to find topic influencers. Just enter your main keyword in a search and then click on "influencers".

TweetReach

While a free version is limited to the last 50 tweets for a hashtag or keyword, it's still pretty useful to get an idea about accounts that get the most re-tweets, the highest reach, etc.

Granted, the time span for 50 tweets usually lasts only a few minutes, so you are not getting the most influential accounts for a hashtag, rather the accounts that had the most influence during those minutes.

They also have a paid version that provides more intel.

Hashtagify

You can go there, enter a hashtag and see the top 5-10 tweeps who are considered the most influential for this topic.

BuzzSumo

Another good tool to find top influencers in your niche. The paid version has a lot of bells and whistles, but even as a free visitor you can see the best performing content for the keyword of your choice, as well as a few top influencers, bloggers and journalists.

Social Mention

This tool allows you to search over 100 social networks and blogs for influencers of your topic. It's a bit less useful for Twitter marketing since the search can be filtered by "microblogs", but not by Twitter. Usually Facebook posts come up more often. It's still helpful if you want to find the influencers regardless of platform.

Social Bro

Social Bro provides real-time analytics to pinpoint tweeps who have been active in the last five minutes. You will have much higher engagement when you send questions and replies to recently active people.

This tool is most useful when you already have a following.

You can quickly see your top influencers and famous social friends.

How to engage influencers and skyrocket your influence

now that you know how to find those influential people, the only question remains: "How to engage them?"

How do you draw the attention of somebody who has thousands upon thousands of followers and is bombarded each minute with replies and requests to re-tweet?

First of all, I don't recommend you actively engage with the influencer until you have at least a few thousand followers. Whether you like it or not, the harsh truth is that most influencers wouldn't bother to reply, let alone engage with you otherwise.

While you're working on that initial following, create a list of tweeps you want to build a relationship with and passively engage with at least 10 of them each week.

Passive engagement is the key. Initially you don't use reply to ask questions, and you especially don't ask for any favors. At this stage you have zero chance to get a positive response to your requests. You will only annoy the influencer, which is not a good start.

The first step is to get noticed. Re-tweet and favorite the influencer's content, recommend him/her to your followers or #FF (one of but a few cases when you are allowed to use a reply during a passive stage), participate in the same twitter chats as the influencer. In chats, ask smart questions, provide thoughtful answers, and be generally helpful.

Add him/her to your list, and follow the discussions. When an influencer asks for help – for example, to participate in a survey, to re-tweet something, etc, - respond.

Here is another method of semi-passive engagement: attach meaningful pictures to your tweets and try to tag influencers in them.

Depending on the privacy settings set by an influencer for picture tags, you might or might not be able to do that. If an influencer's photo tagging is set to "anyone", you are in luck.

If you succeed, the influencer gets notification that s/he was tagged and they potentially could check your profile. Of course, if an influencer doesn't follow you, and his/her setting is set to "off" or to "people I follow can tag me", then this method won't work.

After you passively engage for a while, chances are that an influencer will respond to you in a chat, follow back or otherwise acknowledge your attempts to communicate.

Congratulations! Now you can proceed to a second step.

The second Step is to start actively communicating with the influencer. At this stage you can start using direct replies to comment on the influencer's tweets, ask questions, compliment on a webinar/ speaker gig, congratulate on being featured in the news, etc.

Don't forget to continue Rt-ing, recommending to #FolowFriday, etc.

The third Step – ask for a favor, but the one that will benefit the influencer too. The law of reciprocity works. The overwhelming majority of people want to do something good for those who repeatedly do something good for them.

So after a while you can approach several influencers, inform them that you're doing an article/report, and ask for a tweetable tip. Let them know that the tip will be published on your blog, will include a link (either to their Twitter profiles or blogs), and that you will be actively promoting this article.

Of course, not all influencers will respond, but those who do respond will be more inclined to tweet about your article when it's ready.

Here is a real tweet from one of my followers who approached me after taking time building a relationship.

"We're compiling a list of Mobile Marketing Tips from THE BEST in the biz. Do you have a tweetable tip we can add?"

I responded, and then re-tweeted the article to my 70,000+ followers

Feel free to use this as a template for approaching influencers:

"We're compiling/creating/writing a list/blog/article of "Your Industry" Tips from THE BEST in the biz. Do you have a tweetable tip we can add?"

The fourth Step: relationship building is a never-ending process...

Continue the engagement. There is a good chance that your relationship will grow and the influencer will begin re-tweeting some of your tweets too.

I feel obligated to re-tweet the tweets from some of my best followers from time to time even though they might not be influencers...

Of course, you never should re-tweet just because you're grateful. Only re-tweet high quality content. This is (or at least should be) your unspoken obligation to followers.

So now you have it - the Influencer-relationship-building blueprint:

1) Get noticed through passive engagement

2) Start active (but selfless) communications

3) Ask for a favor that would benefit you as well as the influencer

4) Continue building a relationship

You shouldn't expect that this blueprint will help you to establish contact, let alone build a relationship with every influencer you decide to approach. Some will respond, others won't. Don't be discouraged. It's a numbers game. The more influencers you engage the newer interesting social friends you will obtain.

While it's great to have many influencers re-tweet the content of your choice, it's not an ultimate goal. The ultimate goal is to move the relationship beyond virtual reality: to find a way to collaborate with each other in real life, build business partnerships, participate in professional gigs, form joint ventures, and maybe even become friends.

Friendship and a real-life relationship far outweighs all the benefits of any re-tweet.

Chapter 26

— — — — — ✥✥✥✥ — — — — —

Engaging with your twitter audience

Building a network and expanding it is the most challenging part of marketing on Twitter. It doesn't happen easily. You need to spend a lot of time to achieve it. First, you need to follow the right people and then you need to get them to follow you.

Following the right people

By following the right people, you can view their in your own Twitter streams. This way you learn about them, what they like, what they do, type of links they share, people they interact etc. We need to get the right people to follow. Some tips to achieve it are:

Use the 'who to follow' feature in Twitter: You need to follow people that matter to or are relevant to your business. Please click on the 'who to follow' link at the top right hand corner of your Twitter toolbar. You may choose some of the highlighted topics and/or use your own keywords and start following relevant people. You can search people by their interests, hashtags, etc.

Twitter People Search: It is a great place to search people on Twitter. Twitter searches the real names that people enter when creating accounts. But this may not necessarily the best place to search Twitter for people because we can never be sure that people have put in their real names.

Third party directories like Twellow, WeFollow, Just Tweet it, and many more are available that search for people by their interests, hashtags and many more parameters.

Apps that recommend people to follow based on the people you follow like Twubble, Twitterel, Mr Tweet, etc are great options. These work like matching service. They match other users with the people you follow and recommend other people you can consider following.

It is impossible to create an exhaustive list because new ones are coming up by the day and old ones are disappearing. Simply open Google or any search engine and type in "search Twitter by 'category you want to search by' (like interests, hashtags, location, etc)" and you would find dozens of websites or apps to search Twitter.

Remember, it is important not to follow too many people at once. Ideally, we should follow not more than 20 to 25 people in a day because you need to give people time to follow you back. For instance, if you follow 1000 people in a day and only 20 of them follow you back, it shows you in poor light in Twitter.

Getting people to follow you

Let me share some simple tips to gain followers:

➤ Make your business's name easy to find and follow. For instance, create a page that lists your personal Twitter handle and those of your employees. This way, you give people an opportunity to interact with employees associated with your company. It gives people an insight into your brand and your people. People will relate more to your business.

➤ Place follow buttons on all the pages of your business website, blogs, and other promotions. That makes it easy for people to find and follow your business.

➤ Make your tweets useful for people. People will follow your business if they get value from your tweets. Think about what useful information you can add. The logic is simple. You would not subscribe to a newsletter if you do not derive value from it, would you?

➤ Interact with people you follow but don't follow you back. The key here is to give compliments and feedback to give them reasons to follow you back.

➤ Reward people to follow you or retweet your tweets with a discount at your store or a discount on your services as appropriate. This way, you end up sell your product as well as increase followers.

Tweet something shareable

People tend to share tweets that are useful to them, solve their problems, answers questions they might have, humorous tweets. On Twitter, most retweeted tweets are those that have links, photos, videos, or quotes. Interesting tweets you make have the potential to travel to many potential customers. Some examples are:

➢ Include a photo. A tweet with a descriptive photo can say a thousand words, and probably more. It can mean different things to different people. The possibilities are boundless.

➢ Pose a question through your tweet and answer it using a link. For example, if you are a solar power equipment manufacturer, you may post a tweet "How to reduce your energy bills?" and then answer it with a link to your blog post on solar power for homes.

Or,

If you a car showroom, tweet "which is the best family car?" and answer with a link to a blog post that lists the features of your top selling family sedan.

➢ Share videos on Twitter. Videos are great ways of telling things. A simple 1 minute long video can tell your audience things worth a thousand tweets. As a marketer however, there are certain things you need to keep in mind when you promote videos using twitter:

1.   Twitter doesn't host videos but allow users to link to videos hosted on other websites. These videos then appear as embedded videos that can be played within the tweet.

2.   Instead of embedding one of your existing videos, create a custom video for twitter. Keep in mind that videos embedded on tweets can only be watched on a small 435x244 player. Make sure that the video is watchable on that scale.

3.   Twitter is a microblogging site and viewers have very small attention spans. Keep the videos short. Preferably within 30 seconds.

4.   Tweet your videos as many times each day as possible. Followers would only re tweet recent videos. No one re tweets items that are more than a day old.

➤   Share a quote. Quotations are great ways to engage people. Quotes more often than not encourage retweets and are seen by audiences as useful or entertaining.

➤   Work with others. When Arlington and San Francisco hosted the 2010 World Series, the fans from both cities created a storm on Twitter. The major museums of the two cities also joined the party. Museum of Modern Art San Francisco, challenged Kimbell Art Museum Fort Worth to a tweet-off. The tweet off that followed turned out to be a great burst of publicity for both the museums as the fans of both the teams also loved this tweet off and joined it.

Chapter 27

— — — — — ❦❧ — — — — —

Building your brand with twitter

YOUR MAIN AIM through this whole process is going to be to connect, capture, and convert your prospects through your website or blog, Twitter, and through other social networks, and this involves the following:

•   Connect: Your product needs to be the connection between your prospect and what they need so the first thing you need to do is connect those two things. In order to do this you need to identify who they are, find them out of all the millions of people on the Internet, and then connect with them by offering them something they want or need.

•   Capture: Once you have found them you need to capture them on your website, blog, Twitter, or any other social media platforms. This is so you can continue your relationship with them either by email or through Twitter and communicate your brand message. To do this you need to offer them some sort of incentive so you can capture their name and email address.

•   Convert: When you have captured your prospect you need to convert them into a paying customer by nurturing them and continuing to build a relationship by offering them the content they want through email and Twitter and then moving them toward signing up for a special or exclusive offer.

To achieve this successfully you are going to need to have a well-defined brand, and that brand needs to be communicated through everything you do or say through Twitter, your website, blog, and your email campaign.

Whether you are a one person small business, a large corporation, or an organization, your brand is one of the most important attributes of your business. Your brand is what you want your prospects and customers to respect, trust, and fall in love with so they will buy and continue to buy your products and services. Your brand is what is going to set you apart from any other business and what will give your business the competitive edge.

Never has there been a better time for your business to build your brand and communicate your brand message to your target audience than through Twitter. Your brand is the main ingredient for success, and Twitter is giving you the channel to communicate it. You can literally communicate with your audience every day. If you get it right and connect the right brand experience with the right target audience, you are onto an all-around winner.

It may be that you have a well-established brand already or maybe you have not created your brand yet or it just needs some tweaking or fine tuning. Maybe you are not exactly sure what your brand is, or you feel it needs a complete overhaul. Whatever your situation is, you need to know that your brand is going to underpin your whole Twitter campaign, and it needs to be strong, clear, well-defined, and consistent. Once defined, your business is going to create it, be it, communicate it, display it, picture it, speak it, promote it, and most of all, be true to it. This chapter is going to take you through everything you need know and do to define and create your brand so you can get into the hearts and minds of your target audience by communicating the right message and brand experience.

There are many definitions of the word brand but this is the one I like best because it incorporates pretty much all the necessary information you will need to help you to define your own brand.

Brand, the definition

Your brand is more than a name, symbol, or logo. It is your commitment and your promise to your customer. Your brand is the defined personality of either yourself as an individual brand or your product, service, company, or organization. It's what sets you apart and differentiates your business from your competition and any other business.

Why is your brand so important to your business?

Branding is important because it helps you and your business build and create powerful and lasting relationships by communicating everything you want to say about your product or service to your prospects and customers. A strong brand encourages loyalty and will ultimately create a strong customer base and increase your sales by doing the following:

• Demonstrating to your prospects and customers that you are professional and committed to offering them what you promise

• Making your business easily recognizable

• Creating a clear distinction from your competition

• Making your business memorable

• Creating an emotional attachment with your audience

• Helping to create trust

• Helping to build customer loyalty and repeat custom

• Creating a valuable asset which will be financially beneficial if you sell your business

• Creating a competitive advantage

Your Vision/Your Story

If you want to create a strong brand, one of the first things you need to do is create a clear visual picture of how you see your business now and in the future. This is about daring to see what your business could be without constraints or limitations.

This exercise will not only help you work out what you want to achieve financially and creatively, but it also makes you focus on what really matters and will help you create your own unique voice and story. This is incredibly important when it comes to your branding as this is what is going to make your business stand out from others and give you that edge.

To do this, you need to get away from all distractions and think about how you would like to see your business grow and develop in the next three years. This is more than just putting a mission statement together. This is about your core business beliefs, why you are doing it, what you want your business to be, and how you want to be perceived in your market. To help you do this you will need to ask yourself the following questions and record your answers:

• Why did you originally start your business or why are you starting a business?

• How did your original business idea come about?

• What changes are you looking to make in peoples' lives?

• What are you hoping to achieve?

• What aspects of your business are really important to you?

- What are your hopes and dreams?

- What is your definition of success?

- What sort of turnover and income defines that success?

- How many employees does your business have?

- Why are you in business?

- What are your core values in your business?

- What impact do you want to have?

- What influence do you want to have?

- What sort of things do you want the media to be saying about you?

- What do you want your customers to be saying about you?

- How you want to be portrayed on social media?

- How many Twitter followers do you want?

- What markets are you in? Are you local, national, or international?

Once you have completed this exercise, you will have all the material you need so that you can create the unique experience required to make your business stand out from all the others in your niche. This is the first step toward creating a brand for your business. This is the beginning of your story.

Defining Your Brand

Whether you are responsible for defining, creating, and developing your brand in-house or you are employing a local branding and marketing agency, you will need to carry out an analysis of your business to define your brand. Completing the following exercise will help you define and clarify your brand:

• A factual description of what your business is and the purpose of your business

• Describe your product or service in one sentence

• List all your products and/or services.

• What are the benefits and features of all of your products?

• Which are your most profitable products/services?

• Which are your most popular products/services?

• Who are your ideal customers for each of your products or services? (Consumer or business, age, gender, income, occupation, education, stage in family life cycle.)

• Out of these customers, which ones who are most likely to buy your most profitable products?

• Is the market and demand large enough to provide you with the number of customers you need to buy your most profitable products and achieve your financial goals?

- If your answer to the previous question is no then ask yourself the same question for each of your other products.

- Who are your three main competitors? (Have a look at their Twitter profile account.)

- What distinguishes your business from your competition? What special thing are you bringing to the market that is of real value? What is your unique selling point? What solutions are your products offering your customers that will meet their needs or solve their problems?

- If you are already in business, write down what your customers are already saying about your business. What do you think they would say about how your product or service makes them feel emotionally? (You may need to ask your customers if you do not already know.) What qualities and words would you use to describe the personality of your business as it is now? Here are some examples of words you may wish to use: high cost, low cost, high quality, value for money, expensive, cheap, excellent customer service, friendly, professional, happy, serious, innovative, eccentric, quiet, loud, beautiful, relaxing, motivating, sincere, adventurous, amusing, charming, decisive, kind, imaginative, proactive, intuitive, loving, trustworthy, extrovert, vibrant, transparent, intelligent, creative, dynamic, resourceful.

- Now, whether you are already in business or starting out, write down all the words to describe how you want and need your brand to be perceived and what qualities you want to be associated with your brand in order to match the needs and expectations of your ideal customers. If you are already in business, hopefully this will be exactly the same as how you perceive you are at the current time.

• What is the evidence that backs up what you have said about your brand? This could be customer testimonials or any evidence about product or service quality.

• What is the biggest opportunity for your business right now?

• What products are you thinking of introducing in the near future?

How To Get Into The Hearts And Minds Of Your Target Audience

Your target audience is your most important commodity, as they are the future customers and ambassadors of your business. Every single one of them is valuable, and every single one of them can make a difference to your business. This can be because they are actually going to buy your products or simply spread the word by interacting with you on Twitter.

However, it's a big social world out there. The possibilities of finding new people are limitless, but targeting everyone is not the solution. The biggest mistake you can make is trying to reach everyone and then not appealing to anyone. Your first step is to identify exactly who the people are who are going to be interested in your products or services, and then you need to find out everything about them. You need to get inside their heads and work out what motivates these people, what their needs, hopes, aspirations, fears, and dreams are. Your product or service is the link between them and what they want. When you know this you can tailor every single message or piece of content toward them.

When you know exactly who your ideal customers are, Twitter offers you the opportunity to go find and reach them. It's then up to you to capture them so you can continue to communicate. When you know everything about your customers you are more likely to speak the right language to be able to communicate with them and build trust to the point where the next natural progression is for them to buy your product.

It's only when you truly understand your audience that you can start converting them into customers. Once you know you are targeting the right audience, you can confidently focus every ounce of your effort creating exactly the right content, nurturing them, engaging with them, and looking after them. It's only a matter of time before they will buy your product.

Creating your ideal customer persona or avatar

Once you have done this exercise you are going to own some very powerful information. If you do not do this exercise it is very unlikely that you are going to be able to truly connect with your target audience in the way that is necessary to build trust so that you can ultimately convert them into your customers.

Your answers to the questions in the previous section will have given you a clear idea of which types of customers you need to target to give you the best chance of achieving your financial goals. You now need to find out everything about them so you can get your brand into their hearts and minds. The best way to do this is to create an imaginary persona or avatar of your ideal customer and you can build this picture by finding out the following:

•   Describe your ideal customer and include the following details: are they a consumer or in business, their age, gender, income, occupation, education, and stage in family life cycle.

•   Where do they live?

•   What do they want most of all?

•   What are their core values?

•   What is their preferred lifestyle?

•   What do they do on a day-to-day basis?

•   What are their hopes and aspirations?

•   What important truth matters to them?

•   What motivates and inspires them?

- What sort of routines do they have?

- What are their day-to-day priorities?

- How do they have fun?

- What do they do in their spare time?

- What subjects are they interested in?

- Which books do they read?

- Which TV programs do they watch?

- What magazines do they read?

- Who do they follow on social media?

- Who are their role models?

- What really makes them tick?

- What are their fears and frustrations?

- What are their suspicions?

- What are their insecurities?

- What are their typical worries?

- What is the perfect solution to their worries?

- What are their dreams?

- What do they need to make them feel happy and fulfilled?

Big Questions

To answer the following questions you will need to step inside your ideal customer's mind and imagine you are them.

•　　　　How do you feel when you find your product or service? What is your initial emotional reaction?

•　　　　What are the words that go through your head?

•　　　　How can I justify buying this product for myself?

•　　　　Are you ready to buy immediately?

•　　　　Do you have any suspicions that the product may not be what it says?

•　　　　What are those suspicions? Why do you have them?

•　　　　Do you need more convincing?

•　　　　What do you need to convince you that the product is right for you?

•　　　　What do you feel when you have the product in your hand?

It's only when you have imagined yourself in the hearts and minds of your target audience that you are going to be able to connect with them on any emotional level. With the information from the above exercise, you will have everything you need to produce exactly the right content to match the needs, desires, and expectations of your ideal customer so that you can create the right brand experience and sell your products. This information is like gold.

Communicating Your Brand

Once you have gone through all the processes outlined in this chapter you will have a clear idea about what your brand is, what is stands for, and how you stand out from similar businesses. You now have to work out how to best communicate this to your ideal customer so that when they hear or see your brand name they immediately make that essential emotional connection. This is what is going to make them eventually love your brand above all others.

When you are clear about what your brand is, what it stands for, and how you are going to stand out from other similar businesses, you then need to work out how you can communicate this message in the best possible way. Your main aim here is to create an emotional connection with your target audience that is going to help them grow to love your brand, remember your brand, and remain loyal to it. To do this you need to communicate your brand story through every aspect of your business, including your social media campaign.

With the information you now have you are armed with everything you need to create a consistent brand. If you have not already done so, you can either hand all this information over to a marketing agency or use it yourself to create all the following:

•   Your logo: Your logo will give a clear guideline for all your promotional material, including your website or blog, stationery, templates, or any marketing material that needs to be created for online or offline promotion.

•   Your brand message: This is the main message you want to communicate about your brand.

•   Your tagline: A short, memorable statement about your brand that captures the personality of your brand and communicates how you or your product will benefit your customer.

•   All your 'about' descriptions: You can communicate your brand story through all your 'about' sections on all your social media platforms you are using.

•   The content you create for your business: Every piece of content you create for your business needs to be tailor-made for your target audience. You will need to pick who and what subjects or topics you want to be associated with your brand, as anything you pick to write about will be a representation of your brand.

•   Your website and/or blog: The 'about' page of your website is probably the most visited page on any website and there is a reason for this. People want to find out about your business and what is different or special about it. This is a great place to introduce and expand on the story of your brand. This is where you can really go to town and communicate your beliefs and uniqueness.. Also, the visual style of your website or blog and your individual voice should be evident throughout your site and be consistent with your brand.

•   Video content: Videos are an incredibly powerful way of creating a personal connection with your audience. Make sure that whatever video content you produce and whatever you say is always consistent with your brand.

Chapter 28

— — — — — ❧❦❧❦ — — — — —

Preparing your business for success

WHETHER YOUR SITE is being found through an organic search, an advertising campaign, Twitter, or any other social media platform, all your hard work is going to be wasted unless you have put a system in place to capture leads and convert them into customers. This system has to start from the moment your prospect either hits your website, your blog, or your Twitter profile, and your ultimate goal is to convert your browsers into buyers.

Firstly, the unfortunate fact is that the majority of your website visitors are unlikely to buy from you on their first visit. If you do not have a website that grabs their attention within the first couple of seconds, they will move very quickly onto another site. Secondly, even if your site does catch their eye, they are still likely to check out other sites and still may not return. To make any kind of impact at all your site needs to grab their attention and then capture their email address so you can continue your relationship with them through email. This chapter is going to take you through steps you will need to take, from getting your website or blog ready to setting up and creating your email campaign.

Email is still one of the most powerful ways to convert prospects into customers and has a conversion rate three times higher than social media conversion rates. That is not to say that your Twitter campaign is any less important, as this is where you are going to find and nurture your leads and transfer them to your opt-in by either capturing them on Twitter or on your website or blog. This chapter is going to take you through steps you will need to take from getting your website or blog ready to setting up and creating your email campaign.

Preparing Your Website For Success

Whether you already have a website or blog or you are creating a new site from scratch, you need to make sure it has the necessary features to grab the attention of your target audience and capture their email addresses. Capturing the email addresses of your target audience has to be one of your most important goals when creating your website. Once your prospects have voluntarily submitted their email address, you have the opportunity to build a relationship, communicate your message, and promote your products and services on an ongoing and regular basis. A well thought-out and crafted email campaign can immediately establish trust and favor with your subscribers. Don't forget that it is you who owns your opt-in list and nobody can take it away from you. As long as you are providing your subscribers value with great content, they are likely to want to keep hearing from you. Remember you cannot rely on social media to continue your relationship as these platforms are changing all the time. You need to build your email list.

Once you have completed the exercise in the branding section and have your ideal customer persona or avatar, you will have a clear picture of what your target audience's pain point or problem is and how your product can help solve it or make their life better in some way. If you have a blog, and most businesses today need a blog, you will also have all the tools you need to create the right content to attract your target audience. Armed with this information you are halfway ready to putting a system in place, so your products sell themselves and your website is working like an extra sales person selling your products 24/7.

When your visitor arrives at your site, you have only three seconds to grab their attention. You need to connect emotionally with them and let them know immediately that they have arrived at the right place by communicating exactly how you are going to help them and what it is you are offering them.

Once they are on your site, you then need to win their interest and confidence so that they will voluntarily submit their email address. To do this you will need to create a lead magnet and offer your audience something which is incredibly valuable to them for free. There are numerous ways you can do this and which one you use will depend very much on what type of business you are and what your goals are. If you are a business offering technical solutions, you could offer them a free trial. If you are offering information, you could offer them a free report, a short video training series, or an ebook. If you are selling some kind of product or service, you could offer them a money-off voucher. These work particularly well for restaurants and the service industry as a whole. Whatever you are offering, it needs to be really good to attract your audience and get them to volunteer their email.

Here are the features you need to have on your website or blog or any landing page with a special offer.

• Keep your design simple: Your site needs to have a clean and simple design, and you need to communicate your most important message clearly and concisely to your target audience. Your most important content with any call-to-action needs to be placed above the fold, where they will be easily seen, and your call-to-action should have an easily seen button link rather than just a text link.

• Make your site easy to navigate: Really this is so important. Try to use the minimum number of pages you can and make your menu titles as easy to understand as possible.

• Clearly communicate your message: You want your visitors to subscribe to your opt-in, so you need to place your compelling offer with an image and title of the offer someplace where it is visible. The message and benefit of your offer needs be descriptive and specific.

• Add a clear call-to-action: In order for your visitors to sign up, they will need to be told what to do. Make sure you have a direct call-to-action, for example, "Download your free ebook now" or "Sign up for your discount voucher now." Your call-to-action needs to be clearly visible with an eye-catching button link which is much more effective than a text link.

• Add clear contact information: Make it easy for your prospects to contact you by placing your contact details where they will be easily seen. With the technology available, you can even add chat features so that as soon as your prospect arrives on your site a chat form appears asking if you can be of any assistance. Obviously you need the resources to be able to man this, but it is an incredibly powerful way of quickly building trust and showing how much you value your website visitors by being available to answer any of their questions.

• Email capture form: Your email capture form needs to be as simple as possible, preferably just asking for their name and email. You need to state on the form that their email address is safe with you and will not be shared with anyone. Make sure your form is in a prominent position and consider using a pop-up form that appears 20 seconds after your prospect has arrived on your site. Your email sign-up form needs to go at the top, side, and bottom of your webpage and also on your 'about page,' which is often the most popular page on your site.

•   Privacy policy: You need a clear privacy policy on your website to make it clear that you will not be spamming them or selling their information.

•   Thank you page: Once your visitor has completed the form, you will have them as a lead, but before you let them go you can send them to a thank you page where you can offer them the opportunity to share your offer with their friends by including social sharing buttons.

•   Mobile Friendly: You need to make sure your offer is easily visible and easy to complete on a cellphone. This is incredibly important, as more and more people are purchasing from their cellphone. There is nothing more annoying for the user than if the site is hard to navigate from their cellphone.

•   Don't add external links to other sites. Be careful not to fall into the trap of wanting to make your site more interesting by adding lots of content and links to other external sites, as this will only detract from your main goals and you'll end up sending traffic away from your site.

Landing pages

Landing pages are incredibly effective if you want to promote specific offers for specific products to specific audiences. A landing page is a page that is designed to give information about an offer and then capture a lead with a form for your visitor to complete so that they can download or claim that offer. Landing pages are highly effective in capturing leads because they are designed to be specific in their goal, which is to capture the contact information of your visitor.

The landing page should have a clear, uncluttered design and not have any links or navigation menus that could take your visitor away from the landing page. It should contain the following:

•   A headline (The title of the offer)

•   A description of the offer, clearly detailing the benefits to your visitor

•   A compelling image of the offer

•   A clear call-to-action. This can be in the form of an image or text.

•   A form to capture contact information (The fewer fields required to be completed, the more leads you will receive.)

•   A clear privacy policy on your website that makes it clear that you will not be spamming them or selling their information

•   A thank you page leading them to another offer or social sharing

You can either ask your web developer to create landing pages or there are numerous tools available on the Internet where you can easily create one, for example: www.leadpages.net, www.unbounce.com, www.launcheffect.com, and www.instapage.com

Setting Up And Creating Your Email Campaign

Once you have created your lead capture system on your website, blog, or separate landing page and have your subscribers' permission to send them your email, you are going to need a really good email campaign to convert those leads into sales.

Email is still one of the most effective forms of converting leads into sales, and email is more powerful than ever. Not only is it cost effective but it also provides one of the most direct and personal lines of communication with your customer. Once subscribed, they have invited you into their inbox on a regular basis and producing valuable content for your subscribers will develop trust and deepen your relationship with them. Your email will also work hand in hand with your Twitter campaign. As you build your relationship with your followers on Twitter , they are more likely to deem your emails valuable and open them.

The first thing you need to do is set yourself up with a good email marketing provider and there are many you can choose from: www.aweber.com, www.constantcontact.com, and www.mailchimp.com to name a few. It's important to use a system where you have a confirmed opt-in. This is when the subscriber is sent an email to confirm their email address. This verifies that you are gaining consent and legally protects you. It also helps you to keep a clean list, and it protects you from sending emails to incorrect addresses. You can then automate your emails with an auto responder and send out emails automatically over time.

Your next task is to plan and create your email campaign. Here are a few tips for doing so:

• Be clear about your goals: You need to be absolutely clear from day one what you want to achieve through email. Are you using it to introduce a new product at some time? Are you launching an event? Whatever you do, make sure you know exactly what it is that you want to achieve.

• Keep it simple and in line with your branding: Make sure your email design ties in with your branding. Most email providers offer templates which you can add your own branding to, or you can get a designer to create a particular design. Keep it really simple. Sometimes if things are too fancy they become impersonal.

• Send a regular newsletter: Plan to send a regular newsletter email at least once a month and once a week if you can. You can also plan to send off information about offers which tie in with special holidays and occasions throughout the year or competitions or events that you may be planning.

•   Plan your topics: You need to plan the topics you want to cover in each email, and this should tie in nicely with the plan for your blog articles. You then need to deliver high quality content which is tailor-made to fit with your subscribers' interests, and it needs to be so good that they are looking forward to the next email from you. If you are sending emails about offers then you need to show them clearly how these offers are going to benefit their lives.

•   Attention-grabbing titles: This is where you need to get really creative. Your main goal here is to get your subscriber to open your email, and you need to create a headline that is going to make your subscriber curious and inquisitive and eager to open your mail. Questions work really well as titles, and you will often see your open rates increase. This is because people find questions intriguing and they feel like you are directly addressing them. Try and avoid the words that will trigger spam filters. Simply search Google for a list of these words to avoid.

•   Be authentic and true to your brand: Write your emails in a style that your audience will grow to recognize, 'like,' and identify with your brand. Write so your subscriber feels like you are just writing to them. You need to establish yourself as a likeable expert for your subscribers. Try and create a personal relationship with them by addressing them by name and giving them a warm friendly introduction. Offering them the opportunity to connect with you and answer any of their questions by simply replying to your mail is a great way to create a connection and trust.

•   Keep it simple Make sure your emails are simply constructed and straight to the point so you keep your subscribers' interest and get them quickly to the place you want them to go, like your blog or offer.

•   Include social sharing buttons: Include all your social sharing icons and links in your mail.

•   Make them feel safe: Make sure your subscribers are clear that their email will not be shared and that they can unsubscribe anytime.

•   Analyze your open rates: Most email service providers include statistics in their packages so you can analyze open rates, bounce rates, click through rates, unsubscribers, and social sharing statistics. These results give you the opportunity to find out what is and what is not working.

Conclusion

---- ❦❧❦❧ ----

Now that you are aware of the different details and strategies which can be used for the sake of Facebook marketing, you should be all set to implement it.

Although at first glance marketing via Facebook may appear simple, it is in fact a complicated and difficult venture. As a business, you will want to produce content to post that will increase your sales, develop a strong brand identity and cause your ideas to be spread through the share and like system.

However, this will require strong insight into the way people use Facebook and what has made previous Facebook marketing campaigns successful. You need to develop an uncanny sense to understand what 'good' content is – how to optimize your posts so that they are entertaining and interesting to your customers. Additionally, you need to know every possible trick to cultivate your popularity, using your content in a specific way to get people to willingly spread that content and increase the importance of your Facebook page. On top of this, you must master the myriad of tools that Facebook provides to make your efforts more efficient and more effective. Finally, you need to understand how all this

Facebook marketing actually relates back to increase your business' success through strong brand identity and traffic generation. It is a lot to learn and can be quite daunting.

This guide will make Facebook marketing more accessible and doable for your business. By having read this book, you should be familiar with the most useful and effective Facebook strategies and techniques out there, how to go about doing them as well as appreciate the context of why these techniques are used.

The next step is to start your Facebook campaign or bolster your existing efforts. I wish you the best of luck. With a little effort and some reference to this guide you are bound to increase your level of success.

So, feel free to work upon the different details and implement them. When you are keeping an eye on the insights, it is going to help you immensely in shaping your marketing campaign in an apt manner.

Now, when you have the right knowledge and expertise in this area, you will have to implement the details. Feel free to go through the book as many times as needed because the details listed here are practical tips that are sure to guide you in an apt manner.

Facebook has become one of the most important places for the sake of carrying out marketing campaigns. It is upon you to observe the details, assimilate the points and then implement them to push your business to greater heights.

Use this book as the ultimate guide which in turn will push your business to higher rates of success. I hope you will be able to make the most out of this book and really have an effectively successful marketing campaign.

So, explore the different points and then be all set to enjoy the merits which this book has to offer. Automate the marketing efforts, put in the right budget and watch the results unfold right in front of you.

Is Twitter a part of your on the internet networking advertising and marketing strategy? No matter, with one of the most recent Twitter revitalizes, inclines in multi-screen use as well as continuous showcasing, you'll likely require to examine what Twitter gives the table.

By utilizing twitter, marketers can assemble most recent information about the patterns occurring in their industry. Around a large number of individuals on Twitter so no need of correspondence with every one of these a huge number of individuals. Simply spread the message it will reach to millions. Send a focused-on message to your industry in the event that it is information news it will consequently spread over your industry to your focused on crowd.

You use technology every day, consciously and unconsciously. However, how well you use technology to enhance your business is debatable. Social media, a technological advancement in itself, has shifted the tectonic plates in how business, companies, and people connect and interact. If you think about traditional mainstream marketing i.e. TV and radio ads, newspaper and most print advertisement, and multiply it by 100, you get a glimpse, a brief one at that, of the power of social media.

To say that social media has changed marketing would be understating the role social media plays in modern advertising and marketing. Further, social media is always changing. Today, every new day births a new social media platform that you and I can use to drive our marketing needs. Most of these 'new' social media platforms never make it to the big leagues. What do I mean by big leagues? I mean social media platforms that have stood the test of time i.e. social platforms that are the 'cool kids' on the block. Which social media platforms spring to mind? Most of us will say Facebook. While Facebook is indeed a powerful marketing tool, it does not compare to the infinite superpowers of Twitter. Well, you can only unleash these powers when you truly understand how to use such things like Twitter cards, hashtags, profile optimization analytics and lots of other powerful features that Twitter offers. From a business perspective, Twitter isn't just about tweeting, retweeting, liking, sharing, favoriting and following up on who just had a graduation party, who is getting engaged and lots of other non value adding updates as far as your business is concerned unless your business revolves around that.

Whether you are a complete beginner in Twitter or have been using it for a while as a marketing tool or an informational tool, this book will change your perspective as far as marketing on this powerful platform is concerned. You will soon discover how to make the most use of the 140 characters that you have to use in every tweet.

Most tedious and fascinating piece of Twitter is finding and including contacts. In the event that your message checks followers will consequently added to your follower tally. In the event that you keep up a consistency of refreshing the messages you will get huge amounts of followers.

YOUTUBE & INSTAGRAM MARKETING 2020

Become the best influencer and rapidly discover the secrets of the most watched video channels. Boost your business by creating amazing videos and personal brand

ANDREW PROCTOR

Table of Contents

Introduction

YouTube not only has a high rate of traffic, but the number of viewers is quite high as well. At present, YouTube boasts over 1,325,000,000 users. About 300 hours of video is constantly uploaded on YouTube per minute every day - that is about 5 hours of video content per second. All this points out an obvious trend in the marketing field and that is video marketing. For online as well as offline business owners alike and Internet marketers, YouTube marketing is an important strategy to make the most of the web's incredible shift towards video.

YouTube has grown into an influential social media platform. What started out as a fun medium of introducing the world to three-dimensional interaction has now turned into a powerful tool of marketing. Just like in every other social media channel, the secret to success is getting a following or audience to broadcast your videos to. The more views you get, the more popular your videos will be and the greater success you will have in ranking highly in the search results. Here are some benefits of YouTube marketing.

Audience

YouTube has over a billion users spread across the globe. YouTube is pretty much accessible anywhere and on a range of devices. In fact, at present YouTube is available in over 60 languages and is being used in over 70 countries. The aim of any marketer is to capture and grow their audience. If you are looking for a platform that will provide you with global exposure, then look no further. With YouTube you can reach a worldwide audience, it will help you gain better exposure, viewers, and followers.

Visibility

Google owns YouTube and you can use this to your advantage. Whenever you search for something on Google, you probably might have seen some videos that show up on the first page of suggestions. Well, this is a handy marketing technique and it will help improve your online visibility. If you use YouTube as a part of your marketing mix, then you automatically allow more authority towards your channel. The greater your authority, the higher your page will be placed in search results. If you want to use YouTube to improve your website search results, then make sure that your YouTube channel and the domain name of your website are similar. It will imply that your YouTube channel is an official link to your site. It will increase the relevance whenever someone searches for your brand or anything that's associated with your brand. You need to embed your videos on your website or other websites and it will rank your videos higher on the search engine and it will increase your visibility. When you add keywords to your description of the video, it automatically helps increase your online visibility. Increasing your online visibility is an essential part of a marketing strategy and YouTube will help you attain this goal.

Expertise

A lot of brands and businesses frequently use YouTube to increase their authority in their field of expertise by making simple tutorial YouTube videos. When you do this, it automatically increases your credibility and helps build the audience's trust towards your brand. You can even showcase your products in action through YouTube videos.

Content

You can always repurpose the content from your website and use it to make videos on YouTube. If you have a blog or a website with some content posted on it, then you can repurpose the text and make it into an animation, a video series or even a presentation and post it on your YouTube channel.

Engaging

Videos are an easy way to connect with your audience. Not just that, videos are an excellent means to provide a personal and a more hands-on feel when compared to traditional techniques of marketing. YouTube not only allows you to post videos, but it also offers different features to the viewer. Viewers have the option of posting their comments, sharing the video or even saving the video. It essentially gives your business a chance to interact with the viewers.

Traffic

When you use YouTube to create videos and advertise your brand, it increases the traffic to your website. The popularity of YouTube is one of the main reasons why using it as a marketing tool is a good idea. Given its popularity, it is quite likely that you will be able to create a group of followers for your business or your brand. You can include the link to your business website in the description of the YouTube video. Whenever someone views a video on your channel and they want to know more about your brand, then the link prompts them to visit your website. When people do this, it automatically makes your website rank higher on Google's results page.

Original Content

YouTube provides a brilliant platform to unleash your creativity. You can repurpose content in the form of videos, but apart from that, you have the opportunity to showcase original content that you create. It is easier to make your brand or business more appealing and engaging to the viewers when you post videos that are original and creative.

In social media marketing, Instagram is one of the newer tools that will help you grow your brand recognition. If your goal is to get recognized as a brand or become an online celebrity, then there is no way that you will be ignoring Instagram. Instagram will help you, as it has billions of monthly visitors. Instagram will give you the platform you need to grow and be successful, but do not take our word for it. There are many resources that can show you how many people have become celebrities. That is all thanks to Instagram, and you can genuinely grow it to a multimillion-dollar brand. There are many things Instagram can help you with; let us talk about the basics and go from there.

One of the first things Instagram can help you with is building a great SEO. If you do not know what SEO is, it means search engine optimization. If you want free, unpaid traffic, the best way to go about it is to rank high on Google. Google appreciates it when a website has a bunch of social media platforms they are connected to, more specifically, Instagram. If you have Instagram, and you promote it, the chances are your site is going to rank extremely high on Google. Instagram will not only give you the platform to grow, but it will also give you the free and paid traffic that you have been searching for. Secondly, Instagram will help you tremendously to network with many successful businesses and people. In 2019, many people are resorting to Instagram to connect and network with people. The reason behind that is you can reach many people online; most of them will only connect with you on Instagram. If you are looking at the accounts you follow, you would know that something as big as Nike puts an effort on Instagram, and promotes their products there.

This is the reason that you must use Instagram not only to build a portfolio but also to connect with people and go from there. Many people call Instagram as an entity's online resume, so treat it as such. Another thing Instagram can help you with is to get invited to events and travel opportunities. Building upon the networking part of Instagram, many people who are active on Instagram will get invited to events where they can talk and meet with people. It will help you not only to travel the world but also to grow your business as a brand. Finally, one thing that Instagram can help you with is advertising. Be visible to your target market online so that they can buy your products. If you are in the market of growing your business, there is no better way to reach your market than by using Instagram marketing.

You are essentially paying Instagram to target specific people, which will help you to get more sales. Primarily, every single brand on this earth uses an Instagram advertisement to get more sales. This is one of the essential things you can do to grow your business. Instagram does it all for you. It helps you connect with people. It enables you to build your brand, and finally, it helps you to be the person you want to be. There is no excuse for you not to use Instagram, whether it is for personal use or to grow a brand.

Chapter 1

---- ❧❧❦❧ ----

How to make a youtube channel

There's no doubt that YouTube is one of the top social networks on the web, but how can we set ourselves for success on this platform? To kick things off, we are going to set the foundation for your YouTube success.

Choosing Your Channel Topic

Your channel should focus on something you're passionate about and can create videos about for a very long time. In my case, I'm very passionate about helping people make money with their content, and I can create videos on that topic for a lifetime.

You might be passionate about different things, but start with a channel topic on one of your passions that also has heavy demand. For instance, I am also passionate about running, and while I do see myself creating a channel around that passion in the future, it wasn't something I prioritized at the beginning of my YouTube career. A channel around digital marketing presents me with more opportunities than a running channel based on my current business and demand for topics within both of those areas.

Focusing on one channel and growing that audience first will give you a smoother growth trajectory for future channels you may decide to create. So if you have multiple passions you can make money with, understand that if you pick one but not the other now, you can create a second, third, or even more channels once your first channel gains momentum. One notable fact is that if you wait a while to start the second channel and focus on your main channel, it won't take as much time or work to grow future channels as it will take to grow your first channel.

What To Expect On YouTube

When you commit to creating and growing your YouTube channel, you will have to invest some time on the platform for you to expand your reach. In my experience, it takes around 2-3 hours each week for me to create videos but more time with the marketing.

When you reach the point of YouTube's search and organic traffic taking over, you have the option to dial back your manual marketing efforts and still gain subscribers and views. However, I don't recommend doing that as the more you promote your videos and bring people to YouTube, the more YouTube will reward you.

It's important to focus on a topic you're passionate about because there are going to be some days where you don't get any new subscribers. These days are especially common for most YouTubers when they first start their channels. If you focus too much on the subscriber number but not enough on how much you love creating videos and serving your community, you will not make it on YouTube.

Create great videos, show the love to your community, and get out there and market your videos...and the results will follow.

Video Equipment Set-Up

This is the step of the YouTube process that can greatly enhance the quality of your videos, but it can also hold back a ton of new YouTubers from taking action. I'll share my video equipment set-up shortly, but I want to address new YouTubers first.

When you are first starting out, it's more important for you to create videos and do what you love than it is for you to have the video equipment set-up and solid editing. Just create, create, and create some more.

My first videos were done just with my Mac Book Pro's built-in audio on an ironing board. The audio for these videos wasn't always great. If the computer got hot and the built-in fans turned on, the sound of the fans made it into the video's audio.

When I started recorded videos on my iPhone, the first few didn't have the same sound quality as my computer set-up (at that point, I had the mic, headphones, and all of those things for creating videos with my computer).

I focused on creating content first and then enhancing the experience as I continued along the journey and grew my audience.

A big mistake new YouTubers make is thinking they have to spend a ton of money on equipment and the right camera just to get started. Just use what you have and create great videos.

However, once you have created enough videos and have some traction on your channel, you may want to start thinking about your video equipment set-up. With that said, here are some of my recommendations...

• Blue Yeti Microphone — this is by far my favorite microphone to use. The sound quality is amazing and it only costs around $100. This microphone attaches to your computer.

• Blue Yeti Pop Filter — the pop filter removes most of the background noise and protects your microphone from saliva and moisture damage. Most people don't think about the saliva and moisture damage, and to be honest I surely didn't, but if you want to preserve your microphone and use the same one longer, get the pop filter.

• Headphones — I only use a set of Mpow Thor headphones because they were a Christmas gift. However, any set of headphones will do, even the very basic and common Apple headphones will get the job done. Don't invest heavily in headphones when most of the cheap options work.

• Video Editing — There are a variety of free options such as iMovie, but I prefer to use ScreenFlow because it would take forever for me to get anything done in iMovie. ScreenFlow (or Camtasia depending on which device you use). I personally have never used Camtasia but know that they are both very similar. They also allow you to record your screen, so if you prefer to deliver slides than be seen in your videos, these are both great options for you.

• Lavalier Lapel Microphone — This is the microphone I use for my iPhone. It only costs around $20 and is great if you want to create videos on your iPhone. You'll sound crisper and there will be less background noise. You can also hook this microphone up to your computer or tablet, but I only recommend it for the iPhone. With that said, if you are on a tight budget, it is a less expensive option compared to the Blue Yeti microphone.

You may also want to consider a stand for your smartphone to reduce shakiness in your video. And if you like to create videos on the go, an air vent phone mount will allow you to record hands free quality videos in your car. Air vent phone mounts are the same things Uber drivers use to keep their phones in front of them while they drive. For their purposes, they need the GPS. For your purposes, you can get a better, still angle for creating quality videos on your commute without holding and looking into your phone while driving (which I'd never encourage anyone to do).

Are there more expensive pieces of equipment that will enhance your audio quality? Definitely...but who's going to notice them? There's a point where when the audio is good, you've got rapidly diminishing returns for enhancing that audio.

Just to quickly use some technical terms, 128 kbps is the bit rate of the sound equivalent of what you'd hear on the radio. You could then argue that a file with a bit rate of 1,280 kbps would sound better. Will it? Slightly. Will people notice? Probably not. You'll also make your file much bigger and uploading it will take forever. Most of my files are under 128 kbps because no one's going to notice the difference or think about it unless the sound quality is bad (i.e. too much background noise).

And if you find yourself on a service that has a monthly quota for gigabytes (i.e. Libsyn and other podcast hosting sites have a monthly GB quota, Vimeo, etc.), one file at 1,280 kbps would easily take up your entire allotment. Good luck producing a weekly podcast.

I don't care much for kbps in my videos and don't know my video's average kbps. It's not a metric you should think about.

I just listen to my videos before publishing them, and if the audio sound good to me, I know they'll sound good to the viewer. I'm just using this example to demonstrate that there isn't much of an incentive to improve your audio quality once you have the basic set-up in place we covered earlier. Producing quality videos and doing the marketing is far more important than slightly better audio.

Engaging With Your Community

One of the most rewarding parts of starting a YouTube channel is the community you'll develop over time. You can see how your content is impacting people and get feedback on what type of content to incorporate in future videos.

I love my YouTube community and every comment I get. You can get more people in your community to participate by asking people to comment on something specific within one of your videos. For example, if I'm comparing X and Y in one of my videos, I'll ask viewers to drop a comment and let me know if they like X or if they like Y.

Your YouTube community can also be a great hub for future YouTube video ideas. I often look at the comments and see what questions my viewers have. Those questions often turn into future videos.

One important thing to note is that as your channel grows, you will come across some trolls. You'll have to stay strong during these times and think more about your community that has supported you than one troll with one hateful comment.

And to be honest, trolls are actually good. They indicate you're doing something important, but there's a sneaky element to trolls and using them to your advantage. I'd ignore them in real life, but YouTube is a different story.

Right now, a big social proof indicator is the amount of comments your videos receives. More comments means more engagement which means YouTube will push out your video to more people.

When you reply to a comment, a video instantly goes from having just one comment to now having two comments. This helps the YouTube algorithm. You may want to consider feeding the trolls by replying to their comments. They'll reply back to you, and you can get into a deep conversation with trolls.

It is very important to think before you write these comments because some of these conversations can get heated. However, if you and a troll engage back and forth, you can get 10 or more comments on your video very quickly and YouTube will push it out even more.

This book contains strategies and tactics that won't require you to reply to trolls to boost your videos, but it does help if it's something you want to do. And if you do reply to trolls in this manner, you'll have a deeper appreciation for the community you've built and the people who leave positive comments on your videos. In my experience, you'll get far more positive comments on your videos than comments from trolls.

With that said, you want to focus more of your time on the people who love your content. These are the people who will watch each of your videos, hit the like button, and possibly become customers.

Experimenting On The Platform

YouTube is a platform in constant motion. While the core foundational pieces will remain the same, YouTube will continue making changes to their platform to attract more viewers and retain them for a longer period of time.

As a creator, you need to continue experimenting with the platform. Test different video styles and look at the analytics to get a clear picture of how well you are doing. YouTube is a science that requires experimentation for you to figure out what best works for your channel.

You will get a variety of strategies and tactics that will help create videos, make money with those videos, and reach more people. However, this book will just be the starting point of your experiment. If you decide to take YouTube seriously, I recommend watching other YouTubers in action and pay attention to what they're doing to create more engaging content, monetize that content, and get views.

Combine those strategies and tactics with your own YouTube strategy, and one of your experiments can pay off and result in a surge in your channel's growth. To build up on your YouTube strategy, we're going to take a deep dive into creating videos that make money and get exposure...right now.

Chapter 2

------ ✥❦✥❦✥ ------

How to make good content on youtube

If you want to make good content on YouTube, here are 5 ideas for content types you want to create. First of all, it's a good primer to think about what people are actually looking for on YouTube. Typically, if your audience is the typical YouTube audience, the 13-35 audience, they're looking for engaging content with a lot of value to offer. In order to captivate a younger audience, your content should be more flashy and engaging. If you're aiming for an older demographic, it is possible that these people will watch videos up to several hours in length, if they're engaging.

The King of content length though is the ten minute video. A ten minute video is not too short to be sparse, and isn't too long to be boring. Especially if you pack your video with exciting and engaging content. Hence you should aim for a video length between five to fifteen minutes, but pick whatever is best for your content. If you're making ultra-short comedy videos, these might be less than three minutes in length and if you're uploading your lectures, these might be hours long!

Without further ado then, the most popular types of content on YouTube:

1.   Comedy videos

Some of the most shared videos are comedy videos. They are often used to keep the audience pleasantly occupied. These are often fast paced and very engaging, the energy level within these videos tends to be high. There's two ways to tackle these.

The first method is to just be yourself, but be the version of yourself that's more extroverted and outgoing. It's scientifically proven people are going to listen to things that are loud and also things that change quickly and these are principles you need to embed into your videos. A monotone monologue just isn't going to cut it!

It is a proven fact these types of channels have a higher number of subscribers than most network's comedy television shows, which is crazy to think about.

Though the sense of humor is personal, there are a lot of comedy videos online and you can be sure you will find somebody who matches your style.

Remember, don't be afraid to be inspired by the style of another YouTuber, but add your own personality and flair to your videos. This is how you can be truly unique. This is important. You might not currently be able to beat these large channels on production value, subscriber count or finances available, but what you have that literally no one else on the planet has is your own uniqueness. Find a way to express this through your videos, and you'll be on your way to the top!

2.   Unboxing videos

Though this might come as a surprise, it turns out that there are lots of people interested in watching someone else remove a new product from its packing. Think about when you buy something new that you've been wanting for a long period of time, the excitement that you have when you finally open it, that great feeling of self-esteem and joy.

If you can transfer that through a screen to your followers, you're already on your way to thousands of subscribers.

Finding Stuff to Unbox

The truth is, people do like to see expensive and upcoming items reviewed. A good way to find these items is to type in your product name into YouTube and see if there is a market for it. In addition, if you ever see a video and think 'I can do better than that' then you probably can. This is what finding a niche is all about.

Your product doesn't have to be expensive, in fact it's counterproductive to start reviewing expensive products in the beginning. It's really important that you're very passionate about what you're reviewing. A good example of this is a channel called JeremyFragrance. I was never interested in fragrances until I checked out his channel. The energy he brings and his absolute dedication to everything fragrance really drew me in, and I'm now a loyal subscriber. However, it's also true that people like the surprise and suspense of seeing people.

You can also do product review videos, and this opens up an opportunity for you to make a lot of money in the future by doing sponsored review videos, especially if you have a large subscriber base.

It is a proven fact that most people would love to know other people's opinions about the products they want to buy before they actually buy them. Pick something you know a lot about. People will listen to you if you know a lot about something and can bring that confidence and passion across.

If your video is positive, then they'll want to make a purchase. A good way to leverage this fact to make money is by using Amazon Affiliates. This will be discussed later on in the book, but this is an absolutely incredible way to bolster your income from YouTube.

Since lots of people go on YouTube in search of reviews for the products they want to buy, try making reviews on a product that people don't have videos on. A beyond excellent way to check what people are looking for is type the product in on Google Adsense and check how many searches it has. If a product has many searches on Adsense but no videos on YouTube then you've struck gold. Making a video on this product can increase your view count vastly.

One major reason why YouTube has more advantage over other social media for this type of video is that you can display how you are using the product. For example, how you are applying the makeup, how you are test driving the car, how you are using the new kitchen gadget etc.

3.   Gaming Videos / Let's Plays

If one niche dominates YouTube, it's almost certainly this. Pewdiepie, the biggest YouTuber, started with this niche! This can be similar to an unboxing video, in that you're showing people a game that they've never played before.

What's unique about this though is that you inject your personality into the video to enhance the game. People want to see your unique reactions to whatever is going on. Pick a game, or a genre of games and stick to them. The reason Pewdiepie succeeded is he tapped into the horror game market and humans generally want to see people going through an emotional rollercoaster, if you can find a genre of games that elicits emotion in a similar vein then people will be drawn to your videos. Remember, the most important thing in this equation is you and your reactions.

 A secret technique to increase your viewers and subscribers, especially if you're a PC gamer, is to find an indie game on Steam that is upcoming and message the developer by email asking for a copy before the game is released. You'll be surprised how often they say yes.

Here's an example of such an email:

"Dear Developer

I'm an up and coming YouTuber: [channel link]. I'm looking to review your game. I can make you a quality video showcasing the main features of your game with my commentary over it. I think that this would really benefit us both, and if you like the video, you could feature it on the Steam page of the game.

I would appreciate it if you could give me an early access key to your game so that I can review it before it comes out and therefore have the review ready for launch

Thanks ever so much,

[Your Name Here]"

This is only an example, so do not copy and paste this exact email, and adjust it however you feel necessary. Even if you do not have a lot of subscribers, if your videos are quality then most reasonable game developers will say yes. If they say no however, you can just wait until the game is released and review it then. If the dev features your video and the game is successful, this can increase your subscribers and grow your channel like crazy.

One of my friends made videos on Skyrim Mods on Steam, and he followed this exact process with a very popular mod, and had his video featured by the dev. His video got over a million views and netted him 5000 new subscribers. Remember, for this method to work you need to work volume. Try to message at least 10 developers, the more the better.

One of the most popular video games is Minecraft. The major reason for its popularity is that the game can be modified with ease. In 2018 specifically, this is quite a saturated niche and doesn't leave much room for flexibility, but it's still very possible to be successful in this niche. Here are some top tips for making a Minecraft YouTube channel:

- Stand out from the crowd however you can

- Use unique mods that make your videos more interesting

- Create a Minecraft series with a story and recurring characters (Yogscast style).

- Since your audience is younger, a rapid, louder, more engaging video with more cuts and one that gets straight to the substance is what you're aiming for

- There's an infinite number of cool mods you can showcase and literally all you have to do is Google 'Minecraft mods'.

Livestreaming is also great for creating engagement between you and your viewers. This is excellent for getting donations and live feedback on how you're doing. You don't have to be good at whichever video game you're playing, however this is where your personality really has to shine through. Since this type of streaming typically involves a webcam or camera or some sort, make sure you're confident and comfortable in front of a camera. Remember, practice makes perfect.

4: Vlogs

The classic YouTube videos. The first ever YouTube video was called 'Me at the Zoo', and it's a vlog of one of the creators of

YouTube shooting a vlog at the zoo. It's still available, and you can see how far we've advanced since then.

The concept is simple. You just shoot a video talking to the camera about any random topic. People want a window into your life. They want to know what you're like, all your nuances. The more you're able to open up while keeping the video engaging, the better.

Pro tips for vlogs:

• White rooms reflect light much better than dark rooms, so try and film in a light environment

• Good lighting is a must. You can buy a ring light inexpensively from Amazon, more equipment will be discussed later in the book.

• Be positive. In life, it actually takes effort to be a good person and say positive things on camera, and people want to be uplifted and forget about the stressful day they've had in general.

• Finding a niche is very important, as I've seen channels with really good video quality, but they don't have many subscribers simply because their niche is just too competitive and they're unaware of the tips in this book. A good example here is if you're vlogging and you're in high school, you can make a series of how to cope with exam stress (granted you have to know how to do it yourself), not only is this going to be topical to your life, you'll also able to convey yourself genuinely as this is what you're going through.

5: Educational / How To

In 2017, the amount of traffic to these kinds of videos increased by 70%, that means the views these videos got nearly doubled. Imagine how much this will increase during 2018.

If you're good at something, or know how to do it, you can give tutorials on YouTube. It's simple, in fact, you don't even have to be good at something. Look at How to Basic as an example of this fact. Whether it's Mathematics tutorials (which is a very budding niche on YouTube) or underwater basket weaving, there are nearly unlimited things that people need help on.

Other types of content include haul videos, memes, Top 10 compilations and the infamous prank videos. Of course, there are an infinite number of video types that exist, and if you don't see your type here, don't dismay. The content of this book is principles that can be applied to any type of content you might make!

Chapter 3

————— ❧❦❧❦ —————

Recommended types of youtube videos to boost your following

Content marketing is there to ensure that your audiences are offered with the information they need to make their decisions. The main idea behind any content marketing strategy is to attract customers, engage them and finally convert them into loyal consumers. Basically, the marketing strategy should carry the prospects through the marketing funnel. This is to mean that it should take them through the different product lifecycle.

Video marketing could help you in taking your customers through all stages of your product. This begins by making them aware of the existence of your product/service. Now after your customers have been made aware, they take their time to consider whether or not they should depend on what you offer. This stage is called the consideration stage.

After pulling attention to your side, your customers will begin to question themselves whether your brand has all it takes to be identified as unique. During this phase, a marketer should work to constantly remind the audience of why their brand is unique. While doing this, it is important that they do not appear as too pushy. You should not send a message that appears too obvious you are promoting your brand. First, seek to entertain. Thereafter, win your clients over by delivering your promotional message.

Once your clients begin to consider your product or service, the last stage in the marketing funnel is the decision stage. This is the stage where your prospects make their final decision whether to settle for your product or to keep scrolling other YouTube videos for more convincing brands.

If your leads have been great, then you should expect that your clients will be choosing you over your competitors. Those that are convinced that you are worth going for will make their purchase. But before they do this, they will have to consider the options that they have at their disposal.

In all the stages where your marketing will go through, there are different types of videos that you will be uploading. Without a doubt, you will not be posting an instructional video if your prospects are not aware of what you are selling. Therefore, there are different marketing stages that will affect the type of videos you will post. Keep these in mind.

Marketing Funnel Stage 1: Awareness Stage

The first stage that your product will go through is the awareness stage. Once you have a product ready to market, the first thing that will happen is that your audience will be made aware of its existence. This is the awareness stage. Here, your potential customers are taken through the basics of your company and brand. Your marketing efforts should be on getting them to know more about your name and differentiate it from your competitors. Before your followers understand what you are selling, it is imperative to make them aware of your company as a brand.

A key strategy to enticing your potential customers is by seducing them. In this case, the quality of your content will determine whether you will succeed or not. Therefore, the content you post ought to be informative, entertaining and most of all, appealing in nature.

So, what sort of videos should you be uploading to your YouTube business channel in this stage?

Brand Videos

Just as the name suggests, these are videos that talk more about your brand in general. The main message being driven to the minds of your audiences would be your company values, missions, and visions. The core of your brand should also be reflected in the videos you post. The best thing about using videos is that you get to incorporate images of your brand and tell a story about the journey that your brand has been through. Make sure that your promotional message does not talk about specific products/services that you offer here.

Animation Videos

Remember, we are still trying to seduce potential clients about the existence of your brand. With the help of animated videos, you tap into the minds of your audience through emotional stimulation. Your audience will be left dazzled by the animations that you deliver them. Picture an animated video that left you wondering how a brand was very creative. It left you with a "wow" effect. Your creativity should leave your audience impressed. This is what will keep them coming hoping for more engaging content from your business channel. So, don't disappoint them. If possible, hire an expert to help you customize and create highly engaging animated videos.

Educational Videos

Something important that should be mentioned about marketing is that it aims at creating knowledge. Marketing helps people to learn about new things that they might not have been aware of. For that reason, educational videos featuring your product or service should fall in this category. Your main aim should be to make sure that your potential audience learns about your product faster. This is a stage where you will not want to waste time.

Bear in mind that during this stage, most people are out searching for new information about how to use particular products. They could be out in search of products that help in offering solutions to the problems they face. Consequently, your educational videos should appear here. They should be there to offer them with information they seek.

Documentaries

Just like educational videos, video documentaries will work to inform your prospective clients about something that they are not aware of. They build value. They help them in learning something new that will possibly bear significance in their purchasing behaviors.

Tutorial Videos

Most companies will begin their videos in this section. Obviously, these videos help customers to learn how to use products. They hack into the customers' minds by offering them with a step by step guide on how to make good use of a product. With the help of tutorial videos, you develop a sense of expertness about your product or service. Such tutorial videos fall in the first stage of marketing since most people are not aware of how your product is functional. Equally, they might not be aware of the fact that your product could help them resolve a particular issue they are facing. Hence, it is up to you to deliver the tutorial message in the best way possible.

Marketing Funnel Stage 2: Consideration Stage

From your initial video marketing efforts, the next stage would be the consideration stage. Here, your work is to exploit the leads that you created. You will be dealing with followers that have followed your videos or rather gained interest in what you are offering. Simply stated, you have already captured their attention. So, what you need is to make your followers like you and consider the product or service that you are offering.

Perhaps it is at this stage where most marketers go wrong. Most of them think that consumers need to be pushed to the edge for them to make a decision. Well, this is not the case. In fact, being too pushy will only ruin things. You will be considered as a nuisance to most consumers. It is imperative that you remind your audience about your brand without rubbing on their faces. Just keep them in the know by giving them the reasons why your brand rocks. This is what will make you different from your competitors.

The quality of your content will be of great importance here. High quality content will keep the audience engaged as they would not find any reason to feel less motivated about the products and services that you are offering.

The best videos that you should be uploading to your YouTube business channel are discussed succinctly in the following lines.

Video Emails

Have you ever used email marketing before? Well, the concept is the same. All you need is to make the best out of the contact that you created in the first stage. Once you have your audience subscribing, next you need to contact them with personalized messages. This implies that your videos should be customized to suit their demands. The advantage gained here is that you will be winning over followers in amazing ways. If you send creative messages to your potential clients, you can easily convert them to loyal customers.

Product Videos

Now that your customers are aware of your brand, they need to be made aware of the specifics. What products or services are you offering? How are these products used? What makes your products different from what your competitors are offering? Product videos should answer these questions to your audience. While creating your videos, ensure that you include videos showing how they are used.

Culture Videos

YouTube is a social media network. This means that you could also take advantage of its unique features to interact with your audience on a personal level. As a matter of fact, this is what your audience expects. They expect that you portray your company in a human manner. This means that your promotions should not be just about your brand. Your followers need to feel that they are communicating with a human being behind your brand. Therefore, culture videos will send your brand in a human manner.

The personality of your company should be documented in the video that you post in this section. You could try and incorporate interviews from your employees talking about your company in a positive way. It is important that your employees speak in a natural way. Consumers will be watchful of the tone that you use to promote the culture of your business. Therefore, don't exaggerate that your company is perfect.

Testimonial Videos

Still, at the consideration stage, your customers need to be convinced that there are other people using the product/service that you offer. The last thing they need is to realize that no one out there is using your product or service. So, this is where testimonial videos come to the rescue. They will help your company in developing trust among your audience. Testimonials can also be used to tell more about the unique features that your product has. Again, the testimonials should be documented in a natural way. Your customers don't need to be told that your product is perfect as compared to other brands out there.

What your followers need is a substantial reason why your brand is what they should be going for. Therefore, give testimonials a chance of telling the story to your audience. This way, you leave them to make their own decisions whether or not they should go for your brand.

Public Service Announcements

Your videos could also feature public service announcements. If there are heated public issues that need to be addressed, your promotional messages could take the form of these public announcements. Your main idea is to inform your audience about the issue that might affect them. The good thing about public announcement videos is that they are easily shared by socialites. This is for the reason that they carry messages that directly affect everyone. To you as a business, you will create a positive image in the minds of your audience.

Marketing Funnel Stage 3: The Decision Stage

This is the most important stage in your marketing campaign. At this stage, your customers are about to make their final decision to purchase the product you offer. Here, they might take some time to compare prices with what your competitors are offering. If your potential customers are still hanging on, then it means that convincing them to make their decisions is easy. To this point, your audiences have been motivated that you could be the best brand worth going for. As a result, all you need is a slight push.

There are different kinds of videos that you should post at this stage of your marketing phase. These videos are described as follows.

Frequently Asked Questions Videos

With the effective marketing strategies that you might have implemented, your audience might have questions that they need answers to. As a result, you should research some of the frequently asked questions regarding the product or service that you plan to introduce. The benefit gained here is that these videos dispel any fears that your potential customers might have. It calms them down with an assurance that they are making the right decision. In the end, they would be motivated to make a purchase without looking back.

Demonstration Videos

Another important question that your customers would want to ask is whether you will be there to help them use your product. Remember, they are new here. As a result, they don't want to learn by making mistakes. This means that you need to upload demonstrational videos. These videos should feature guides on how to use your product. If it is a service that you are providing, the videos should inform your customers how to access the particular service.

Personalized Videos

Your YouTube videos need a personal touch to guarantee that you are not only winning followers but that you are also keeping them engaged. Why is this important? Giving your posts a personalized touch makes your audiences feel special. It is worth pointing out that personalized videos could be incorporated at any stage in the marketing channel. This is for the reason that they highly motivate customers to keep relying on your brand.

At the final stage of your marketing process, personalized videos are crucial to ensuring that followers are converted into customers. As your followers contemplate on whether to choose your brand or not, sending them personalized videos will surely win them over.

Beyond the Marketing Funnel

So, after your leads are converted into reliable customers, this is your end of your marketing campaign, right? Definitely not! You still need to keep your customers engaged. Your brand is still young, and chances are that you need your customers in the future to secure that your brand takes over as the market leader.

After you have won a number of clients to your side, there are certain videos that you need to post to ensure that you cement your brand name in the minds of your audience. So, which type of videos should you upload here?

Thank You Videos

After clients have purchased your products, they would be glad if you keep pushing them with your highly appealing content. Don't give up just yet. Post thank you videos to appreciate your audience for their support. Without them, chances are that you would not even have that social media presence you are boasting of.

Thank you videos will transform your customers into loyal clients. These are the people that will stick with you in good and bad times. Other marketing strategies that you will employ to promote such loyalty include adding your customers to your mailing list. Equally, you should use Facebook, Twitter, Instagram, and other social media pages to continuously interact with them.

From the look of things, knowing which type of videos to post at every marketing stage is very important. The last thing that you need is to deal with confused customers. Therefore, it is essential that you handle your marketing campaign strategically by making sure that every step is not neglected.

First, start by making your customers aware of what you are selling them. Next, help them out during the consideration stage. Give them a reason why your brand stands out from the rest. Thereafter, make certain that your videos also motivate them during the decision stage. This is a crucial stage that will determine whether they will opt for your product or not. Most importantly, understand that this is not the end of the marketing line. Your marketing efforts should go beyond converting your leads into customers. You also need to have loyal customers behind you. As such, it is imperative that you keep on keeping on.

Chapter 4

─ ─ ─ ─ ─ ⟪⟫ ─ ─ ─ ─ ─

Find your niche and channel branding

Your YouTube channel is like a storefront! Gift the perfect look that would flaunt your style, and make sure you brand it like a pro!

When I say brand here, I mean the literal Branding - the usage of icons, banners, thumbnails and so on! This will give your channel the right look. So, how can one create a sensational look with their Branding?

Content is important - The brand designs must be relevant to the kind of content you generate. You would certainly wish the Brand conveys what your viewers can anticipate to see.

It must be familiar - The Brand design you choose must depict the style of your channel in a consistent and logical manner. It must convey the channel's core message to the viewers so they know what they are getting into. You can just keep it simple. Ensure all your videos, including the channel trailer correspond to your Branding.

Must be easy to find - The Brand designs of your channel should make it seamless for the channel visitors to search and find your channel. When tagged using metadata right, and posting your videos on the right social media platforms, your channel brand design will help your viewers in recognizing your channel easily.

The Channel Icon

Your channel icon will be the face of your YouTube channel everywhere across YouTube and Google, you can see this image in the top right corner of the page when you're logged into YouTube. Ensure that the icon looks great both small and large. It will also appear on the left-hand side of your YouTube banner as an overlay, and also on watch page. It could also be displayed on the right-hand side of other channels' pages if you've been chosen as one among their featured YouTube channels.

First, you should ensure your icon is either a rounded picture or a square one which can render at 98×98 px.

The best image you upload must be an 800×800 picture in either BMP, PNG or JPG formats!

Channel Art

This one is the banner right at the top of the channel page. This is a great place to showcase the personality of your channel.

Also, the channel art appears on every platform where the visitors watch your channel, be it TV, tablets or Mobile phones.

Make sure you upload a picture of resolution 2560×1440 px.

Description of the Channel

The Channel Description will be displayed in the About tab which will give the viewers a brief overview of what could be expected of the channel. It also gets displayed when viewers hover above the channel icon on watch page. You can write up to 1000 characters and can also include links.

Your channel description must tell viewers what your channel is about. You can also consider mentioning the kind of content you would be producing, what your upload frequency would be and the like.

Custom Thumbnails

These are a really good way of packaging your video series with consistent feel and look. It would also help the visitors choose your video out of a plethora of thumbnails. Recently, a question came to me of a person who attended my seminar, asking how thumbnails would make a difference. I was prepared for this question since I was anyway going to explain the importance of thumbnails. I showed five packets of different colors but of same size, to the attendees. I asked them which packet would they choose. While a few chose yellow, some chose blue and so on. Once they were done choosing, I showed them that all the packets had the same Chocolate wrapped in different colors, nothing more!

The subtle learning here is that even if your content is at par with similar content, some might choose the latter just because they can! So, how do you grab their attention? By thumbnails!

Your thumbnail must flaunt the content that you have! A picture can speak a thousand words, so make your thumbnail talk! Choose a bright, bold as well as legible font for your thumbnails. You can also consider conducting separate photoshoots rather than taking a screenshot from the video that you've made!

Make them bright, bold and legible.

Watermark

This is a logo that is embedded on each of your YouTube videos, and you can enable them so they appear on the bottom right hand side corner of the videos. The Watermark will help you in promoting your brand all across the video. While watching on laptops and desktops, this watermark will even let your viewers subscribe to your YouTube channel without pausing the video or leaving it. Your viewers will be able to recognize that a certain video is from your channel the moment they take a look at the watermark.

In order to make the most out of your watermark, consider the kind of visual message you want to send out with your watermark. Do you wish to use the channel's logo or rather include an image which would invite the visitors to subscribe? Make your pick!

To set the watermark, click on YouTube settings → View Additional Features → and then Branding

Make sure to select Entire Video for Display time.

Channel Trailer

The moment someone opens your channel page, the first video that shows up is your Channel trailer, that is if you have it. This video should be less than 2 minutes. It will give an overview of what your channel is about. It would be the first thing the unsubscribed user sees when your channel page is opened. Hence, you need to ensure you make long lasting impression and compel these users to subscribe to your channel seeking for more!

To set the Channel Trailer navigate to Channel Home page → Click on Customize Channel → Click on For New Visitors you can set it from here

Finding Your Niche

YouTube is no small community. There is an abundance of creators as well as viewers, all of them with variegated interests, passions, and needs. This comes into play while you decide to make your videos or upload content through your channel. It is normal to feel that making videos about the most trending and wide-reaching topics will make your videos better and will reach a larger number of people, but many a times, it has been seen that videos that cater to a niche audience perform better than generic ones. In fact, many YouTube channels have achieved success by making videos for a niche audience. They will see whatever is trending and decide to put out videos that fall into the particular category. Similarly, look for videos that you think are doing well. However, you will have to make it extremely good as there is already a lot of competition for it.

The great thing about finding your niche and making videos about it is that you are actually interested in the topic, and this makes it that much easier for you to create the video. You are more driven and passionate about it. You can connect better with the fans. All of this leads to a higher success rate. So, instead of following the herd, try and make videos about something that you love and care about. You may think that a particular topic is too obscure to be liked by too many people, but sometimes it's surprising how many people are interested in such topics. There is no point in giving people something that they have already seen. Try offbeat topics and things that will easily grab people's attention. You cannot play it safe if you wish to make it big. Choose topics that you think will draw in crowds that like to view different things.

Chapter 5

———— ❧❦❧ ————

Secrets to producing more effective videos

In the world of YouTube, one thing that you will want to learn is creating a must-see type of videos. These are videos that are highly attractive. The videos will make your brand stand out in ways you never anticipated before. Also, the exceptional videos that you create will generate the sales that you expect. There are important considerations to guarantee that you master the art of creating such videos.

The way in which you create your videos should not be similar all through. You have to be creative and produce videos that are diverse in nature. This section takes time to identify pointers that should help you in creating effective YouTube videos for your marketing campaign.

Get the Technical Details Right

Perhaps you might have been thinking that all you need when creating a video is a camera and good lighting. While these are necessary requirements to create a good-looking video, it takes more than just that. You need to be aware of the technical details required to shoot a quality video. The video that you will be creating should be stylish. It has to feature the best visual details that will keep your audience impressed.

When shooting your video, also consider the fact that you are producing for a particular medium. Clearly, what works on television will not work on a web browser. So, if a video expert shoots a video knowing that it will be aired on TV, the video will not work on web browsers. Accordingly, you need to differentiate the technical details of the video you will be shooting.

Consider YouTube Standard Display

Most of your viewers will be watching your videos on their smartphones or their computer screens. This means that they will not be watching your videos on large screens as you had expected. You should have this in mind as you shoot the videos meant to be uploaded on YouTube. The standard YouTube display should be carefully considered as this is where your content will be uploaded. Depending on the tool that you will choose to shoot your video, ensure that you shoot it right.

For those that would use their webcams often, the subjects need to be closer to the lens for good visibility. On the other hand, if you will be using a camcorder, zoom in to capture only the subjects. Other objects or people that are in the way should be removed from the frame. Getting close up shots will help you in creating effective videos that your audience would love to watch.

To boost clarity, you need to choose ideal scenes that will make the video worth watching. Adequate lighting is necessary to give your videos an uplift. In situations where you have to use a webcam in a dark environment, you should purchase lighting equipment that will light the room.

Slow and Steady Shooting

There are certain video effects that will only leave your audience clicking on the next video in line. Shooting your video too fast will bring in effects that could affect your audiences' eyes. Your followers don't want to watch videos of people moving too fast on the camera. There is nothing to see here. Consequently, they might decide to move forward and look for better videos. This is how brands lose followers. Keep your video effects at minimal too. Give your consumers an easier time watching something that is clear and fancy to watch.

Quality Equipment is Vital

With the digitalized environment that we live in, you need to also make your videos digital. Don't shoot your video with an old camera that has limited features. Finding a good camera these days is easy. There are numerous people with high definition cameras. These tools could be rented if at all you don't have access to one. You could also use high definition smartphones in some cases where you are shooting personalized videos. The videos should simply have the right quality to spark interest from your audience.

Re-Edit Old Videos

Re-posting your old company videos could be a great way of cutting on your marketing costs, right? Well, not necessarily. Yes, you might cut on your marketing costs, but you need to re-edit the old videos. Remember, content needs to be updated to meet your consumer requirements. Also, if the video quality is low, you need to upgrade. You should not allow yourself to be blinded by the tight budget that you plan to stick to. Embrace the idea of creating quality videos regardless of the financial situation that you are in. Undeniably, there is always a good option for you that is affordable, and yet it delivers.

Work With an Expert

There are many production companies that you can turn to these days. These companies compete amongst themselves for clients. Consequently, if you do some digging, you will find yourself a company that meets your expectations at a considerate price. The importance of working with an expert is that they assist in bringing the video production experience that you lack. Ultimately, you will add a touch of professionalism to your brand. Stylish videos uploaded to your YouTube channel will portray your brand in an ideal manner.

Think Outside the Box

The tips discussed in creating effective videos should not derail you from trying something unique. We live in a digitalized environment where creativity is highly appreciated. Consequently, if you are thinking of adding something impressive and unique to your audience, do it. Take risks here and there. You never know what to expect from your audience until you try.

Moreover, depending on your followers, you can choose to think outside the box and do things differently. For example, if you are dealing with a young audience, they might still get your message if you use a shaky video. So, you should also consider your audience when shooting your videos.

Improving your YouTube Video Content

Part of making your YouTube videos more effective begins with your content. Top class videos will not get you anywhere if they lack the right content. Sometimes having great content could help in compensating for your poor quality of videos. Content is vital to selling the message about your business. If the content sounds stupid, then rest assured that this is the assumption that your followers will have regarding your business. At the back of your mind, you should have the mentality that you want your prospects to come back again. You need them to share your content to increase your brand awareness. Keeping this in mind will warrant that you focus on creating content that is captivating.

So, how do you go about improving the content of your YouTube videos?

Entertain

A rule of thumb when creating YouTube videos is that you need to be entertaining. Your content should be enjoyable for your audience to watch. Think about this: what would you want to see in a video? Without a doubt, you need to be entertained. Therefore, give your audience what they need. Entertain them.

You might claim that your product or service is not entertaining. One fact is that it does not matter what you are advertising. There are creative ways of crafting your message to entertain your followers. A funny video will keep your prospects glued to the video and as a result, would watch the video to the end. To you, this is a good thing as you will get better rankings if people watch your videos to the end.

Inform

Apart from creating content that is entertaining, you also need to inform your audience about something that should help them. Talk about your product benefits to their lives. If they are going to choose your brand, what's in it for them? They should be aware of the fact that they stand a chance to lose if they fail to use your product. The art of convincing your customers is not easy. However, if you understand your audience's demands, you will serve them better.

Keep it Short

People browsing over the Internet have a short attention span. One minute they are watching a particular video and the next minute they are browsing through other social media pages. It is rare to find an individual having a single tab over the Internet. You need to take advantage of this. Post short videos that will appeal to your audience within the shortest time possible. It's funny that a 10 second video will greatly entice your audience as compared to a 10 minute video. Quantity is not quality. Keep your content short for the best results.

Stay Focused

Don't try promoting ten varying products in a single YouTube video. You will only confuse your customers. Stick to one message about a particular product that you are promoting. Your customers don't need to know about the entire line of products that you are dealing with. What are your customers looking for? Keeping your message focused gives your followers the opportunity of relating to your brand on a personal level. They would feel as though you understand their tastes and preferences. Thus, staying focused will aid a lot in improving your content quality.

Stay Away from Hard Selling

Take your time to scroll through different YouTube videos that market products and services. An interesting thing that you will realize is that soft sells perform better than the hard sell. You don't need to be too pushy with your marketing message. Quite likely, your followers are aware of the product you offer. They only need a small push to agree to purchase from you.

Keep your Content Fresh

There are thousands of videos being uploaded to YouTube on a regular basis. This means that you need to constantly update your content. Whatever you posted yesterday might be replaced by something that your competitor posts today. You need to ensure that your YouTube channel is up to date with videos that feature the latest information. The last thing that you want is to lose your viewership. Therefore, you need to keep posting on a regular basis. There are times when you don't have time to post content to your channel; in such cases, you should rely on tools that will automate the process. You could also hire a trustworthy individual to do the task for you. Before hiring any person, make sure that they have the right experience for the job.

Keep Your Message Clear

If your audience fails to understand the main thing that you are promoting, then your videos are not clear. You are not communicating to them about what your product is all about. After watching your video, your prospects should list down the benefits that they can gain by using your product. Before uploading any video to YouTube, you could seek help from friends or other professionals. Have them watch the videos that you plan to upload. Ask them questions about whether or not they get your marketing message clearly. If the content is clear, you can move forward to edit your videos further on areas that you think are necessary.

Be Funny

The aspect of being funny is closely related to being entertaining. However, the two are different things. You can be entertaining, but you are not funny. So, it is imperative that you create content that is funny. Who doesn't like to laugh? People will always remember the funny things that they watched on YouTube. In fact, most of them share funny videos with their friends on other social media pages. Hence, it makes sense if you improved your video content by choosing to be funny. In this case, you will never go wrong. Funny videos require creativity. As such, you need to invest your time researching what makes your audience tingle. Don't just post anything because you think that it is funny to you. You are crafting the message to impress your customers and not yourself.

Judging from the details provided, producing quality videos is not as challenging as you might have thought. The tips provided are simple things that you might have neglected as you create your videos. Most importantly, you should never neglect the message that you intend to reach your audience. Paying too much attention to delivering quality videos might blind you from realizing the importance of the message.

As pointed out, delivering quality content will help in compensating for the poor quality of your videos. This shows how essential your content is. Improving your content quality is also quite straightforward. You need to focus on your message while making sure that your video is short. Similarly, as a marketer, you should aim to inform. Make an assumption that people are not aware of your brand. Therefore, talk to them briefly about what your brand entails. A winning strategy that you should always remember is to be funny. Give your audience a reason to recall your videos. If they find your content funny, they will share it all over. Before you realize, you will be hitting the headlines.

Chapter 6

---- ✦✦✦✦ ----

How to generate youtube video ideas

Content creation for YouTube requires a constant supply of ideas. When you are creating videos on a regular basis, it's not uncommon to run out of ideas. Viewers can detect stale content or topics that you milk to the hilt because of popularity and controversy.

To make sure that you have a steady stream of fresh ideas, you have to create a content calendar where you plan things ahead of time and schedule the publishing of your videos.

But before you can do this, you must first get ideas. No matter how creative you are, there will be times where ideas don't flow and the creative juice dries up. The good news is that you can get ideas and topics from a lot of sources. You'd be surprised at how easy to fill a content calendar with all the ideas you'll get.

Google and YouTube Search Autocomplete

As you type keywords or phrases on Google's or YouTube's search bar, a list of different suggestions appear that autocompletes what you have typed in. These suggestions are based on what people are searching for on Google or YouTube.

Keep in mind that what appears in the autocomplete suggestions are simply the kind of search string people look for. There's no confirmation that it is based on search volume or popularity.

For Google search, you can scroll down at the bottom and you'll see searches related to the topic you are looking for. Different variations of your keywords are displayed with different topics. From the suggestions, it would be impossible not to find something that you can make a video about.

Trending Topics

Popular topics that are being talked about on different social media platforms are free ideas you can build your video content around. What's great about getting ideas from trending topics is that you can ride the trend. If you can hit it at the beginning of rising interest, your videos will have a better chance of getting massive views which will send a signal to the algorithm that your videos could be worth suggesting.

Timing is of the essence if you want to ride the trend. This means making videos and publishing them while the topic is still hot.

YouTube Trending

When determining trending videos, YouTube considers view count, velocity, age of the video, and where views are coming from. The goal is to surface videos that appeal to a wide range of viewers and showcase a diverse group of video content creators.

The chosen videos represent the extent and coverage of what's happening in all of YouTube. It has less to do with what video has the most views, but more of what videos are relevant to viewers. The tending videos are updated every 15 minutes so videos move up or down or stay in their positions.

This is a minefield of content ideas that YouTube is giving you on a silver platter. Right in front of you are videos that have been handpicked by YouTube based on metrics that indicate what viewers are watching. If you create your content around those topics, you are guaranteed views and engagement.

Twitter

Twitter is not as forthcoming when it comes to how it determines the trending topics. The algorithm determines the tweets and hashtags that would be included in Twitter trends. It's safe to say that one of the factors is the number of tweets.

Trending topics are based on your location, your interests, and who you follow. This means it's relevant to you and people who share the same interests. You can get ideas from this if your niche is based on your interests.

Google Trends

Google Trends is also a great source of ideas for your videos because it analyzes the top search queries across regions. The popularity of topics is usually attached to a triggering event that sparks search inquiries on Google.

News Apps

News app is the perfect source for numerous video ideas that will also get you more views. It doesn't matter if you're an Apple or Android user, there will be tons of news app to download.

With most news apps, you can configure what kind of news stories the app sends you. You can set it up to include topics you want to cover on your channel based on your niche.

Here's how to get the most out of this method. Choose a story that has audience potential to gain traction. Ask yourself the likelihood of a particular story gaining a lot of traction. You can confirm this by searching in Google Trends. Or you don't have to look far and just look at YouTube's trending topics.

Reddit

Content creators are always searching for the next great idea and they always find inspiration from Reddit, one of the most popular websites in the planet. With over 330 million monthly active users, Reddit is a gold mine for video content ideas. It's also a place where fandoms congregate and talk about things that they're into. Even the most obscure topics are being discussed in this site so it would be impossible not to find potential video content ideas.

Typically, Reddit users would submit breaking news, ask questions, share stories, and look for suggestions in the subreddits (topic-specific forums). You can go to the subreddit that aligns with your niche and join the discussion. Look for the posts that ask questions. List down the problems and struggles. Those deeply engaged in the conversation will suggest different solutions. Take note of them and think of ways how to expand the answers and how you can be more helpful. When you have enough information, you can start creating your video

Ask Your Followers and Subscribers

YouTube Community allows you to interact with your followers or people who watch your videos. You can start a discussion or create a poll to get the pulse of your audience. You can also pin a comment asking them what topics they are interested in.

You'd be surprised at how helpful that would be in coming up with new ideas for your video content. Since the ideas are coming straight from your audience, there's less guesswork and you'll know that they will be more receptive to your video content.

Look to Your Comments

YouTube's comments section may be a source of negativity and snide remarks but it is also a treasure trove of ideas. The good thing is that inside the YouTube admin, you can search the comments for specific words and phrases. You can track down questions that viewers are asking and you can create a video to answer those questions. With tons of questions, you'll never run out of ideas for video content.

Spy on the Competition

Check what the competition is doing. Look at the channels, websites, and social media of companies or people who are in the same niche or industry as yours.

If your niche is gaming, you can check out the popular gaming videos of your competition. See what's trending in the gaming niche and piggyback on that popularity.

If you're in the cooking or baking niche, see what popular vloggers are doing in their channels. Make a similar video but make it better by adding more information or exclusive footage that will draw more viewers to your channel.

You can use two tools to spy on your competition:

Tube Buddy

Tube buddy is a browser plugin that can be integrated into your YouTube account. It adds a layer of functionality that helps you gauge how your videos are performing. It is essentially a third-party video analytics app that gives you useful information at a glance. It gives data on total views, estimated earnings, engagement rate, number of comments, subscribers, views, tags, and watched hours, among other things.

Tube Buddy also has a built-in keyword planner. This allows you to put a word or a phrase that has something to do with the type of content that you make and then Tube Buddy will generate different ideas based on things that people are searching for. It will also show your chances of ranking for that particular keyword or topic.

VidIQ

Another tool to use is vidIQ. Just like TubeBuddy, vidIQ shows metrics, analytics, and important data that can help you get more ideas for video content.

What's great about vidIQ is that you can analyze the videos of your competition (or related channels). You'll see the level of engagement for each video as well as its velocity, which is the views per hour. Videos that have high velocity are videos you want to get ideas from. You can create similar but better videos.

Doing so will increase the likelihood of your videos showing up in the suggested videos section, which generates massive traffic to your videos and channel.

Survey Your Audience

It doesn't matter how big or small your audience is, you are encouraged to ask them questions about the kind of content they want to watch. When you survey your audience, you're getting video ideas that your audience already cares about. You can pin your question on the comment section so they can reply to that thread.

You can also use polls. It's extremely easy for people to participate when they don't have to think too much for an answer because all they have to do is to just choose. With multiple-choice questions, you can get tons of engagement. This removes guesswork and wrong assumptions on your part.

You can also do a Q & A video. What people ask about you or your channel or niche will give you an idea of the type of content that your audience wants to watch. Use the community tab on YouTube to tap into your followers' pulse.

You can also use SurveyMonkey for your survey. This is only if you feel that a YouTube poll is kind of limited. Alternatively, you can use Google surveys, which is free and quite easy for people to submit information. You can get insights into not just a video idea, but what people are dealing with, their problems, pain points, or challenges.

How to Shoot A High-Quality YouTube Video

Video content is taking over the Internet. More and more people are preferring to consume information through videos on YouTube because they are more engaging, more urgent, and more entertaining. It becomes necessary to produce high-quality videos to attract more viewers and grow your subscriber base.

Set-Up

There are different ways to record a video for YouTube. The method would depend on the type of camera you have and the kind of video you intend to shoot. There are so many options when it comes to the type and brand of camera to use for recording videos. Instead of contemplating and worrying about camera brands, lens kit, and accessories, focus on the content and just use what you currently have. It could be an entry-level

DLSR, a smartphone, a handheld camera, or a webcam. As long as it can record in high definition, it would do.

The important thing is to understand and master the basics of video recording. You only need to have a foundational knowledge of the camera and equipment to get started with video recording.

If you're just starting and don't want to spend a lot of money, you could buy the camera that's within your budget and just upgrade to a better camera that would satisfy your video recording needs.

Cameras

In choosing a camera, you must first decide what kind of video content you'll be doing. If you are doing mostly a talking-head video where you're just talking to the camera, you don't need a full-featured camera. What you intend to do with your videos will help you decide which camera to use.

Here are the types of cameras you can choose from:

•   Point-and-shoot cameras

These no-fuss cameras are so easy to use that you can use straight out of the box. You can select one of the many presets available depending on the type of video you're recording. They deliver full HD image quality and are ideal for vlogging.

- DSLR cameras

This is the camera to use if you want high-quality images in full HD. While it has the most professional-looking results, here is a learning curve before you can operate the camera properly. You have to learn how to focus the lens and be familiar with the settings. DSLR cameras are typically used in shooting scenes with cinematic effects. Videos shot with DSLR look more professional and well-thought-out.

- Smartphone Cameras — Although phone cameras now deliver high-quality images, they don't quite match up with standalone cameras. Many YouTube creators use their smartphones when they are vlogging. They use the selfie mode to record themselves as they go through their daily activities.

- Webcam – These are tiny cameras that you can use if you're doing video game walkthroughs, demos, and screenshare.

- Action Cameras – These are small compact cameras used to record first-person point of view of events. They are best used in capturing fast movement because of their superb image stabilization system. They are ideal for recording extreme sports and underwater shots.

Microphones

Your videos must have clear sounds. Viewers may tolerate shaky camera shots, but they can't stand poor audio. That's why it's important to use a microphone when shooting a video.

Cameras have their onboard microphone, but you would have to stay within three to four feet from the camera to capture the voice and sound. This setup wouldn't work if the subject you're filming has to be talking from a distance. An external microphone will help boost the audio quality.

Types of microphones

•   Shotgun – This microphone has directional recording so they are effective in picking up sounds when pointed directly at the source of the sound.

•   Lavalier – This microphone can be clipped onto your clothing (also called lapel mic). It's best used for interviews or when the subject is far from the camera.

•   Boom — This microphone is used to capture dialogues or conversations among several people. It's connected to a long pole so that it can be held above the frame of the scene. This is used in filmmaking because it can capture natural sounds effectively.

Lighting

Lighting is important in creating high-quality videos. This is something that many creators take for granted. Lighting is more than just making sure viewers see your subject, it also creates the tone and mood of the video.

Different kinds of lighting setups and techniques can influence how your video would be perceived by the viewers. If you want your viewers to feel a certain way when they watch your videos, lighting can help give tonal cues that will match the message that you're trying to convey.

Lighting can also be used to guide your viewers where to look. It can naturally draw their eyes on the specific part of the video you want them to focus on. High contrast images can make objects in your videos stand out. Although you can make adjustments in post-production, it will save you a great deal of time and grief if you start with proper lighting. With great lighting, your videos will look professional and pleasing to the eyes.

Here are the most common lighting setups that can make your videos a whole lot better.

•   Two-point lighting system. This uses two light sources at opposite ends. The first light source is the "key light" which provides the primary lighting to the subject. The second light called "fill light" balances out the shadows.

• Three-point lighting system. In addition to the key light and the fill light, this setup uses a backlight that splits the subject and the background.

• Natural light. There's nothing better than natural light coming from the sun. You can record outdoors at certain times of the day when the light is at its brightest. Alternatively, you can record near a window so you can take advantage of natural light coming in. The downside to this is that it's a little trickier to control, but it can be done.

Accessories

• Tripod – Unless you really intend to make shaky action videos, you must use a tripod to stabilize your shots.

• Teleprompter – A video teleprompter is not required but it can help you create more content faster. You can structure your content so that you don't waste time going off-topic. Since you're reading from a teleprompter, you can minimize mistakes. The fewer mistakes you make, the faster the editing can be done.

Techniques

Even if you're just new to video content creation, you can follow these simple techniques to improve the quality of your videos.

1.   Lighting

When it comes to filming videos, lighting is extremely important. Whether you're using natural light or artificial light that you've set up in your room or studio, it's important to understand how it should be used or manipulated in order to get the best effects.

If you're more into video blogging you're most likely filming yourself a lot of times in your room. In this scenario, window light is the best light to have because it gives a nice soft light coming in from a natural source. It illuminates nicely and the shot comes out looking all clean and evenly lit.

When you have the right lighting, it gives you a wide range of capabilities when you're editing the video. It's much easier to make a color correction. There's little need to adjust the brightness level because the video just comes out nicely as it is.

You'll know that you're not having enough light when you're losing some detail. When you're in a room with insufficient lighting, there will be some color drain and the image looks a little muddy and grainy. But if you film with light coming from the window, you can immediately see the difference.

When working with window light, all you have to do is to move closer or further away from the source of light to get the right lighting for a particular time of the day. When the light is too harsh, you can shoot in the corner of a room or move as far away as possible from the light source. Your positioning makes all the difference in how the video quality is going to be perceived by the viewers.

The same principle applies when you have a DIY lighting setup. The overall look of your videos will be a lot better if you just focus on how to get the best lighting from the get-go. It will prevent reshoots and it will save you time on editing.

2. Proper Music and Sound

If you watch videos on YouTube, you'll find that it's quite obvious that people don't put a lot of thought on the music and sounds they use in their videos. For some strange reason, the music and the video content don't match up. This creates a dissonance that will just confuse your viewers.

Never underestimate the power of music to elevate the quality of your video as a whole. It changes the way viewers see your content and the content creator (that's you!).

Think about it, if you use the wrong track for some incredible footage, the video will not have the epic impact that you're going for. It's all about the music or song choice. The music sets the tone to your narrative or whatever message you are trying to send across through your video.

The music choice is a big factor in how your video will be perceived by the people. If you use an epic music for a footage that does not deliver an epic content, people's expectations would be subverted and not in a good way.

In terms of ambient sounds or sound effects, the use of a good microphone makes a huge difference. This is because it gives rich audio that captures authentic sounds. It engages the audience because the video has all the right visual and sound effects to create an immersive experience with the clip or the footage.

You must match the visuals to the audio. It's highly recommended to edit your video to the music. If you do this, you will enhance your video substantially and it will resonate with your viewers. If you provide the right music and the right sound effects that match the footage, you are giving your audience the full experience. Music and sounds are often overlooked but they make videos a whole lot better

3. Master the Video Editing Software

Whether you're using a sophisticated video editing software or something that has a lower learning curve, you must learn to use it properly. You can watch tutorials, attend training and seminar, ask a friend to teach you, or look up how-to videos on YouTube. Do whatever it takes to master your editing software of choice.

Why? Because it's going to help you plan out how you are going to shoot your videos especially when you are shooting in the field or shooting on location. If you know the features and limitations of your editing software, you can plan your shots ahead of time. You'll know beforehand the things that you can do to digitally edit your clips. This way, you can shoot according to your requirements, taking into account what your editing software can and cannot do.

For example, if you're going to do a transition and you don't want to include some dragging clips, you can easily bring them into the software and edit the transition to make your video snappy and energetic.

If you don't know what your software can and cannot do, you will end up shooting unnecessary scenes or you might fail to shoot scenes that you need to make up for the limitations of your software. Knowing your editing software will help you figure out how to get the most out of your raw footage.

4.   Motion in shots

This is perhaps one of the most overlooked things by video content creators, more so by beginners who are just learning the ropes of filmmaking. More often than not, they will just set their camera up on a tripod and start filming whatever it is they need to film. Then, they move to the next shot doing the same thing. So what happens is that they have a sequence of static still shots. They are not only boring to watch, but they also don't have any impact at all. They are no different from images being shown on as a slide show.

If you're filming an event, don't just throw the camera on the tripod and hit the record button. Moving the tripod to different locations and doing the same thing to capture other activities is not really giving the viewers the atmosphere of that event. It's just like you're letting people watch from a distance. There's no story to tell.

Motion in shots is so important because it could turn even the most mundane things into something fun and utterly engaging. If the camera is moving, it's helping you move the story along. You are capturing more movement and more emotion thus giving the audience more cinematic feel.

With more moving shots, your video is going to look more professional because you planned it out and put more work into it. The results are definitely a massive improvement over someone who just puts the camera on a tripod.

5.   Good Location and Time of Day

Location matters when filming your video. If you have an incredible landscape in front of you or you are in a picture-perfect location, it will look incredible on video. However, you're most likely be holed up indoors at home or at the office. But keep in mind that the same rules apply whether you're shooting indoors or outdoors.

The angle of the shots matter. You have to think about the best parts of your location and make sure that you are capturing them. For example, if you are outdoors, you must use the right angle to capture the trees and plans. Angles must not be too high to lose focus on the subject and it must not be too low to miss out on the nice views of the surrounding.

When you're indoor and filming yourself talking, think of the best angle for the location you are in. A low angle does not work because nobody wants to see a lot of spaces that don't add value to the video. Nobody wants to see the ceiling or the walls when you're talking. If there's nothing interesting above, there's no need to use a low angle.

If the angle is too high, people will wonder why it's too high and lose interest in what you have to say. The key is to make the necessary adjustments based on where you're shooting from.

Another quick tip is to remove the clutter from the background. They are distracting and will take your viewers' focus away from you. So clean up the background. Move objects that are not relevant to the video or to the setting you are going for. Get rid of any clutter.

The time of day is also very important when you're choosing a location and what you're going to shoot. The best times to shoot are early in the morning or in the evenings to later at night. Early in the morning is optimal because the light is usually the softest during that time. The Sun hasn't come all the way up and the light isn't harsh yet the colors are usually nice and vibrant.

One of the best times to shoot is during the golden hour where the residual light from the sunset is still illuminating the sky. The colors are going to be significantly better than they would if you were shooting at high noon on a sunny day. Your videos will be more exciting and vibrant. With great location and time of day, you wouldn't have to make a lot of adjustments and fine-tuning.

To summarize:

•   If you want good light, find that window light or set up some studio lights

• Use good music and you want to edit to the beat. You want to keep those sound effects in mind for ambient noise.

• Know and master your editing software so that you know what shots you want to get and what you can edit out based on your software's capabilities.

• Pick a good location and a good time of day to shoot your videos.

• Keep motion in mind when filming. Static shots are boring.

Smartphone Video Recording

If you have a limited budget and cannot afford any of the shiny new cameras for your video production, you can get started using your smartphone.

People often start with just a smartphone and that's perfectly fine. You don't need to have an expensive camera right off the bat (if you can't afford it). Once your channel starts to earn some serious money, you can invest in a high-end camera.

Here's a breakdown of how to shoot a video for YouTube using a smartphone. It doesn't matter if you have an iPhone or an Android phone, the principles and techniques are essentially the same.

1. Before you lock down your shot and set up any gear, put your phone in selfie mode and get a feel for the room. Walk around to see what the background is going to look like with you in the shot.

You don't want the background to be too busy so either you clean up the background or find the spot where the background is not too cluttered.

2. Get your gear ready. Aside from the smartphone, you would need a tripod, a lighting kit, and a microphone.

3. Lock down your shot. Decide if you want to do the selfie mode or the normal camera mode. It is recommended to use the normal camera mode setup because the normal camera on most phones is superior to the selfie camera.

TIP: If you want to use the selfie camera, do not look at yourself, look at the camera lens so you'll be making eye contact with the viewer.

4. Lock in your video settings. Before you start to shoot, set your to 1080p because it just looks better on YouTube, thereby helping you get more views and build your brand faster

5. Plan and outline your topic for discussion. Before you even sit down to record the video, rehearse what you're going to say. Do your research and go straight to the point. Break down your

discussion into points and in easily digestible chunks. This not only helps you record the video better, but it also allows your audience to follow along with the video all the way to the end.

6. Edit. You're not going to get things right on the first take. It's guaranteed that you'll have tons of blooper reels, outtakes, and B-rolls. This is where editing helps. Use free or paid apps and do the editing on your smartphone. You don't need to transfer huge files to your laptop or PC because you can do all the editing on your smartphone.

Notable video editors for smartphones are iMovie, KineMaster, and PowerDirector.

Chapter 7

---- ✥✥✥✥ ----

What matters most for getting subscribers?

When you are building a business, you have to draw in your audience using more than basic sales tactics. Trust matters a lot when you want to draw in customers. If your customers don't respect or trust you, you aren't going to have any luck. Therefore, you have to take the time to build up trust and rapport with the audience and customers. When you do this, you will have an advantage over other businesses and help your list of subscribers grow. When you upload video content to YouTube, you are giving your customers reasons to evaluate and look at your products and services.

Credibility and YouTube Marketing:

Credibility arises when someone has all the information needed. There isn't a more direct, more easily absorbed, or simpler way to show information than using YouTube videos. Just 20 seconds of content is a lot more engaging and offers more value than a whole page of text or marketing content.

- Showing Satisfied Customers: The best way to build up your credibility and trust using videos is to put videos up on your channel of people recommending your product and proof of client engagement. For potential customers, a satisfied client giving their opinion is the most convincing piece of evidence that your brand is worthwhile.

- Winning New Clients: Proving the way you respect and treat your existing customers is going to help you gain new ones. Videos which show customers enjoying your brand or showing how good it is will engage new viewers and subscribers. Testimonials on your channel will build up trust by demonstrating and displaying the value in a way that is engaging and meaningful in a way that other ads could never be. Small or large, any business needs to use video content to build and establish their business and products.

One simple method for doing this is putting a video up that has instructions or information steps, targeting your audience with success and accomplishing a set of actions or tasks. As newer social networks, such as Blab and Periscope pop up, older websites seem to pale in comparison. YouTube is an example of this, in some cases. Although it's still wildly popular, people might fear that YouTube isn't going to be as popular pretty soon.

The fact is that YouTube has existed for very long, leading people to believe that newer websites make more sense to put their time and effort into. Although the newer sites are valuable and useful in their own way, it isn't smart to exclude YouTube from your current strategy of marketing.

The Three Most Important Factors on YouTube:

If your desire is to create a YouTube channel that is successful and shows your niche, you must already know how to create a successful brand and channel. To be more specific, you have to be aware of the three consideration that is most important on YouTube.

1. Your Quantity of Subscribers:

A lot of interested, quality subscribers and viewers is your ideal YouTube audience. Quality, interested subscribers, means anyone who is already interested in the niche you are involved with. They are already subscribed to other channels that are somewhat related to the niche you're in and like watching a lot of videos about that subject.

- Appeal plus Marketing: Attaining a higher number of subscribers means creating a channel that is appealing and combining that with the correct form of marketing. It does help to have an existing audience outside your videos, but you don't need this. It's possible to leverage the audiences of other people's challenges by interviewing experts in your niche, leaving comments on related video content, and more. However, when you choose to try to go leverage the audiences of other channels, you can only enjoy success if you choose to have a "win-win" attitude.

- Commenting on Videos: You can get more exposure by commenting, while your comments offer more social proof and exposure for the videos. This is a win-win situation for you and the video creator.

- Interviewing Experts: Seeking out information from existing experts in the field will help you get more exposure and credibility (especially if the person also does promotion for the interview). This offers a win-win for you and the expert. Other methods exist for getting a higher number of subscribers, but the best approach is to find a couple that work best for you, then focus on those.

2. How Long the Videos are Watched:

YouTube has intentionally emphasized that when they think about videos viewed, they are also considering how many minutes of video are watched. This is partially to help against spam since people can just purchase views. These fake views are dishonest and make video content appear better to possible audience members. But these videos will likely not appear high up in the search results of YouTube. To get a higher rank, you need to make videos that people want to watch all the way through, or at least, most of the way through. You can do this with two different methods:

- Creating Compelling Content: The first way to get people to watch your videos all the way through is to create compelling content that makes people want to watch. How is this done? You can check out what your successful competitors are doing and look at what works here. Next, check out the retention rate on your own videos to see what works. Don't check out the retention rate of your videos until you've gotten past 100 views. If your retention rate is based on just eight views, this isn't enough information to form any conclusions.

- Making One Longer Video: The other method for increasing the length of time your videos are viewed is to of course create a valuable video. However, how long your video is matters, as well. Retention rate determines how long someone sits through your video, but how many minutes they watch for matters more. If you want one specific video to get great ratings, you can make it a bit longer.

You can do plenty of planning to prepare for your video if you want to make one specific piece of content longer. For instance, you could do an instructional video on how to develop an exercise routine and make it 25 minutes long instead of four. Using advertising's help, you can get people to watch this video for thousands of minutes. Your average watch time for your videos will go up due to having a longer video that people watch for longer.

It won't matter whether the longer video and another shorter video get the same amount of clicks, but it will matter that people spend more time watching the longer one than the shorter one. Make sure you make compelling content, but for some of them, make longer videos to add to your overall minutes-watched score.

3. How Consistently you Upload Videos:

If you are more consistent with uploading videos, you will also be likelier to gain attention from those subscribed to your channel. A lot of people subscribe to a channel and then forget about it unless you make sure you are consistent with putting out content. The thing about publishing and uploading videos is some audience members will have email notifications turned on, so that each time you put something up, a group of viewers will know. Your subscribers are likelier to remember you if your videos come out on a regular basis. If your videos are uploaded once a week, on Friday afternoons, your audience will be more likely to remember that you and your channel exist.

Some of your subscribers are going to look at your channel regularly to find what you have released most recently. These audience members will usually engage with, watch, and even comment on your video. When they do this, your video will go up in the rankings on YouTube, bringing more traffic through the search engine, too. The audience members are the ones who will get this momentum flowing for you. But for them to be able to do this, they have to be able to remember your channel, meaning consistency of uploading is key for you.

The Powerful Video Platform:

In our modern world which is increasingly full of social networks, YouTube remains a very powerful platform for your videos. Since we have covered the factors that matter most for building up your subscribers, you can build your channel and videos using this information. Obviously, the most important factor of all is that you create valuable content, but you also need to know how to do this as it relates to SEO on YouTube. Experimenting with plenty of ideas will allow you to find out what works best.

How to win and keep subscribers on youtube

Videos are leading the scene of content marketing as of this year. YouTube is in the lead as far as video blogging goes, along with video marketing and video sharing. The platform is free and offered by the giant search engine, Google. People absolutely love YouTube and use it all the time. Twitter and Facebook have also tried to join the game of video marketing recently but as of yet, have only a tiny fraction of the impact of YouTube. If you already have a channel on YouTube, you might be curious about how to draw more subscribers to your brand as well as increasing how far your videos reach.

Since YouTube has at least a billion visitors each month, a gigantic potential exists for building up your audience, each time you make a new video. This can be a fashion design review video or a skateboard trick tutorial. Either way, YouTube is where people go to find the videos they want. Plenty of brand new YouTube stars are being made every day, so for those seeking publicity and online marketing expansion, it's a must. YouTube is the best way to expand your reach across the online world as a blogger, increasing your connections with readers.

More Tips for Getting Subscribers:

The chances for bloggers to make use of YouTube and bring more traffic to their site is high. In order for this to occur, however, you first need to know how to bring more subscribers to your channel. This detailed section will show you just how to do that. If your main business goal right now is to build up your channel, these tips will help you see tremendous growth within a matter of months.

Make a Script and Plan:

The initial step to making your journey on YouTube successful is to have a plan for your channel and video content. The next step is then to structure how your videos will go. Choose what you like to create and work on getting the skills related to that. Although we mentioned drawing inspiration from your competitor's channels, don't copy what they do. Sticking to what you are passionate about is key for enjoying success with this platform.

- Writing a Script: Your video creation will go much smoother if you actually write out a script since this will keep you on track as you speak and make organization much easier. When you make a script to stick with, you will stay on task instead of getting lost in rambles. This will keep your events flowing perfectly and make your video focused. When you write your script, include the main points to cover, calls to action for your audience (such as subscribing or liking the video), how many words you'll say, and what actions you'll perform while on camera.

- Identify the Target: You need to also identify the target audience, structuring your script on their current understanding and level of information. If you're doing tech videos, are you speaking to tech beginners? Are you talking about Americans or non-native speakers of English? Are they intermediate or experts in the field you're discussing? Are you trying to be informative or funny to suit their tastes? Using the right language for your target audience is a must!

Making Entertaining Videos:

We've already discussed the importance of making videos that are valuable to your audience. This is an obvious one, but your content has to be informative, engaging and also entertaining for viewers. And this has to be the case throughout the whole video, not just the intro or ending. If you lose your hook right in the middle of your video, you're going to lose viewers.

- Informative Video Content: Content that is most valuable to viewers is both informative and entertaining instead of being just one or the other. With all types of marketing, this is the standard, but with videos, it's especially important. Think about it, if someone wanted to find something out just for its informative properties, why wouldn't they just read an article or get a book on the subject? They are watching videos to receive information in a new, more engaging way.

- Evergreen and Burst: More specifically, try to upload a mix of evergreen and burst videos. The burst videos are popular for a short time to get you hits in the short term, but won't stay popular past a certain amount of time. Evergreen content, however, will stay relevant for a long time and get you valuable archived YouTube views. If you can, attempt to make content that is mostly evergreen. If you have a hard time being comfortable in front of a camera, do screen casts, which involve giving information with other images shown.

  However, whichever type of videos you focus on, always ensure they are both valuable and highly engaging before you publish them.

Aim for making More Videos:

This might be simpler to say than to do, but it's very valid for the future success of your channel. One of the main reasons people subscribe to YouTube channels is because they appreciate what they see and are expecting more of it.

- Don't be Forgotten: Subscribers on YouTube won't usually appreciate channels that are dead or don't make a lot of videos. In our modern age, especially, consumers are always looking for more entertainment, and you must be ready to follow these demands to stay relevant. As we've already mentioned many times in the book, consistency is the only way to create a valuable, lasting relationship to your audience.

- Stick to Your Schedule: Try to release your videos according to a strict schedule. One each week is ideal, but you should go for a minimum of one each month. Stay with that schedule and try not to upload anything between, which could hinder your YouTube reputation. People enjoy watching TV series because they can look forward to episodes on certain days. Following this structure will help you be more appealing to viewers.

Be Ruthless in your Editing:

With your YouTube videos, you need to be ruthless with your editing. The famous photographer, Thomas Hawk, says that for each picture he publishes, 10 have been rejected. This should apply to all areas of editing, videos included.

- Don't Rush the Process: Be ruthless with your editing to make sure that what you publish is only your absolute best. If you rush through this for the sake of sticking to your publishing schedule, it's going to hurt your business over time. Instead, adequately prepare and give yourself plenty of wiggle room as far as time goes, so you can select the best content.

- Ask a Friend: If you can't tell which shots of you are best for your final video, ask a friend to watch with you and help you decide which ones are upload-ready.

- Do Plenty of Recordings: Whenever you decide to shoot a video, do plenty of recordings and only select the best ones. Take a lot of shots until you find one that you are confident about. You can edit with Adobe Premier for Windows. The right editing tools will help a lot with this and depending on how serious you want to get about it, you could hire someone to help you edit.

Always Explore and Experiment:

This is meant to be a fun experiment, so don't forget to keep exploring to find what works best for you, personally! Someone else's methods may not work the best for you, so find your own. Experiment with backgrounds, camera angles, thumbnails, and the rest of the methods given to you throughout this book, then track the changes you make and how they impact your audience's reactions. Stick with your business and brand, always staying true to it. Keep in mind that creating something valuable using YouTube requires perseverance, time, and effort. But if you're committed, you'll see the benefits in no time.

Chapter 8

————— ❧✦❧ —————

How to leverage youtube analytics to grow your channel quickly

YouTube Analytics

If you want to crack the code on how to grow your channel, you need to understand YouTube Analytics inside and out. The best way to do this is to know what the key YouTube metrics are and how they are interpreted.

To some people, they are just a bunch of vanity metrics that make your channel look successful to other people. While this is true to some extent, what you need to be focusing on are the actionable metrics that can help your channel grow and attract audiences.

YouTube Analytics is your window to how your channel is growing or failing. It gives you insights into how each of your videos is performing. The stats can be intimidating but you can start looking at a few key statistics that show how your videos are doing.

YouTube Analytics is essentially a gateway to determining your channel's success. By understanding how the analytics works, you can learn to uncover trends and movements to see what's working and what's not working from YouTube's standpoint. With all the data you have in your arsenal, you will be able to determine who's watching your videos, what your viewers are likely to watch, and which videos can potentially make you the most money.

Key Statistics

Looking at the statistics can be overwhelming. If you're not accustomed to looking at graphs and numbers, you're most likely to be intimidated by them. To make things a little more manageable, you must think of YouTube Analytics as a necessary tool to grow a healthy YouTube channel.

If you don't know where to begin, you must focus on a few key statistics and determine if there is an upward or downward trend. When you see a pattern (good or bad), you'll begin to form questions that will help you dive deeper into the analytics of your videos. As you search for answers, you'll begin to get more insights into what's driving your channel's growth or what's impeding its success.

The key statistics to monitor and analyze include watch time, number of views, reach, number of subscribers, traffic sources, and ad revenues. By looking at these key statistics, you can immediately see if there is an upward or downward trend.

The best way to approach YouTube Analytics is to answer these key questions:

1. How is my channel performing?

Your channel's growth hinges on the number of viewers, subscribers, watch time, and audience engagement. Your channel can be considered successful if it is making progress in these key metrics and meeting the goals you have set out for the channel.

2. Who are watching my channel?

Your viewers matter that's why you need to get to know them so you can get an insight into what they are interested in and what would compel them to keep coming back to your channel. If you are able to have an accurate profile of your viewers, you'll have insight into how to tailor your videos to match their preferences.

3. How engaged are my viewers with my channel and videos?

This tells you how the engagement level of your viewers. You can determine if they are binge-watching your videos or engaging in different ways like commenting, liking, or watching the ads on your videos.

4. How much money am I making from my channel?

If YouTube is your business, you'd want to know if you're efforts and hard work are paying off. With analytics, you can easily determine which of your videos are generating revenues and which ones are not performing well in terms of financial returns. You can also identify when your channel is generating the most money.

YouTube Analytics Dashboard

The dashboard is the interface that you'd be looking at when you want to see statistics pertaining to your channel's performance. It gives you the overview, reach, engagement, audience, and revenue.

The three main parts of the channel dashboard are:

- Real-time – This shows the number of people watching your channel and also displays the top videos with real-time views. You'll get an idea of how many viewers are actively watching at certain times of the day.
- Watch time reports – This is where you'll find all the key metrics related to watch time. Information in these reports will tell you about who your viewers are, how long they are watching, where they are discovering you from, and what part of the video is getting their attention.

- Interaction reports – The reports show you how your viewers are responding to your videos. It tells you if they are engaging positively or negatively. It also gives insights into their behavior when it comes to commenting, sharing the videos, or interacting with the videos.

Reach

By looking at the Demographics report, you will have a clear idea of who you are reaching with your videos. Data is categorized by age, gender, and geography. What this tells you is that you can focus on making videos that cater to the type of viewers you are reaching. If you find that most of your viewers are outside of the United States, then you might want to consider adding closed captions or translations on your video. You might even add localized metadata so that it can be accessible to your viewers from a specific geographical location.

How to improve your reach

For you to reach more target audiences, you need to learn how to read impressions and click-through rates. It's suggested that for you to improve your reach, you have to optimize your title and thumbnails. Even if you think that you have optimized them, you might want to make some adjustments if you're not reaching enough people.

In your analytics, go to Reach Viewers, where it will show you data about impressions and click-through rate.

Impression is essentially the number of times that your video is shown to an audience. It does not automatically mean that they're clicking on the video. It just means that YouTube is putting your video out there and showing you how many times it shows up on someone's page. In less formal terms, it's the number of "eyeballs" your video gets. For example, the video may appear on the YouTube search results, but it's not guaranteed that the person who made the search query will click on it. You have to make your video difficult to resist by just looking at the thumbnail and reading the title.

Click-through rate is the percentage of people who saw your video and actually clicked on your video. Next, click on Overview and choose one of the most popular videos and then it'll show you the data within this video. Then compare it to another video. If one video has a higher click-through rate, it's highly likely that the video is attractive to the audience which compels them to click on it. The first things they see are the thumbnail and titles.

When you are evaluating the thumbnails or the titles, you also want to look at your click-through rate. A really great example of this is testing titles and thumbnails and seeing what converts better.

What click-through rate is telling you is that people are compelled to click on our video by just looking at either your thumbnail or your title. This is a great analytical tool for you to gauge the effectiveness of your thumbnails and titles.

Watch Time

Before you can even begin to grow your channel or scale up your business using YouTube, you need to understand watch time as a key metric. Watch time is extremely important for content creators because it's the metric that YouTube uses to evaluate videos and channels.

Watch time is the total number of minutes a viewer spends watching your video. The longer your watch time, the more likely that YouTube will push out your videos and your channel in front of target audiences. This means that your videos will be included in the recommended list for a particular topic or keyword.

A strong watch time performance indicates that you are creating video content that are incredibly engaging that's making your audiences stay on YouTube longer. YouTube rewards content creators who have the ability to keep viewers engaged for as long as possible. YouTube would much rather keep all traffic within the platform than away from it.

To better understand watch time, you have to look to your audience retention report. You can leverage this key tool to improve your content so that you can increase your watch time.

The audience retention can tell you a number of important things: average view duration and average percentage viewed.

The data will be different for everyone depending on the length of the video. If you have a one-minute video and everyone watches the one minute of that video, your average percentage viewed is going to be 100%.

For an hour-long video, there's a great possibility that viewers will only watch the first five minutes or they will skip to certain parts of the video. The longer your videos are, the smaller the percentage will be.

What you need to look at is your audience retention report per video. You can see the video's performance in terms of absolute audience retention and relative audience retention.

Absolute Audience Retention tells you at what point in the video when viewers start dropping off. It means this is the point when they lose interest and move on to the next video that catches their attention.

Relative Audience Retention, on the other hand, shows you how your video compares to other videos on YouTube with a similar length. You'll know how your video is performing relative to other videos with similar video length. You can determine which parts of the video are performing excellently or poorly. It's normal to see your video performing below average towards the middle or the end either because of short attention span, boredom, or unengaging video.

What you need to monitor is the Absolute Audience Retention because this key metric will help you to understand how you can improve your content from the performance of your existing videos.

What's great about YouTube Analytics is that you'll see where the retention takes a dip and you can click on that dip from the chart and it will redirect you to the exact mark in the video where viewers are dropping. This way, you can review your video and see where it went wrong. Perhaps it's because the intro was too long or you digress from the topic or you're not giving the audience what they came to watch your video for. You can take down notes to ensure that you don't make the same mistakes in your future videos.

On the flip side, you have to look at the peaks within your watch time graph. A peak indicates that viewers are rewatching sections of your video. There can be a handful of reasons why they would go back to a specific portion of your video. Just like in the dips, you can click on the peaks to get redirected to a specific mark. Perhaps viewers are going back to the section where you provided valuable tips. Or they may have been going back to sections where controversial statements are made. It could be anything. But whatever it may be, you have to take notes.

The dips usually happen when you're close to the end of the video. In this case, it's normal for people to leave. But if your viewers are dropping midway through the video, there must be something causing that.

What are the key takeaways from looking at audience retention report?

- If there are major drop-offs at certain points in your video, find out the reason why. Analyze your video content and identify possible mistakes. Perhaps people don't like long introductions or they don't agree with what you're saying.
- When viewers are rewatching parts of your video, ask yourself why. Examine the video and figure out what makes viewers go back to that point in your video.

How to Increase Your Watch Time

With the help of YouTube Analytics, you'll be able to determine the type of content you should be posting. If you know how to read your traffic sources, you can find potential content ideas that you can use for your channel in the future.

Traffic sources enable you to understand how exactly people are finding your videos. More often than not, people are finding videos through search. They type in words or phrases and they browse through the search results. If your video ranks for certain keywords, chances are, it would be on top of the results.

Other times, people browse through the suggested list. These are videos that are related to the video that you are currently watching.

If you want to understand what else you can be posting about in terms of content, you can click on YouTube Search, which means that you want to understand how people are finding you on YouTube through the search bar. Through this feature, you'll know which search terms and keywords are sending you views.

Understanding the traffic sources helps you capitalize on the data that you get from YouTube Analytics. It will encourage you to create more engaging content that will compel your viewers to keep coming back for more.

Best Time to Post

YouTube Analytics can also potentially answer the question "When is the best time to post my videos?"

Without looking at data from YouTube Analytics, you should choose the day and time to post based on your ability to stay consistent with your posting schedule. For the YouTube algorithm to favor your video, there needs to be as much engagement as possible within the first 24 hours of the video being uploaded. As long as you can stay consistent and active during the days and the times that you choose to post, you can stick to that schedule.

However, if you want to take it a step further and leverage analytics to choose your post times, you need to learn how to read your demographics. The demographics data will tell you all about your audience. This will give you an insight into when to post your videos on YouTube.

When you click on Geography, you'll see all the different countries that your audience comes from. If you want a much more specific data, click on the map icon and it will show you a map where the majority of viewers are based on State.

For example, if you click on United States, t's going to show you which state your audience is in. This helps you in determining what time zone to post your videos. This means people are awake and active on YouTube or social media.

If you see that the majority of your audience is on the East Coast, then you should be posting videos during peak times in that time zone. If your viewers are mostly from other countries, you have to post on the times they are actively engaging in YouTube or on other social media platforms.

What social media platform to promote your videos

If you know where your traffic is coming from, you can determine the best social media platform to promote your videos. Currently, the most popular platforms are Facebook, Instagram, and Twitter.

If you have data about your traffic sources (or where your views are coming from), you can identify which platforms are the best use of your time to promote your videos to the right audience in order to drive traffic to your channel.

If you're just starting, you may not have enough data to see a pattern that you can confidently base your analysis on. In that respect, you will need to do some experimenting. But as you gather more data, you'll see a clear pattern so you can do away with trial and error.

What you do is you want to go back to your traffic sources and got to External. This shows you all the traffic that you're receiving from external sources. These sources are everything outside of YouTube. It can be your website, blog, Facebook, Twitter, Pinterest, or Instagram.

If you are heavily promoting your videos on Instagram but more viewers are coming from Facebook, it means, that Instagram may not be the marketing route to go. Instead, focus on promoting more on Facebook.

Data on traffic sources a great way to understand where your traffic is coming from. Not only that, you can identify which platforms are performing well and performing poorly as a traffic source. What you think is true can be tested by the data you have. By knowing the best traffic source, you can focus your promotional and marketing efforts on those social media platforms.

Revenue from Monetization

Video content creators who use YouTube as a source of income would be very interested in how their videos are performing from an income standpoint. Your audience contributes greatly to your revenues. That's why if you want to be profitable in the platform, you have to focus on reaching more audiences and catering to their viewing their likes and preferences.

Once your YouTube channel is approved for monetization, you can enable all types of ad formats on your videos so you can earn revenue from them. Aside from that, you can earn from Super Chats whenever you go on live stream.

YouTube Analytics will show you the Revenue Report where you get an overview of your estimated income from different revenue streams. This includes your estimated revenue from YouTube Premium.

The Ad rates report, on the other hand, gives a breakdown of how much income each type of ad is bringing into your YouTube channel. You can get a sense of how well certain types of ads do in the ad rates.

You'll also get data on where your revenue is coming from based on geographical locations. You may be surprised to find that your ad revenue comes largely from countries outside of the United States. Without analytics, you will not know this and you would probably just assume that your revenues all come from the United States.

You can use the revenue data to know where to focus your promotional efforts on and help maximize viewership. As far as YouTube revenue system goes, more views and longer watch time lead to more money for your channel.

Revenue changes over time. You might find that as you grow your channel, you'll experience peaks and dips in earnings. Many factors can contribute to your revenue performance and you'll be able to know what they are when you deep-dive in your analytics.

If you can find patterns when your revenues are on the decline, you can make adjustments in the content you're creating. It's much easier to address the issues if you have data that tells you where you're doing right and where you're doing wrong. Use the insights derived from the data to make mid-course corrections or completely change your video content strategy.

Chapter 9

---- ❧❦❧ ----

Measuring the ROI

From time to time, you will want to find out whether your social media marketing campaign is getting you the results that you anticipated or not. Certainly, you can't argue that your marketing campaign is successful without proper evaluation. It is imperative that to prove to stakeholders that your investment in social media is paying off. This, therefore, makes it important to measure your return on investment (ROI). This chapter takes a look into why measuring ROI is important and how you can successfully do so.

The value that you generate from your marketing efforts on social media can be measured through the use of ROI. This is a common metric used by marketers to gauge how well they are doing with regard to their marketing campaign. So, why should you measure the ROI of your social media campaigns?

There are several reasons why measuring ROI in any social media marketing campaign is essential. One of the most important reasons is the fact that it shows the value gained from using social media as a marketing channel. In addition, through the metrics that are used in ROI measurements, marketers get to prove that marketing on social media is indeed effective. Additionally, it also helps to indicate the specific marketing tactics which are generating admirable results. At the same time, marketers can use insights to determine marketing efforts that are not yielding good results.

Judging from the above reasons, you can conclude that ROI matters a great deal in your social media marketing campaign. But, the question that you might be asking yourself is, "How do you do it?" Well, here is an outline of what you could do.

Define Your Social Media Objectives

Most people will want to jump into the conclusion that your ROI tells you a lot about how much money you are making from your social media campaigns. The truth is that not all brands use their social media pages to boost their revenues. Some use them to increase their brand's awareness whereas others use social media to increase their engagement with their audience. In addition, there are those who use social platforms as an ideal channel to offer customer service.

The point here is that there are many things that social media can help brands to achieve. For that reason, when measuring your return on investment, you should start by defining your objectives. The significance of doing this is that it gives you an idea of how much you are ready to spend on social media.

Set Practical Goals

Next, you should consider setting practical goals. Goals help to tell you more about how you will be using social media to achieve set objectives. Setting SMART goals here is very important. Say your social media objective is to increase your brand's awareness, a well-structured goal will take the form of: 'Increase brand's social share by 10% in three months.'

Track Performance Metrics

After clarifying your goals and objectives, you will want to find out whether you are achieving these goals and objectives or not. This is where performance metrics come in. There are several metrics that you will have to track and analyze including likes, shares, reach, traffic, engagement, revenue generated, and so on. More about these metrics will be discussed later in this section.

Know Your Social Media Spending

As part of ensuring that you accurately determine your ROI, you should pause and go over the amount you are spending on different social media platforms. In this regard, you will want to measure your returns against several aspects including:

- Cost of Social Channels

Contingent on the social media networks that you will be using, you should strive to find out how much you are getting out of your investment. This applies to situations where the social media platform you use has to be paid for.

- Social Ad Spending

You should also measure your returns against the amount of money you are spending on ads either on Facebook, Twitter, Instagram, etc. The good news is that this is a straightforward process since there are tools which will help you in carrying out the analysis.

- Content Creation

Did you spend money on content creation? If so, how much did you spend? It is important that you include your content creation expenses to make sure that you are getting accurate results on your ROI.

Now that you understand the importance of measuring ROI, let's take a closer look at some of the things that you will be measuring.

Awareness Metrics
Awareness metrics will tell you a lot about the audience that is aware of your brand. Some of the specific metrics that you will be tracking here are as described.

Brand Awareness

This metric illuminates the attention that your brand gets on social media during a specified period. There are several metrics that will help you evaluate your brand awareness including shares, mentions, impressions, and links.

Audience Growth Rate

This metric measure how fast your audience is growing on social media. Essentially, it defines how fast your brand is attracting followers.

Post Reach

This metric will tell you more about the number of people who saw your social media post since it went live.

Potential Reach

Unlike post reach, potential reach tells you the number of individuals who would have seen your post at a certain period. This metric is essential since it helps marketers to continuously expand their audience. Therefore, by measuring potential reach, a marketer can gauge their progress.

Social Share of Voice

When tracking mentions, you will also want to know whether there are more people talking about your brand compared to your rivals. To measure this, the social share of voice metric will help you. It is a competitive analysis of how visible your brand is on social platforms.

Engagement Metrics

Metrics here will tell you more about how your brand interacts with your prospects and customers on social media. Below are some of the metrics that will help you measure social media engagement.

Likes and Shares

The number of likes and shares that you get on your social media page will show you how people are interacting with your posts. It is quite simple to track these metrics since the number of likes or shares is displayed on the social platform that you will be using. When using YouTube, for instance, likes are displayed under the video posted on the platform. The same case applies to Facebook and Twitter.

Audience Growth

It is also imperative that you keep track of how your audience is growing within a specified timeframe. The audience growth metric shows you the rate of your audience growth in a month. By utilizing the insights that you will be getting here, you can increase the number of posts if you notice that there are many people who like what you share. Similarly, if there is a decline in your audience growth, this can be seen as a red flag explaining that your target audience is not impressed with your posts.

Followers

An interesting thing about marketing on social media is that you will only be followed if you follow other people. Therefore, you should look for influencers who could be interested in the products that you are offering. In addition, following some of your customers will also help in getting the word out there about your brand.

It is vital that you find a balance between the number of people that you follow and those that follow your brand. Remember that having many followers doesn't mean that you have an added advantage over your rivals. Quality is more important than quantity. Therefore, it is better to have a few followers who will find your content relevant, rather than having thousands of followers who are rarely moved by your posts.

Clicks Per Post

Businesses will want to share blog posts on their social media pages. The links shared on social media can be tracked to determine the number of clicks people have made to reach the business website. More clicks will indicate that people are interested in what you share. Content is what motivates them to click and follow your brand.

Conversion Metrics

The main reason for posting on social media is that you want to get more conversions. A high number of conversions shows that your social media engagement is highly effective. Key metrics in this category include:

Conversion Rate

A high conversion rate will indicate that your social media campaign is effective. It shows the rate at which your audience are taking the desired actions on your posts. For instance, after viewing your social media ad, they went ahead and purchased a product from you.

Click-Through Rate

The number of times your audience click on your call to action links is measured using the click-through-rate metric. This metric takes your audience to other pages where they can view more content. A high click-through-rate shows that your content is quite compelling.

Bounce Rate

This refers to the percentage of individuals who click on a link on your social media posts, but then quickly leave. A high bounce rate will indicate that you are targeting the wrong audience. Conversely, a low bounce rate will imply that your content resonates with your followers.

Customer Metrics

These are metrics which will provide you with the information you need on how your target audience perceives your brand. Some of the metrics to track here include:

Customer Testimonials

Simply put, these are comments or reviews that talk about a particular brand. It goes without saying that good testimonials will demonstrate that people love your brand. Moreover, if there are several recommendations for your brand, it shows that people are happy with your products/services. If you are looking for more testimonials regarding your brand, you should ask your audience to leave a review behind. When doing this, you should never make the mistake of rewarding the people who leave behind testimonials. Some of your followers will end up concluding that your brand lacks credibility.

Customer Satisfaction Score

The level of satisfaction that customers get from your brand is measured using the customer satisfaction score. To track this metric, you have to create a survey on your social media page to ask customers about how they rate your service provision.

Certainly, you must have come across a survey asking you to rate the level of customer satisfaction you gained by depending on a particular brand. The advantage of using this metric is that it is easy to understand and incorporate into your social media marketing campaign. People find it easy to fill out the survey since it doesn't take a lot of time.

Tips to improve your social media ROI

Besides measuring your social media returns on investment, you should also learn how you can improve ROI. There are several considerations that you should bear in mind here.

You Only Improve What You Measure

Despite the fact that there are numerous businesses which use social media to market their brands, few of them get good ROI. This occurs because most businesses fail to understand the importance of measuring their return on investment. Successful social media marketing is not just about posting content on social media and engaging with your followers. You have to gauge whether you are progressing or not.

When businesses fail to measure their ROI, it means that they are unlikely to improve in their marketing campaigns. Perhaps this is one of the main reasons why brands find themselves struggling to penetrate the noise on social media and reach their intended audience. Therefore, before you think about improving your social media marketing campaign, you should start by measuring your ROI more often.

Understand Who is Engaging with Your Content

Your social media ROI can be improved greatly if you invested time in getting to know the people who interact with your content. Knowing your audience helps you to determine the best metrics to measure your performance.

Define Relevant Metrics

The last thing that you should do is to use particular metrics just because your competitors are using them. This will only mislead you as you will end up measuring statistics which are not relevant to your business. For that reason, you ought to take a step back and evaluate the metrics that work for you. The best way of doing this is by choosing metrics which are in line with your set goals.

Post Frequently

Regular posts are more effective compared to infrequent posts from brands. There is a good chance that customers will want to follow a brand that engages with them more often. When striving to capture your audience's attention by posting regularly, you should make sure that you deliver the right content to them. More importantly, posting at the right time will make a huge difference as it will guarantee that your posts can be seen by your target market.

Choose Ideal Social Media Channels

Choosing the right social media channels to reach your audience is something that should be prioritized above anything else. This is where your audience spends most of their time. Therefore, it is crucial that you make the right decision regarding the platforms that you will be using to post your ads. Posting your social media ads on the wrong platform will only render your marketing campaign ineffective. This is because no one will see what you are posting.

Your first step in your marketing campaign should be to understand your audience. This includes knowing the social media platforms that they use. Targeting them in the right places will boost your chances of improving your ROI.

Create Quality Content

Creating and sharing quality content will also have a positive impact on how people engage with your brand on social media. Your customers expect your content to entertain and educate them. Don't focus too much on selling your brand. Social media requires that you bring in the social aspect of your marketing campaign. As such, humanize your brand by showing people that you can interact with them on a personal level. In the end, they will not hesitate to recommend your brand to their friends on social media.

Motivate Your Social Media Team

Your social media team will greatly influence the success or failure of your social media campaign. If you keep your team motivated, they will work diligently to accomplish your marketing goals and objectives. Motivation here can come in the form of showing your team that you are working with them rather than pushing them around. If possible, ensure that you train them regularly on vital social media marketing tactics that they should implement.

Push for User Engagement

There is no greater feeling than making your audience feel like they are valued. Surprisingly, this is easily achieved by engaging with them. Brands often ignore their customers and give excuses like they lack time to reply to all their customers' comments or complaints. User engagement is key to winning over the hearts of your customers. Therefore, you should think about hiring a team that will specifically work to make sure that your followers are paid attention to.

Always Experiment

Thriving in your social media marketing campaign also calls for experimentation. You have the freedom of trying out different marketing strategies and finding out whether they are effective. You can also experiment by changing your brand's voice and gauging how people respond to the adjustments. It is from such experiments that you can gain a unique marketing strategy that guarantees you accomplish your marketing goals within a short period of time.

Use Real-Time Apps

Customers will fancy the idea of using your social media business app to gain a better engagement experience. This is because there are more customizable engagement options when using your social media business app. Accordingly, you should consider the idea of developing apps which can help bring together people who are not only interested in your brand but those who are looking to connect with your followers.

The bottom line is that measuring your social media marketing ROI ascertains that you know the direction that your social media campaign is taking. Ideally, it is the best way of knowing that you are not operating blindly as you promote your products and services on social media.

Chapter 10

---- ❧❧❧❧❧ ----

Using social media to promote your channel

The impact of social media on your YouTube subscriber and view count is of such tremendous importance that this entire chapter is dedicated to using social media successfully to your advantage.

The primary goal of using social media is only to increase your view count in your videos and develop a strong fan base that favors your videos. This doesn't directly give you any profits, but it helps build a solid viewer base and reaches out to those who do not know about you or your videos. In the end, it all comes down to your view count and ad clicks on your videos, which significantly affects your profit.

If used in the right way, social media can help boost your view count several fold. As mentioned before, your YouTube videos have their unique address or "URL." Copy this URL and paste it in your Facebook, Twitter, or any forums you frequent. Any user who clicks this URL will be directed to your YouTube video, at which point, if it interests the person, he will subscribe and add to your pool of views. Make sure to include these URLs only in places that do disturb or annoy the other users.

Try and convince your family and friends to see your videos beforehand when you start out. It is important to get someone's opinion as it may be different from yours. Try to correct your mistakes before using social media platforms to promote your videos and channel. If you end up uploading a mediocre video in your initial stages, your audience will get an impression of you being a mediocre video creator. Under no circumstances should this happen. So, take precautionary measures, and make your first few videos the best before promoting them.

Given below are some of the most widely used social media platforms to effectively promote your videos and channel. Read on to know how you should go about promoting your videos and how you can gain a larger audience.

Facebook

Facebook, as an example, is the perfect place to paste these URLs on your own timeline or on a Facebook page that you have created to promote your channel. This way, only people who are interested can view your videos. Unnecessarily posting URLs and videos on another user's page or private chats could take a turn for the worse as it builds a bad reputation.

Facebook has the additional option of paid marketing. You pay a nominal price, and your videos will be displayed at the top of the user's homepage. This means more traffic as your videos have more chance of being watched if they are placed first. Despite nominal prices, you might not want to use this option initially until you have enough subscribers and a steady view count. Using YouTube for profit requires zero initial investment, and hence, you should be able to pay for the marketing from your profits and not your pockets.

Despite this, many viewers stop watching your videos after clicking on your link. To overcome this, link the URL of a playlist of your videos that are related in some way or the other instead of a single video. This helps the viewers get interested and stay interested.

Instagram

Not many YouTube video creators consider using Instagram as a way to promote their videos, but it is an absolute fun and easy way to do so. As with Facebook and Twitter, you need to link your Instagram account as well on your YouTube channel and vice-versa. Instagram should be used to give regular updates about your life, if you want to of course. Most people like to know about the daily life of YouTubers, and you should get a good number of hits on your Instagram profile, which means you also have a chance at gaining more hits on your

YouTube channel and videos. Apart from this, you can and should upload teasers of your next video. It should not contain the essence of the video itself; rather, you need to post pictures that make the audience hungry for more. This way, you are guaranteed a good number of views on your videos if you make your Instagram posts enigmatic. A good idea would be to release a teaser the day before you upload the actual video. This ensures your viewers are still interested. Setting up an Instagram account is fairly easy, and you can update your posts on it regularly with just your smartphone, which saves a lot of time.

Twitter

Twitter also holds great potential in increasing your view count. Hashtags are your greatest weapons; use them right, and you can easily set a trend that helps with promoting your video. Make sure to reach out to people with similar interests as you, and give them shootouts in your videos and request them to do the same for you. This ensures that their fans, subscribers, and viewers know about you, which once again spells nothing but profit.

Being interactive is one of the best ways to sustain the interests of your viewers, and Twitter chat is the best way to interact with your viewers. Create a custom hashtag, tell your viewers the exact date and time you will be online to chat, and start chatting! Interact with your viewers, respond to questions, figure out what they expect more from you, build some trust, and lastly, always thank them for spending their precious time to view your videos. This not only helps create more interest, but also a higher number of viewers as everybody likes their opinion being considered. This can sound slightly arduous and time consuming, but Twitter is very smartphone-friendly. You can perform these actions while travelling or when you have free time, saving you time that can be used to create content for your next video or to go about your daily life. While Facebook should be the primary platform through which you get the support of viewers, you should aim to provide regular updates on the topic of the next video via Twitter. Note that your tweet is limited to 140 characters, so it only makes sense to keep your updates as short and mysterious as possible to provoke the interests of your viewers. Always link URLs to your videos at the end of your Facebook post or Twitter tweet.

Blogs

If you are a blogger with an already well-established audience, promoting your YouTube channel should be much easier. Simply include URLs to your blog on your YouTube channels and to your YouTube channel in your blog. This leads to more traffic in both places and hence more income. Creating videos related to the article you blogged about and pasting their URLs in your article is the best way to increase traffic. A video demonstration or tutorial or summary is always preferred to a written one. A blog requires you to regularly update the content; else it loses the interest of viewers. This gives an incentive to update your YouTube videos and stay ahead of others in trending topics to tremendously support your blog and vice-versa.

If you are not interested in creating a blog and maintaining it or feel that it takes up too much of your time, then it is a good idea to look up bloggers who create similar content to your videos. You can then request them to link your videos or your channel in their blogs for a small fee (only if the blogger has a large fan base, of course) or you could strike a deal where you link their blogs in your videos and they link your videos in their blogs. This is a great way to set up mutual trust and gain each other's followers.

Google+

YouTube is owned by Google, so why not use Google's own social media platform, Google+, to promote your channel? The great thing about Google+ is that you don't have a character limit like Twitter does. It is a great replacement to blogging, and you should consider it as a miniature blogging platform. All you need to do is create your own personal logo, a custom look on the channel, and give your Google+ page a personal touch to let yourself be more easily recognizable. You can include your video links in your posts to gain more support. Unlike Facebook, a large number of Google+ users use it for marketing. You should try to find out similar individuals or professionals in the same niche and engage with them. Try to share their posts if you feel the need to do so, and you increase your chances of them sharing your content. It is also a great place to get feedback and advice from professionals who have already been down the road you are taking. Like Twitter, hashtags are used in Google+ as well but just not to the same extent. Use precise hashtags to get more hits and never give your posts innumerable inaccurate hashtags as it is an indisputable way of bringing forth hate comments from your audience.

MySpace

MySpace is another popular social networking website and can be used extensively to promote your YouTube channel.

The Share Trend

Sharing is an amazing way to rally more viewers. All it requires is you to ask your viewers to share your videos if they liked it with their friends and family. It is a given that most of them won't. But once a few people start sharing and your videos get around, it's only a matter of time before it is trending.

The idea behind sharing is to get you introduced to people who do not know about your videos yet. They view your videos and, in turn, share them, which leads to a hopefully never-ending cycle. Shares are the best way to get your videos around. What this means is your videos gain more traffic.

A requirement to this is a lenient privacy setting on your social media pages like Facebook and Twitter. You want your videos to be watched by people other than your friends. Make sure your videos are visible to the public at large, and you have a shot at gaining the large number of viewers that you want. Keeping your settings secured eventually will lead to a loss in your subscriber count as your videos will not be going around the social media platform as much as you would like them to. For this reason, it is optimal to create a different account or a page in the social media platform dedicated only to your videos. You can link back to your personal profile which you will be keeping secure and tell your viewers to personally give you requests and feedback or so there. This helps with security as well as getting you the maximum shares possible.

Social media is all about a person's opinion being heard. You may upload videos and promote them with all your resources, and they will not generate the expected traffic if you do not take some time to respond to your viewers. This is the most important part of using social media to promote videos. Always remember to ask people to like, subscribe, and comment. This will give you a general feedback. Ignore the mean posts if they do not have any constructive criticism. A good idea would be to upload a "Q & A" video where you answer some of the questions asked in your previously uploaded videos. This serves a dual role of making your viewers feel appreciated and increasing your income.

Effectively utilizing the social media available to you almost guarantees in gaining never-before-seen traffic and subscribers. It also ensures you have active and not passive subscribers, i.e., those who subscribe to you and view your videos regularly.

Chapter 11

———— ❧☙ ————

Reach your target audience

To reach your target audience, you have to know who they are. And to know who they are, you have to think about their age, their location, their relationship status, their agenda, the personality, their interest, their education, and their career. You need to ask yourself what do your audience want and how you will give it to them. You need to ask yourself what they need and if you can provide that thing. You need to ask yourself which problem do they have and if you can solve that problem. You need to ask yourself what their dreams are, and can you help them to achieve those dreams. How will they be entertained and can you entertain them?. Most importantly, how are they going to follow you? You need to know what are your target audience's biggest motivations are.

The biggest shift in moving from having a typical account to having an account that will generate revenue from for you is to shift your perspective from being self-centered to being audience-centered. First of all, you need to answer these above questions even though you will realize some of the questions require more specific answers than others. For instance, you might not want to target only one gender, but at least you have thought about it and you have explained why you don't want to target only one gender.

The point of all this is for you to be as intentional as possible about your target audience. You need to constantly ask yourself, why don't I know my target audience. If you don't know your target audience, then you need to think Deeply. You can create some imaginary people that you think would be your perfect followers. Give them some backstories. Give them a hair color. Give them names. Give them different names. Have a solid visual perception of the people that you are creating your content for. You might even find out that your target audience is very similar to you. If that's what you found out, then that is great because you already know yourself better than everyone else. You need to think about all your dreams and visions and all the answers to the questions that you mentioned above. And how to target your target audience.

You should think about the Instagram account that you enjoy looking at the most and ask yourself what do I like about this Instagram account and why do I even like it in the first place? Why or ask yourself why don't I like this account in the first place or why does it bother me?.

If you don't know any Instagram account that you enjoy him, then you should go to your niche and look at all the Instagram account that you follow and write down all your thoughts and opinions about the Instagram account.

Go where they are

Now once you have nowhere your target audience is. You should go where they're hanging. They are already hanging out somewhere. Your mission is to find those pages that they are following. Find the Instagram accounts that they are liking. Find those topics that they are commenting on. Find out where they are. Find their favorite pasta. Find out their favorite account. Find out their favorite Instagram account. And then start following them. Start building a relationship with those accounts. Get to know their hashtags The hashtags are usually the best place to start looking around those pages and you find the accounts that are already big players there.

Organize your marketing goes

Once you have decided to work on Instagram, then you have already switched into the world of marketing. And all you need to do to go is to change your thought process and start thinking like a marketer. Do you know that you are already officially a brand once you create an Instagram account so every decision that you make needs to be in line with this brand? Brands have their rules, algorithms, and regulations, so you need to have your own rules and regulations.

Instagram rules are always changing, they are never permanent and it can make life difficult for you. But your goal is to change no matter what Instagram throws at you. The basis of marketing will always remain the same, and the basic principle of effective marketing is for you to go where they already are. Know what you want them to do, and know who you want to reach. And you need to know what you want to do with them. You need to allow them to know what is in for them and what will be easy to make them act.

You need to be patient and flexible with them. You got to understand that no two accounts at the same even if they look very similar. This means what will work brilliantly for one account will not work for another account, even if you create 11 different accounts that are nearly identical in the same industry and you're targeting the same audience and using the same voice to target all the audience.

You still cannot use one strategy for all account, because the same thing will not work for different accounts. There are many Instagram experts out there telling you to use one certain strategy, but you have to understand that one strategy will not work for all. Even if you get progress today, it doesn't mean that you will get progress tomorrow, because things might change. Even if you copy the strategies that big account uses, it might not work for you.

You might read a strategy that somebody used to gain 20 followers in 5 minutes but when you try the strategy, you might only get one follower in 5 minutes, and that will unfollow you shortly after. Then after some months again, you might try that strategy and it will work. After some time, you will discover that all your old tricks are no longer working so you will have nothing else to do. So you should never get too comfortable with Instagram, you have to be changing and you have to be trying things out and testing things out simple ideas and don't expect anyone to work for the long-term.

Just constantly watch your results and keep on brainstorming new ideas or new approaches.

Determine your vision

You need to ask yourself questions about your product and your brand. If you are marketing a product to your followers that you haven't released yet, then you can ask one of your followers to test that product out. For instance, if you are marketing a seasonal product from Starbucks, you can also use it as if they are excited to be part of it. Asking your followers to comment on their favorite post or product is a great way to encourage engagement with them and to market your product. But it will also encourage them to leave positive comments rather than negative ones.

You could simply ask your followers simple questions like what will you wear with those blue shoes. So try to create a vision for your Instagram account to determine what you want to be over time. And what you want your account today and exactly what you want your account to say. The time in which you want to post in the morning, and exactly what you want to post in the night and determine who your account is going to help, and who your account is not going to help. So that you won't once people come to your account they will already know if the account is for them or if the account is not for them.

They cannot instantly know if they should follow you or if they should not follow you. If you check your current Instagram account or any of your social media accounts I'm sure you will see tons of people that are not your target market following you. You will see people that can't even speak your language following you, and this is bad for business. If you are trying to build an Instagram page that is able to generate money for you, then you need to be able to specify a target audience. You don't need a general target audience for your Instagram account, you need a very specific audience .you need specific people who are coming to look for specific kind of results to follow you, you don't want just any random person to follow you.

If you are building an Instagram account that sells clothes, then you need people who are interested in fashion to follow you. If you are building an Instagram account that sells shoes, then you need to sell to high-class ladies that are interested in shoes to follow you. The same thing, if you are selling watches on your Instagram account, then you need people that are interested in luxury things to follow you. If you are trying to sell high fashionable clothes or a 2020 model type of clothes, then you wouldn't want somebody that is 60 years old to be following you. The same thing applies, if you are sending women shoes, you wouldn't want men to be following your Instagram account.

You will only want women to be following your Instagram account. So you have to determine your vision for your Instagram account. You also need to determine where this account will be in the next 5 years. Are you going to sell it off? Are you going to start an affiliate marketing? Are you going to start drop shipping products? Are you going to sell digital products? What exactly do you intend doing with the Instagram account?

You have to determine all that upfront, even before you create the Instagram account, even before you click on the sign-in button on Instagram; you have to determine exactly where your account is going to lead to. Because if you intend to sell affiliate products on your Instagram account, then you will manage it differently than if you want to drop ship products on your Instagram account and you will manage it differently if you want to sell digital products on your Instagram account. Also, you need to determine which name is going to be using. You need to determine all of this upfront.

Direct users to clink your profile

Even if you're utilizing the clickable link in your bio, you have to update it to the current all relevant content and make your users know that you have updated the link in your caption. You could say something like, want to learn more about this link, then click on my bio. This is great especially when you're posting the video or a photograph of a product and you want users to be able to engage with the product and buy from you. You could also put a shopper bill link in your bio and write something like, "to shop this product, then follow the link in our bio." Try to offer additional insights to the link, or supporting data. This is no brainer especially because the caption is the best place to be able to capture your followers and provide them with more information on the content of the photograph or the video or to provide them with unique insight or supporting data that they may have not known before.

You could also post the photo of a member of your team or an industry leader, and when you post their photography, you also want to include the names of the people in the caption and provide more information about those people. You could also post their achievements, and who they are.

Encourage action

If the image that you are posting features a particular product, then try to encourage the users to purchase the product by telling them to get their hands on it. And then provide additional information to the link of the website that you want them to purchase it, and also the price of the product that you want them to purchase. You should also encourage them to take action by donating if you are a non-profit company, or you could also post the link for them to attend a brand-related event. To do that, you just need to post the image of the shot or the venue, the image of the setting, and say something like, "join us today at 2.pm time, for more important connections, interesting conversations, and great refreshments." Always use fill in the blank sentences.

A great way to be able to encourage engagement with your post and your followers is to offer them insights and to use fill in the blank statements by saying something like, "my favorite way to start the day is blank, and then use the photograph of somebody that is enjoying your product in the morning. That way, followers will be able to state their own personal routines under the comments section, and this will make your followers be able to associate your product with their morning routine without you even being aggressive or too forward about it.

Chapter 12

------ ❧❧❧ ------

Set up your business profile

In order to get popular on Instagram, you should have a great account with amazing pictures, a few other tricks up your sleeve, and you're set. There are millions of users who have an account on Instagram and you need to put in some effort in order to be amongst the best of them. If you put up the right posts at the right time, you're quite likely to get popular in a short time. As you read on, we will guide you to create an Instagram profile that will be the envy of others.

➤ Your first step in creating an account is choosing the perfect username. Your name should be catchy and should catch the eye of other users. Try not to make it too long or have too many symbols in it.

➤ The second step is choosing the perfect profile picture. Putting up your own photo is the best option so that people will connect your profile to your face. Find a fun, good quality picture of yourself to use for this purpose or take a new one.

➤ You should now give careful thought to choosing a theme for your Instagram profile. It has been noticed that pages with a particular theme get more followers and likes on their posts.

This is because the followers will know exactly what the page is about and follow based on their interest. You can also choose to post whatever you want outside of any specific theme that limits you. However, a themed page has more chances of becoming popular. For instance, if you are someone who loves food, make your account food related. If you are interested in fashion, focus on that. This allows users to have an idea of what they'll be seeing in their feed by following your account. In fact, your theme can have variations other than a subject area. Your theme could be a color, where all your pictures are black and white or have a pink hue. It could also be random pictures of different places with your dog in all of them. Get creative with your theme and make it uniquely yours.

➤ After you have decided a theme, start clicking some great pictures. Learn how to use your camera in the best way possible to get the best shot. You can go ahead and click a hundred different photos of the same subject to get the best angle. This is worth it even if you just end up using one image you think is perfect. Get a firm grasp on how the editing options in Instagram work as well. This will help you enhance your images and give them the best visual possible.

➤ Build a portfolio before your start working on getting more followers. There are a lot of tricks you can use to generate traffic to your profile but very few people will follow you if your profile is empty. So start by uploading a few great pictures that will make your account look good and make users anticipate better posts in future. Don't upload a meaningless, bad quality post. Quantity is not what you are aiming for, but quality definitely is. Work on getting these pictures up and then get those followers.

➤ Find out what the best photo editing applications are. Download the ones that suit your purpose and theme. Utilize all the amazing options available. Different applications offer different tools to make your photos better or more creative. Some will let you adjust the brightness, saturation, etc. Others will allow you to insert text in different typography on the photo. Use these for posting great pictures on your Instagram account.

➤ Give some thought to the captions. You can choose to have short or long captions. However, these should be to the point and not some boring narrative your followers lose interest in reading halfway through. Your captions could be inspiring, funny, sarcastic, or just about anything that inspires some type of emotion. They should, above all, relate to the photo and not be completely out of context. You can tell the story of your picture using its caption. This will help your followers relate more to your content.

➤ Be personal in your posts. After all, your profile is entirely yours and should be distinctive from others. Other users will choose to follow you only if they feel your feed is distinct from other run-of-the-mill accounts they have no interest in. Your followers should be able to feel a connection with you. It doesn't mean that you have to have some kind of emotional outburst in every post. Getting personal means the user feels that they are seeing bits and pieces of you in your photos and not just a random cup of coffee. Your coffee picture should narrate a story of whom you are having it with or where you like it best. That personal touch can make a big difference.

➢ Link your Instagram profile to any and every other social media accounts you have. This could be your Facebook account or any other blog you have as well. This will help you generate a greater number of followers from there to your Instagram. If you have a huge following on Twitter or any such network, just update a post and let them know you are now on Instagram as well. Most of them will definitely follow through, if not all.

➢ Make your Instagram site unique as compared to any other social media account you have. Give your friends and other users a reason to follow your Instagram account specifically. Why would they do this if all your content were the same on every online profile that you have? If you have a popular Tumblr account, your followers would follow you on Instagram as well if they felt there was something more or different to see on Instagram and not just the same thing in a different format.

➢ Follow other users and like their posts as well. Other Instagram users usually want the same thing as you, even if they aren't going about it the same smart way as you are. However, liking the posts others put up will adds a lot of brownie points for you. Find other people's accounts where the posts are similar to yours. See who follows these accounts and then follow them. Once you appear on their news feed, they will probably check out your account and follow you back. You should also like the posts of the people you follow or else you will just look as if you are a ghost account. You can also choose not to follow these people and just like or comment on their pictures. This will also get their attention if you don't want to follow as many people as you want followers. Your comments will not only be noticed by the owner of the profile, but also other followers of the same person.

➢ Interact with your followers and other users. Comment on pictures other users put up. Most people appreciate comments more than likes on their pictures. You can be among the select few who make this effort. This will definitely make the user interested in your account and maybe make them follow you as well. You should also make it a point to reply to all the comments people leave on your posts. This will encourage them to continue commenting and liking your other pictures. It also builds a loyalty following for you because of the interactive effort you made. This will help build your own Instagram community.

➤ Use hashtags to direct people to your photos even if they aren't following you. The main way in which Instagram users discover each other are by searching for tags on categories that interest them. You should also pay attention to which hashtags are trending during that period and use them on your posts. This will allow more likes to be generated on your post while that particular tag is trending.

➤ Contests are yet another great way in which you can engage with other Instagram users. You can also hold your own contest at some point on your page when you have a lot of followers and a particular theme to your page. This will, in turn, direct more traffic to your Instagram profile and allow you to gain more followers.

➤ Do not post too many pictures too often. Your followers don't want just your posts to flood their feed. Make sure to pay attention to quality over quantity. This will see a much more positive reaction from the user base. Post one good picture a day instead of ten bad pictures that have no point.

➤ Make an effort to find out what kind of posts people like more often. While you should stick to your unique theme, you need to give this some thought if you want a huge number of followers in a short time. Posting such content will only work to your benefit. For instance, most users have noticed that pictures taken at the beach or have sunsets are very popular and get a large number of likes as compared to others. By uploading such content, you will surely see more followers on your account faster than if you posted other pictures all the time. You should keep posting what interests you, but also make a conscious effort to put up pictures that interest the audience you want to keep engaged in your profile.

➤ Yet another thing that you should keep in mind, your profile should be public. The privacy setting should not be switched on to the private account tab. This will definitely not work in your favor if you want more number of followers on your account. It will actually make it harder to attract new follower when they can't even see what your profile contains.

➤ Give a moment to write a good bio as well. You can make it short, yet effective in order to gain people's interest. Make the content meaningful or catchy. It can be a brisk description of who you are or what your interests are.

Chapter 13

─────── ❧❧❧❧ ───────

Get more followers

Tips and Tricks to Increase Your Followers

Brands desire to have a large following on social media. It is a general belief that more followers mean more engagement and higher chances of making sales. Therefore, they do everything humanly possible to gain new followers. However, there are different tricks you can apply to increase your fans. These tricks are meant to be followed religiously. You are guaranteed massive followers if you adhere to every instruction.

Create Quality Contents

Before you can be regarded as a thought leader in your niche, sufficient evidence of your posts needs to exist. Users would instead not follow an account that barely has engaging contents. You should post quality and relatable contents that can spur engagements. Users can post their reactions in the comments section. Also, they can tag their friends on posts they think is worth sharing.

Visit Pages with Similar Niches

It is recommended that you take a gander at what they are up to. You can get one or two insights there. Also, you can drop honest and intelligent opinions via the comments section. Other users who have noticed your comments would likely follow you because they believe that you possess a vast deal of knowledge in their field.

Share Your Profile Link on other Social Media Accounts

This technique has been known for its effectiveness. Followers on other social media accounts may be newbies who might not have an idea of who to follow. Posting your links on other social media accounts might make them click on the link and check your profile. If they deem you worthy, you may earn a follow.

Share Your Instagram Link on Your Website or Blog

If your website or blog boasts of a significant traffic every day, you can post your Instagram profile link. People who visit your website or blog can be redirected to your Instagram profile via the link, and you might earn yourself a follow or two.

Upload Multiple Photos

Photos attract a vast deal of attention. You can post multiple photos if you want to garner attention and follows. Users can swipe through pictures and click on the Follow button when everything goes on well.

Write Short and Witty Captions

Your captions need to be kept short because the average person has a low attention span. Therefore, you need to compose a caption that will grab attention in an instant.

Mention and Tag Other People in Your Posts

When you tag other people in your posts, it is visible in a section where tagged posts appear. If the person you tag is an influencer, more people can view your post through this medium, and they can even follow you if they find your content interesting and engaging.

Comment on Blogs Related to Your Niche

You can visit a blog that shares similar interests and leave comments. Remember to include your Instagram profile URL in the comments. This way, more people will be able to connect with you.

Create an Email Newsletter

This doesn't apply to your followers only. Gather email addresses any way you can and create newsletters that you can send out periodically. You can use apps like Mailchimp to set up your newsletter. You should note that the newsletter needs to contain solutions to a general problem. However, these problems can be the ones your brand can solve using your products and services. Also, you can offer professional and not-too-personal advice from time to time. This is a way to show you do care. Always include the URL of your Instagram profile in the newsletters so they can click directly from the mail and connect with you.

You Can Suggest Your Profile to Your Contacts

There are many communication tools used nowadays. It isn't surprising to see someone use WhatsApp, Telegram, and the likes. You can suggest your profile to your contacts too. You might have a large contact base. You should maximize this opportunity. It isn't limited to WhatsApp and Telegram alone. Even your mail contacts are not left out. You need to tell them the value you are creating and convince them that following you is quite beneficial to them.

Use Popular and Relatable Hashtags

This one cannot be stressed enough. These hashtags have the power to place you on the world map. That means you should really use them. They are like fuel to the growth engine in a post. If you include the popular and relatable ones in a quality post, you are guaranteed more engagements and even follow. New users can click on your profile and scroll through your posts. Jump on favorite conversations that are being talked about while you are planning to create your content.

Post Contents Regularly

Many brands are skeptical on posting contents regularly in a bid not too appear lousy. However, this is a very wrong notion. Brands should not be afraid of posting regularly. You need to be active at all times, and regular posts are a way of showing your regularity. People do not like following inactive or less active accounts. However, you should refrain from posting uninspiring, dull, and attractive posts.

Attach Your Page Link to Every Marketing Material

Marketing materials are likely to attract more followers. They are sent to a wide range of people, so it doesn't hurt to include your page link in these materials, including your business cards, signature, handbooks, souvenirs, etc.

Organize Contests on Your Page

The average human loves freebies, so you should use it to your advantage. You can organize competitions on your page from time to time. It can be in this form:

"What year was our Instagram page launched? Five lucky winners get blah blah blah. Winners would be picked randomly. Remember to include #XYZ. You need to be following to be eligible."

The above example shows that something is up for grabs. They will most likely jump on it. Your comments sections will be filled with answers from various people. You have also indicated that you will pick winners randomly. Therefore, everyone thinks he or she stands a chance to win a freebie. The comments will not stop trickling in. The next instruction says that they should include a hashtag. This is an effective way to promote a hashtag. Since they are eager to win the freebie, users will add the hashtag to avoid being disqualified. The last instruction reads that they need to be following your account. Non-followers will undoubtedly follow the account since they do not want to be ineligible. Comments achieved, hashtag promotion achieved, more followers gained. What more do you want from this promotion?

How to Create a Top-Notch Instagram Contest

Before you set up your contest, you need to ensure that you are not violating any Instagram policy because it would be a fruitless effort setting up a game only for the post to be taken off the Instagram app by the developers. You should note the following:

You must include rules, conditions, and people who are eligible when setting up a contest.

You need to clearly define it that Instagram is not the sponsor of your contest.

You should include a peculiar hashtag in your contest. It has to be only associated with your brand. This will promote brand visibility. You can even add the hashtag in your bio. There is an emphasis on "peculiar" because numerous individuals and brands can adopt other hashtags, and it cannot be linked to you. However, you can also include generic hashtags in your post(s) to increase popularity.

Set up your contest using a quality photo, video, or GIF. Your contest has to be enticing and engaging. Therefore, you need nothing short of quality. You can search for design templates on the internet. You can also brand these visuals as a way of promoting your brand.

Give away a brand-related prize. As much as cash giveaways are the trends, you need to consider the value such giveaway would add to your brand. For example, if you are a travel or tourist agency, you can give away free travel visas or discount prices to winners. These winners will share their testimonies on their page after having their fun moments.

Interact with Influencers

You can visit the profiles of influencers you can identify on Instagram and turn on their post notifications. Whenever they post contents, ensure you like and engage them with comments. They will notice your activity if you do it frequently. This can endear you to them. Influencers do free promotions on certain days, so you stand a chance of being a recipient. Also, some users go to influencers' page to build their followers. They follow accounts that have liked and commented on posts.

Also, you can pay these influencers to post a screenshot of your account on their feeds. Instead of posting your contents, they can post screenshots and attach your username as caption, asking followers to follow your account.

Go Local

You can look for posts uploaded from places around you. You can tap on the Search icon, click on the Places tab, and input the particular area you are looking at. It can be a neighborhood, town, city, state, or country. Comment on posts you are conversant with. It can be a topic peculiar to this location. Input your opinions, and you might start a conversation. Other people who have different ideas and opinions can chip in theirs too. At the end of the discussion, you can follow them, and they shall reciprocate because of the kind of relationship you have built.

Add the Share and Like Buttons to Your Website and Blog Posts

You can add the share and like buttons to every post on your website or blog. When viewers click on these buttons, it will be shared on their social networks. Their friends can view these posts and click on the links provided. When they read the posts, they can be intrigued and check your profile. Since you have the link to your Instagram profile embedded in your website or blog, it is easy to visit the profile and follow your account.

The Follow-Unfollow Technique

This method is a proven method of gaining more Instagram followers. Almost everyone is doing it. In general, when people follow you only to unfollow, it is not because they are not interested, it is because they are also trying to build their brand just like you are also trying to do. People follow others so they can notice their pages and follow back. Some people even go as far as sending direct messages only to let you know that they have followed you, and they expect a follow-back. Often, people glance through their accounts and follow back. However, people who gain followers rapidly might lose count of accounts following them, so they might not notice. Honestly, many people are not even interested in your account. They only need you to add to the numbers. You won't even know that until they unfollow you a few days later.

How This Technique Works

First, you need to find various accounts with a large following who share similar interests with you. You can even turn on post notifications. Every time these accounts post new contents, like and also post comments. Then start following everyone who likes these posts and check the comments sections and follow those who post comments too. The instruction is so particular on similar interests because you do not want to amass followers who do not care a hoot about what you do. They will be there to add to the numbers, but they will give you little or no engagements.

Be consistent with the follows. At least 30 percent of those you have followed would follow you back.

You should note that you can only follow 7,500 accounts at a time.

After forty-eight hours, you can follow those who did not follow back or unfollowed you. There are many third-party apps on whatever mobile OS you are making use of. Instagram does not support these apps, so they find ways of taking them down. Find different apps from time to time. Unfollowing them is a way to even out the followers' ratio.

Shoutout-for-Shoutout Technique (S4S)

This is a technique where two or more users have agreed to post each other's contents and give shoutouts, asking followers to follow the accounts.

This is another technique that has had positive impacts on those trying to build their Instagram accounts. There is nothing special required. All you require are popular accounts that share the same niche with you. All you have to do is share an engaging post created by them on your feed. Ask your followers to follow the account too. In the same vein, they can reciprocate the gesture. This is a way to increase your followers.

Some Other Things You Need to Know

To make it fair and enjoyable, you can request for shoutouts from accounts that have a similar number of followers as you. It is very commonplace to see accounts with over 40,000 followers add phrases like "S4S 40k+" to their bio. This means that accounts with less than 40,000 followers should not even consider contacting them for S4S. However, if your followers' number is close to 40,000, you can still message them. They might consider.

Users who are up for S4S add their email addresses to their bio. This means that they want you to message them privately for details. Also, you can send them private messages via Instagram Direct. For business pages, the Contact button is available if you need to talk to them. This means that if you need to send a particular picture or details to the target user, you can use the call-to-action button made available, or you can send a direct message. Also, you can send emails.

You should also note that some accounts would agree to do S4S with you, but the condition is the post would be on their page for a limited time. It would be deleted after the stipulated time. You do not have much choice. Even worse, some people sell shoutouts. This is just to let you know the hustle is real. People do pay. Branding must develop.

If you see a profile that has "S4S" embedded in it, you can send a message and make the proposal. They can ask you some questions, and if they feel confident doing business with you, they might agree to a deal.

Why S4S Works

A lot of people question the efficacy of S4S. It is quite useful if you learn the ropes and act appropriately. An Instagram with a large follower base is not required before you can use the technique. No matter the number of followers you have, look for similar accounts that have almost the same number of followers and engage each other. You can join these accounts, develop a relationship, and show them you do care about their developments.

The more the numbers grow, the more you need to reach out to other accounts solely for S4S purpose. Since your follower count is increasing, you can reach to accounts with the same numbers. As a brand, you need to pay more attention to growing your Instagram audience. S4S is a feasible way. If you churn out quality contents regularly and you want to increase your follower count, you should do S4S. However, it requires consistency, hard work, and patience.

The S4S is an easy technique that you can adapt for your rapid growth. Many of these big accounts have used this technique. Some of them still do. The question is, Why shouldn't you?

Regular Update of Your Profile

Everyone likes quality. This why you need to churn out excellence in all areas. You need to update your profile regularly. Your profile picture needs to have a high resolution. It needs to represent your brand too. Your brand logo is recommended. Also, you can use branded hashtags that resonate with your brand's products and services. This hashtag can be put in the bio too.

Using Instagram Stories

What is the best combo you have ever come across? Chicken and chips? There is something way better: Instagram stories and hashtags. Have you ever realized that the ten-second video you posted on Instagram stories might be the game changer? It is a powerful concept that only requires simple steps: post your stories and add relevant hashtags. You can do mini research of the relevant and trending hashtags you want to input.

Each time you post a new story on Instagram, you can input a generic hashtag to the post. You can make it visible by laying it over the photo or video. Below is a step-by-step instruction:

Find Hashtags

You need to find the right hashtags to use. They need to be the popular ones. Click on the Search icon, and you will see hashtags with a high volume of posts. You can make use of them.

Create an Engaging Story

Ensure that the story you are about to post will strike a lot of engagement. No one wants boredom. Therefore, give people reasons to look forward to your posts. Video clips are the recommended contents for Instagram stories. They do not have to be too many. Post a few every day. That should work out fine.

Sit back, relax, and watch the views start rolling in.

Chapter 14

––––– ❧❦❧ –––––

Organic traffic and growing your page

Perhaps the essential part of being on Instagram is growing your following so that you can have an audience to market to. You have contributed to your ability to grow your following and increase your outreach. There are still several things that you can do to improve your Instagram account. Start seeing higher engagement rates. In this chapter, you are going to discover what it takes to grow your following and start generating success through your Instagram account.

Encouraging Engagement on Your Page

The first thing that you can do to start increasing your audience is to encourage people to engage with you on your page. Remember, the Instagram algorithm favors it when people engage on other users' pages, which means that if you can get your followers to start engaging with you, then that would be good. You can feel confident that they are going to start seeing more of your content, too. You can encourage engagement in two different ways: engaging with others and asking for engagement from your followers.

When you engage with the people who follow you regularly, they feel more inclined to engage with your posts because they begin to feel the development of a relationship. The back-and-forth support between you and your audience becomes a regular part of your relationship. When you go out of your way to go through your follower list and start engaging with people, you actually "break the ice" between yourself and them. This makes them feel more comfortable and engaged with you and your brand. You can do this by regularly going through your list of followers and tapping on random accounts and engaging with their content. Leaving a few heartfelt comments and liking some of their recent posts is an excellent opportunity to start engaging with people. This also inspires them to like back your content the next time they see your content. As you post, you can also ask for engagement by saying things like, "We love summer! Do you?" This encourages people to speak up. You can also increase engagement by writing captions that say things, like, "Comment with your favorite _____!" or "Tag a friend who would love this, too!"

Asking your followers to engage with your content in this way helps them break their thought process from mindless scrolling. Instead, you help them choose to participate in your content. Another great way to encourage engagement is to run giveaways on your page. This allows you to set rules that require individuals to engage with your post to enter the giveaway. Often, companies will decide on what they want to give away. Then they will set the requirements for individuals. For example, "Follow us, tag a friend, and share this post to your stories to enter in the giveaway!" Then, they will leave the giveaway for a certain period, allowing them to experience plenty of engagement from their followers. This type of behavior drives up engagement on that one post, but it will also support you in driving up engagement on the rest of your posts as well. You do not want to be engaging in too many giveaways, however. Two to four giveaways per year are plenty, and this is a great way to get involved with more followers.

Regularly Updating Your Following List

The people and the hashtags whom you follow are the ones that populate your main home screen, which allows you to see images that everyone you are following shares posts regularly. You want to ensure that you are regularly updating your following list so that you are only seeing people who reflect those that are actually associated with your branding or positioning. You might feel inspired to follow personal interests on Instagram, but this is typically best reserved for private personal accounts instead of business accounts. You want to ensure that your time spent scrolling through your followed accounts is spent investing in the growth of your business so that this becomes productive in the long run.

You can update your following list by going through the people you follow and unfollowing anyone who does not make sense to your brand. This way, you are not seeing content that is entirely irrelevant to you or following accounts that are unlikely to provide you with any return on your engagement. You can only support or unfollow up to 60 accounts in an hour, so take your time with this, and do it regularly so that you do not have many changes to make to your account. It would help if you were doing this every week so that you are staying relevant in your industry and seeing the latest trends and people who are coming up. Once you have unfollowed everyone who is not connected to you, you can start going to your most popular hashtags. See if there are any new hashtags or followers for you to pay attention to through the top posts in these searches. This way, you can start following new users who may support you in bringing more attention to your account each time you engage with their content or interact with them.

In addition, when you follow new hashtags that are trending in your niche, you can keep tabs on what's hot. You can also go ahead and start using those hashtags on your photographs so that you can stay relevant, as well. This type of research creates two powerful opportunities for growth in one move, so it is worthy of your regular attention and time!

Saying the Right Thing at the Right Time

On Instagram, you need to make sure that you are answering the right thing at the right time. By posting the right content at the right time, you can ensure that you stay relevant and that your content relates to what your audience is going through or thinking about. Your audience will be likely paying attention to and engaging with your content. The easiest way to say the right thing at the right time on Instagram is by following your audience.

Paying Attention to the Trends

Pay attention to the latest trends, concerns, and issues. That may be arising that people are paying attention to. For example, if you are in the blogging industry and you blog about current events concerning famous people, you would want to stay up-to-date on all of the latest trends and gossip. You would also want to blog about them as soon as they reach your eyes. The same would go for any industry that you are in. The moment you see a trend or topic waving through your industry, you need to be prepared to get on board with it, customize how you share it according to your unique brand, and offer it as soon as possible. In addition to following unexpected trends that arise in your industry, you also need to be following expected trends like holidays or scheduled events that are relevant to your audience. For example, if you are in the fashion industry, you should be paying attention to popular fashion events like Fashion Week and the Victoria Secret Fashion Show. If you are in the tech industry, you should be paying attention to the latest device launches and information regarding events that are big in the tech industry, like the annual E3 event.

These types of events occur consistently, and they are extremely helpful in allowing you to stay relevant in your industry. Pay attention to the information being released by those who drive the industry like influencers and developers. It is important that you avoid talking about things out of season or out of turn, as sharing information too long after the event occurred can result in coming across as irrelevant or outdated. Typically, people who see companies sharing outdated information will believe that this company is not paying attention and does not care enough to stay in the loop with what is going on in their industry. As a result, people will not follow you. Remember, we live in the digital age where information can become available fast, and trends can rise and fall even more quickly. It would help if you were ready to get into these trends and start creating your brand's name in the heat of the moment, not after the trend or information has already started declining in popularity.

If you find that staying with the trends is harder than it looks, try finding three to four people or blogs. Follow those who are always quick to jump into new trends, and pay attention to these individuals or resources. This way, you are not overwhelming yourself by trying to follow too many people at once, becoming lost in what is relevant, what is a trend, and what is entirely irrelevant to you and your audience.

Targeting Your Audience Through Your Words

You now know that Instagram's biggest way to target audiences is through hashtags. This is how you can reach new audience members and start growing your audience fast. However, there is another verbal element that comes into play when it comes to creating an impact through your captions and writing. This is by having words in your captions that resonate with your audience.

You do not want to be using words that do not make sense to your audience or that sound completely irrelevant or outdated. This will lead to your audience becoming disinterested in reading what you have to say and struggling to actually "follow" what you are trying to tell them.

The best way to speak like your audience is to pay attention to what they care about by following them back and listening to how they are speaking. Regularly scroll through your feed and read what the people you follow are saying so that you can get a feel for what their language is like, how they tone their messages, and if there are any unique slang words, phrases, or acronyms that they are using to connect with their audiences. The more you read your niche's captions and comments, the more you are going to become familiar with how they are speaking, what they are saying, and what they are reading.

This way, you can begin emulating their language through your posts and saying things in a way that makes sense to your audience.

When you do start emulating your audience, there are a few things that you will need to refrain from doing to avoid having your audience tune out from what you are saying. One thing to remember is that you need to prevent emulating your audience to the point that you lose your authenticity because you sound like you are identical to those whom they are already reading. Make sure that you pay attention to your brand's voice and your mission statement and adapt the industry's language to meet your tone and not the other way around. If your mood seems too off-base for your industry, you can consider casually adjusting it slightly to fit the industry's needs more. But do not begin changing your approach too frequently, or you will come across as fake and untrustworthy. The second thing that you need to avoid doing is creating messages that are filled with industry jargon that your general following is unlikely to understand.

If you attempt to use industry jargon that is commonly used between those who sell products and services in the industry, but that is unlikely to be recognizable by those who purchase in or follow the industry, you may lose your following solely because they do not understand you. You do not want to be creating gaps and confusion in your marketing by using language that your audience does not know because this can make it unnecessarily challenging for people to follow you and support your business. Keep it simple, speak in a way that your audience will understand, and adapt the industry language to suit your brand's message and purpose.

Leveraging Instagram Stories

Instagram Stories are a powerful tool that can be used not only to nurture your existing following but also to attract new followers for your business. When you use your Instagram stories correctly, you can create a significant influx of engagement from your followers and add a personal opportunity to connect with your brand. It also allows you to create a more interactive page overall. On Instagram, people love interacting with the brands that they love and consuming as much of their content as they can, and Instagram offers plenty of ways for followers to do just that. As you upload stories throughout the day, you create the opportunity for your followers to feel like you are genuinely thinking about them throughout the day, which establishes a connection of care and compassion between you and your followers. Not only will this help you maintain your existing followers, but it will also help new or potential followers see how interactive and intimate you are with your following, which leads to them wanting to be a part of your audience as well!

The reason that stories work is simple. People are nosy, and they like to know the insider's information. This is not a bad thing either, but rather just a simple human experience where we all desire to be a part of something bigger than ourselves. And we want to connect with those around us to become a part of that "something bigger." You can position yourself as the facilitator of that "something bigger" by turning your brand into an experience that people can enjoy and an entity that they can share an intimate and compassionate relationship with. Stories give you a great option to do that because every picture or short clip you share reflects a part of your personal behind-the-scenes experiences. You can also curate your story feed to offer an even more exclusive and intimate feel by purposefully sharing things that will allow others to feel like they are genuinely connected with you through your feed.

The key to making your stories intimate and leveraging them to attract new followers and maintain your existing ones is to make sure that the content you share in your stories is exclusive and unlike anything that you are sharing anywhere else. Be very intentional in sharing things that are more personal and "private" than what you would share on IGTV or on your feed itself because this way, people feel like they truly are getting that private insight into your brand. Instagram stories are already somewhat exclusive because, after 24 hours, they are gone and cannot be viewed again. You can play up that exclusivity thing by sharing the right content, mentioning things that you shared previously that new followers can no longer see, and even by suggesting outright that your story feed is exclusive. Say things like, "Keep your eyes on my stories because I will be announcing an exclusive offer here first... Get it three days earlier just by watching the story!" or something similar to this. Another way that you can leverage Instagram Stories is by making story highlights which can enable your new followers to see exclusive tidbits of your previous stories.

So, if you are someone who regularly travels, and you often share intimate travel experiences with people, such as the restaurants you dine at or the people you meet, you might consider sharing these in your stories. Then, you can create highlights of certain moments from your travels that were most exciting or interesting so that your new audience can glance back through your stories and start feeling more intimately connected with you right away. Leveraging your highlight reels in this way is a great opportunity to show your new followers what to expect, give them that feeling of having known you and your brand for a long time already, and increase their interest in you right from the start.

Using IGTV to Increase Your Following

IGTV is a great way to increase your following. These videos stay in place for as long as you leave them up, which means that followers can look back through your IGTV channel and watch stuff that you put up days, weeks, months, or even years ago once it has been around long enough. You can leverage IGTV to create new followers by creating excellent IGTV videos and then promoting them elsewhere on the net so that people are more likely to click over to your channel and watch. Once they see your video and the quality of the content you create, they can choose to follow your page to get more if they decide that they like you. The big opportunity with IGTV is that you can promote your IGTV channel just like you would a YouTube channel or any other free video content on the net.

By creating great content and then sharing it around the net, you can encourage individuals to go over to your Instagram to be able actually to see the video. This means that you can funnel people from Facebook, Twitter, Snapchat, email, and any other social media platform to Instagram so that they can catch your free content and learn from it. To make your content accessible, you need to make sure that the IGTV videos you make are worthy of receiving views. In other words, you need to create high-quality and engaging content. Your audience wants to pay attention so that when you share it with other platforms. They are more likely to click through your channel and watch the content that you created. The best way to create valuable content is to offer entertainment, insight, or guidance concerning your industry so that your audience is more likely to pay attention to it and watch it. For example, if you are an astrologer, you can create daily videos offering the astrological forecast for the day. If you are a sports announcer, you can create a daily video that highlights the most memorable sports moment of the week or the latest stats of famous players or teams based on the sport that you announce. If you are an educator of sorts, you can create a simple ten-minute or less tutorial on how your audience can do something for themselves that ties with your industry or your area of expertise.

By creating valuable content like this, you make it easier for your audience to understand why and how they are gaining value from your IGTV, which means that you will have an easier time promoting it and getting traction from that offer. Once you have created fantastic content, make sure that you leverage it in every way that you possibly can. Share it across all of your other social media platforms, talk about it in your stories, write about it in your latest post, and make sure that you save it for a future date. If you create timeless content, you can always use it as a reference to older videos when a few weeks or months have passed so that you can use them as a marketing opportunity all over again. For example, if you are a make-up artist and you did a specific tutorial, you can promote the video as soon as you make it, and then refer back to it if you notice someone famous wore a similar look in a recent event. This is an excellent opportunity to create one piece of content that has maximum impact, meaning that you can gain even more followers just from one excellent time investment. When it comes to marketing, that is really what it is all about!

Leveraging Influencers the Right Way

Brands and influencers go hand-in-hand, as they are both responsible for helping to generate success for the other. If you are not yet aware, influencers are individuals who build a trusted following in a particular industry and then advertise for industry-specific brands to their existing audience.

A great example of an influencer, or a family of influencers rather, would be the Kardashian-Jenner-West family, who is known for becoming and staying famous for the reason that most people cannot understand. This is because this particular family blew up around the same time that influencers were becoming a thing, and they leveraged their star power to begin making brand deals and endorsing companies. At this point, most individuals in the family have their businesses, although they still make money by supporting other products and marketing these products to their respective audiences. Influencers are solely focused on generating a massive following of people who like and trust them in a specific industry that interests them the most and then marketing to their audience for the products and companies that they want. As a brand, you can leverage influencers from your industry by having them test out your products or services and market them to their audience. Since their audience is already established and trusting in the influencer, you can trust that once the influencer has tried and endorsed your products, your recognition and sales will increase as well. The key here is making sure that you are working with influencers correctly. On Instagram, there is an unfortunate trend of companies that are attempting to work together with influencers and who are going about it in the wrong way, which results in losing a lot of money in this area of potential growth.

These companies, not knowing that they are making such drastic mistakes, find themselves attempting to work together with low-quality influencers or individuals who are not yet authentic influencers, which means they are not making a massive impact. Rather than having their products in the hands of people who can make a difference, they are attempting to get their products into the hands of people who do not, indeed, have an impact on their target audience. Typically, they will do so by encouraging potential "influencers" to buy their products and then make money anytime they purchase the products. In the end, the most significant way that the company is making money is by having the would-be influencers buying products and not by marketing the products to their target audience. When companies use this method, they end up looking spammy and careless, which results in them being seen as low-rate companies that are not worthy of being trusted or invested in. In the long run, this leads to an unsustainable practice, which can also lead to the premature demise of a company that could have otherwise succeeded in the online space. If you want to leverage influencers, you need to make sure that you are getting your products or services into the hands of people who can have an impact on your growth because they are already so connected with your target audience. Although you may lose some money by giving products away for free to these influencers, you will ultimately end up gaining cash because they will drive a lot of traffic to your page and your website. To create this positive and sufficient momentum in your business, you need to ensure that you are plugging into deals with the right influencers. Be very intentional and cautious about whom you offer your products or services to, and make sure that every single influencer you work together with can genuinely make a positive impact on your business.

Also, approach them professionally through their messages or email if they provide one and not through their comment's section on their photographs as this also comes across as unprofessional and spammy. If you want your company to look poised, respectful, and worthy of trusting and investing in, you need to make these long-term investments properly.

Increasing Your Posting Visibility

When you are posting on Instagram, you want to make sure that your posts are getting seen so that you can maximize your visibility, engagement, and traction overall. Instagram's algorithm favors individuals who get a lot of traction on their posts quickly and will ensure that even more people see these posts by placing it in more favorable viewing spots. If you want to gain these more favorable viewing spots, there are a few things that you can do to maximize your posting visibility and earn more followers overall. As you already know, a posting schedule is a valuable way to start increasing your posting visibility. It enables you to be put at the top of search feeds around the same time that your audience would be looking for your types of posts.

You can also ensure that you are engaging with other people before you post so that you appear higher in their newsfeed with your new posts as well. Another way that you can increase your posting visibility is by choosing hashtags that are only used 300,000 times or less overall, as these make it easier for you to be posted in the "top posts" section of the hashtag. Most people will browse these posts first, so being seen in this section ensures that you are going to be seen more frequently by people in your target audience. Another way that you can increase visibility is by creating high-quality posts and posting them consistently between one and three times per day. The more you post, the more you will be seen, and if your content quality is high, people are going to continue following you and paying attention to your page. When you post content, follow all of the strategies to ensure that you are creating content that people want to pay attention to and engage with. Never post a photograph that is too low in quality, as this will result in you having fewer followers or people unfollowing you because they may think that your standards are going down. You may notice that more significant influencers and brands do occasionally post lower quality photographs, and the reason is that they can get away with this easily. They have a huge following already, and they are unlikely to be impacted by one image. You, however, can be affected early on in a massive way. You want to avoid having people think that you are, in any way, posting low-quality content as this can lead to the loss of credibility and, eventually, followers. Lastly, if you want to maximize your visibility, make sure that you are engaging specifically with the people who are following you. These are the individuals who already see you in their newsfeeds, which means that they are the ones who will be most likely to engage with you quickly when you post new content. If you can get your real following to join soon, it will be easier for new followers to find you in their discover pages or on the top post tabs, which makes it more likely for you to be identified and followed by your target audience.

Engaging With Your Followers

This is a great way to maintain your existing following, but it is also a great way to discover new people who will want to follow you. Think of it this way. Your current following is already a part of your target audience, which means that they likely connect with people who are a part of your target audience by going to your followers' pages and connecting with them through their content. You establish a greater connection with your following, which is also increasing your ability to be found by their followers and friends. When their audience sees you commenting on their posts, if they are interested in what your brand has to offer, they may then click through your page and locate you. So, not only will this improve the way the algorithm works in your favor, but it will also add another avenue for people to discover you on Instagram. Another way that you can leverage your existing following to gain more followers is to go to your followers' pages and click onto pictures that are relevant to your industry. For example, if you sell bikes and your followers post an image of the mountain biking on a cross-country trail, this would be relevant to your industry. You can then look at the list of everyone who has liked this picture and begin engaging with these individuals by going to their pages, liking their content, commenting on a couple of images of theirs, and then following that individual.

This shows genuine interest, helps you stand out to that individual, and increases their chances of following you back. Of course, Instagram only allows 60 new follows or unfollows per hour, so make sure that you leverage this tool carefully to avoid being seen as spammy or overwhelming to the algorithm or your audience. Once these new individuals follow you, your process of going through your followers and engaging with their content will further support you in maintaining and building your following because it makes it clear that you care.

If you engage with someone to earn their following and then never engage with them again, people will start to see your brand as superficial, which can lead them to unfollow you or no longer engage with your content. Keep yourself genuine and connected as much as you reasonably can so that you are always building better relationships with your existing audience and new relationships with your potential audience. Lastly, anytime your audience connects with you by commenting on your pictures, replying to your stories, or messaging you, make sure that you engage with that individual. This shows that you genuinely care about them and what they have to say, and it creates a positive relationship between you and that individual. Take some time out of your day each day to respond to all of these forms of engagement to make sure that you are investing in building a meaningful audience. On Instagram, which revolves around its social experience, a little bit of returned engagement can go a long way when it comes to building lifetime fans and relationships with your audience.

Analyzing Your Results to Increase Your Growth

Finally, you need to make sure that you are analyzing your results on Instagram to encourage higher growth on the platform! You can analyze your results either through the in-app analytics provided through Instagram itself or through a third-party application if you choose to use one of those. You can do this; however, you feel most confident, as long as you are regularly checking in to see how your content is performing. By periodically checking in, you can ensure that you can track trends in what your audience likes the most, what content gets the best engagement, and what earns the most likes on your page. As you monitor these trends, it becomes easier for you to understand what types of pictures, content, and offerings your audience likes the most, which means all you need to do is start creating more of that type of content for your page. Your analytics are not only going to support you in discovering what kind of content you need to be creating for your page, but it will also help you determine what you should be creating and offering more for your audience. These numbers will tell you exactly what products or services your audience enjoys the most and what they are buying the most, which allows you to begin offering the same types of products or services. If your business is solely on Instagram, you can create offerings that are specific to your Instagram audience and focus on expanding in the area that your Instagram audience seems to support. If your business exists on several platforms, then you can pay attention to your analytics across all platforms and incorporate this into all of your future offers.

If you find that the analytics vary from platform to platform, consider creating a variety of offers and then selling the offers that sell best on each platform exclusively on that platform. So, if you are a computer technician, and you find that Instagram users seem to be more interested in purchasing tech products and accessories from you and Facebook, individuals seem to be more interested in buying your actual services. You can market, respectively. Any time you have a new product available, emphasize your marketing around that product on Instagram and market only slightly on Facebook. Then, whenever you have a service to offer, place emphasis on your marketing for that new service on Facebook, and only refer to it a few times on Instagram. This way, both audiences know that there is more to your business than what you are sharing exclusively on that platform. Still, you are not bombarding either audience with content that they do not typically pay attention to.

The last part of your analytics that you need to pay attention to ensure efficient growth is how your audience on Instagram is relating to your actual target audience. On Instagram, a few accidental mistakes can lead to your audience being entirely off the target, which can lead to you having a tremendous following that is filled with people who are not interested in purchasing anything from you or your company. If you notice that your target audience and your Instagram audience are wholly misaligned or that your Instagram audience seems to engage with your content but never actually purchases anything, you need to start addressing your strategy. You want to make sure that you are putting your emphasis on the parts of your audience that are going to support your conversion ratios by becoming paying clients; otherwise, your time spent on Instagram will be pointless. If you do find that you do not have the impact that you desire, go back to the beginning of this book and start reviewing the chapters where we discuss carving out your niche and finding your audience on Instagram. Refreshing yourself on this information and moving forward with a renewed perspective can support you and connect with the people that you mean to communicate with.

Chapter 15

———— ❦❦❦❦ ————

Using hashtags: the power of hashtags

This chapter is on the power of hashtag. We can't talk about Instagram without talking about the hashtag. The hashtag is the symbol followed by a word that describes a post for what it is. They are the controversial description of any Post. When it comes to using Instagram for business, you need to use hashtags even a single hashtag could increase your chances of getting more engagement on your post. Hashtags are an effective way to drive traffic to your content. Now when using hashtags, you have to use a hashtag that really fits your company and a hashtag that will get you traffic.

Using a hashtag like a summer or love can bring you more traffic, but it is not relevant to your brand. So you don't really want to use those kinds of hashtags, they are not specific hashtags and they just attract the general audience. So the more specific you can get on your hashtags the better the most specific you can get on a hashtag; the better you'll be at attracting and engaging your audience. So now how do you find the right hashtags to use, while you wait to do that will be to review some of the most popular companies in your niche and check out the hashtag that they are already using? Don't try to reinvent the wheel. Just copy or model what other successful companies are doing and do it.

After you have done that, the next thing will be to create a list all hashtags and start using them on all your posts. So that you'll be able to know with hashtag works and which hashtag does not by varying the degree of each hashtag, the more specific you can get on the hashtag, the better. After you have made a list of all the hashtags, you will now start testing different combinations of the hashtag on your post.

So keep track of everything. Keep track of the hashtag. Know which ones are working and which ones are not. Sometimes it might seem frustrating to type all the hashtags and test all of them out but you have to do it if you really want to grow your Instagram page.

You could also type out the hashtag on your laptop so that you will be able to work seamlessly between your mobile and your laptop. Also, type out the hashtag on your laptop so that you will be able to work seamlessly between your mobile and your laptop.

The highest hashtag you are supposed to use on any Post is that if you use more hashtags, then Instagram and delete your comment so start using the hashtag slowly. Don't Many hashtags at once. Find out the hashtag that works for you and then build on those hashtags. Now besides using hashtags to grow followers, you could also use the hashtag as a powerful marketing tool so among. Create a hashtag that is a signature of your brand and use it on your post.

Invest in hashtags

Investing in the hashtag is a great way to get more eyeballs on your post. So you need to find the right hashtags to use that are the hashtags that you know that your followers are already using and will definitely be searching for them. Instagram normally allows about 30 hashtags per post. So use every single one of them. Utilize the space for every hashtag. If you go to the search bar and search for a hashtag, you will be able to see how many posts are already using that hashtag. Your main goal is to use a hashtag whereby you can get in the top post. You want to also use a hashtag that is popular enough to attract many people because of more people. You want to also use the hashtag that is popular enough to attract many people because the more people are using the hashtag the better.

So try to balance things up when starting out use hashtags with a low post count and then as your followers grow use hashtags with more post counts. When starting out, you could use the hashtag with under 100,000 posts and then as you start to gain more followers, you can gradually increase it and start using hashtags with about 500,000 post count. As you start using this strategy, you will begin to see the minimal results at first, but as time goes on, you will start to gain momentum. Now you should know how to find your first tags. Think of any basic word that describes your niche and type it into the search bar, when you do that many suggestions will come up.

When that happens, write down every tag that has over 100,000-post count and then takes those tag and start applying it on all your post. Organize the tag list from the smallest to the biggest post count. For instance, if you're in the travel niche, you could type the word travel into the search bar and many travel suggestions will come up. Write down all the tags that have post count under 100,000, then search for more travel-related words like nomad explore, and adventure. Keep doing that until you have it ready to go. Now, as you start using the hashtags, pay close attention to the last two or three hashtags on the list. That is the one with the most competition at once. With the highest post count, the ideal hashtag collection will allow you to get into the top post of the first post. When you start to rank for all the 30 tags, you can start aiming higher.

Now once you run this for some time, you can find other slightly bigger tags to add to the bottom of the list and remove some of the tasks from the top of the list. Now try to update your list every 3 to 4 weeks. Now some people claim that using hashtags for every post will affect you in the Instagram algorithm, but this isn't true. If you use hashtags on your Instagram post, you won't notice any drop in engagement. But just remember that you need to watch your own result and make decisions from the hashtag. This is a vital part of Instagram because they allow you to be able to search for different images and topics and to participate in conversations. So including the right hashtag on your post will allow you and your post to get seen by more people.

Which hashtags are right for your brand?

So this section will show you which hashtag is right for your post and your Brand. And how to get the maximum engagement for your account. Now a hashtag is simply a string of words or a word that followed a # sign. People can click on the hashtag or search for a hashtag in the explore tab to see the collection of every post that contains the hashtag. now, you can decide to use emoji's. Have you ever notice that you cannot use special characters in your hashtags?. Now Instagram has limited the hashtag to about 30 for every post; if you try to use more than 30 hashtags on your post, then the comments won't show up. Using Instagram hashtags correctly will allow you to increase the potential view of your post and help you to gain more followers and find more people on Instagram with similar interests.

It will even help you to be able to do market research on your competitors. So using the hashtag will allow you to gain new followers increase your visibility and increase your post engagement.

How to use trending hashtags

The next section is to search hashtag best practice and how to use trending hashtags. Hashtags have become more popular. Now I'm sure you have heard of the word trending hashtag before. Simply put a trending hashtag is a hashtag that has become popular in the Instagram community and a lot of users are using it at the same time. There are many trending hashtags related to different events and topics in society and in the media. There is the trending hashtags for politics. There are trending hashtags for social trends and their trending hashtag for anything. The mannequin challenge became a social trend the hashtag. Now trending hashtag does change and they are very very time-consuming. You don't want to post a trending hashtag after it has stopped reigning because people have already moved on from that trend and to other trends.

If you use a trend that has stop trending, then you will confuse your followers and it makes you look out of touch with your audience. Now the power of a trending hashtag differs because some trends tend to stay longer than others. So when using the trending hashtags, make sure you check if it is still trending. There are many ways that you can check a trending hashtag on Instagram but unlike Google Plus and Twitter. Instagram does not show the trending hashtag on a site, so the best way to find trending topics for Instagram is to check trending topics on Twitter because they are social media platforms.

You could also check Google Plus to find other trending topics that are more niche specific to your brand. Now you have to realize that the fact that a tag is trending on Twitter doesn't automatically imply that it is also trending on Instagram too. Now many resources allow you can use to find trending hashtags on Instagram.

Trend Map

One of them is the trend map, which is a site that allows you to view a visual map of the geographical trending tags on Instagram. This is going to be very good for you if you are a local business, or if you are running a brand-specific account. It is good to know what is trending in your area so that you can use it to gain more followers on Instagram and on other sites. You can also use the site hashtags.org, which is a site that allows you to find all the declining constant and trending topics, and as well find out the metrics on your social media account.

30gram.com

The next one is 30-gram is a site that allows you to search for Instagram hashtags, and it even suggests alternative hashtag words so that you can use it on your post to gain more followers.

Using trending topics

Now next question is, how do you use these trending topics to grow your brand and grow your business on Instagram. Now when you look through the trending hashtags, you should be able to identify the hashtags that are related to your business or that you feel you can somehow connect it to your business. Using humor creativity is also a great way for you to use a popular trends to gain more exposure related to your brand. You can take advantage of a trending hashtag like the final of a television show to gain more followers. Using a trending hashtag is a very valuable digital marketing tool that you should add your Arsenal because it will allow your message to be seen worldwide by a massive audience without you needing to put in any extra work or spend any extra money.

How to find related Hashtags

The next tip is how to find related hashtag. Now you have to notice that hashtags differ. Not every hashtag will be that effective the #london hat will not be as effective as the hashtag Fashion Week or Super Bowl. If you use a hashtag without relating it to your business, then it will be harmful to your brand as it will appear as if you are trying to use some marketing gimmicks, and as if you are desperate for followers.

You have to be very selective in the type of trending hashtag that you use. While it may be tempting to use all the trending hashtags as possible, you do not want to use too many trending hashtags in a short time. Unless you want to come across as a spammer and can get your account banned, you need to put a lot of thought and consideration into the hashtag that you use. Only use hashtags that will be effective and worthwhile for your Brand and then disregard the hashtags that won't be effective for your brand or that that will not really resonate with your followers.

Try to be thoughtful and considerate with every hashtag that you use. Timing is a very important factor when it comes to using trending hashtags. If you can capitalize on a trending hashtag on time, you'll be able to make your brand memorable and gain a higher engagement. If you don't jump on a trending hashtag early on, then you shouldn't even use it at all because at that point-in-time time, your followers will already be experiencing topic fatigue and you don't want to seem out of touch.

Now while you can sometimes use mainstream trending hashtags like Fashion Week or Superbowl to gain wide exposure, you should try as much as possible to use niche trending hashtags that are related to your industry or your brand. If your company is in the art niche, then use hashtags that are specifically targeting the art community, so that you'll be able to increase your popularity among your target audience resonate with your followers and strengthen the tie with your community.

Campaign hashtags

The first hashtag is campaign hashtags. Now campaign hashtag is hashtags that are created by you and unique to your brand. But the difference between campaign hashtags and brand hashtags is that campaign hashtags are not permanent hashtags like a slogan or a company name, but instead, it is specific to a product launch or a marketing campaign. Now campaign hashtags are usually for the short-term, they are not for the long-term like a brand hashtag. The best hashtag to use will be the one that simply states the name of your marketing campaign or short-term contest now just like brand hashtags. You want your campaign hashtag to remain unique. You don't want to confuse it with another brand. If not, it will make it look like you're copying another campaign from another brand.

It is very good for you to search the potential of a hashtag that you are planning to use and see if it has been taken up or not. Campaign hashtag is extremely beneficial as they will make your followers aware that you are running a new campaign and help to gather interest among the whole Instagram community. And also help your followers and your customers to be able to engage with the campaign using the hashtag so that they can help to generate awareness to their own followers too.

A good example of a campaign hashtag was used by the brand home people when they started their college football season to celebrate football. And also showcase how their product was being used by their customers. The brand promoted the winners of the contest on their various social media channels and on his website.

Content hashtags

Also, use content hashtags that are related to a specific post or a specific content and that is not really Branded. They may not even be related to your brand at all. now, most times content hashtags are not really popular or trending, they are simply common and they relate to your posts like #travel, #beach and #nature.

The content hashtag helps to improve your SEO because they allow your post to show up whenever users are searching for a specific type of content. Also, when users are searching for your product type, your post will show up when you use a content hashtag. Examples of content hashtags are lifestyle hashtags event hashtags, location hashtags and product hashtags.

Product hashtags

Product hashtag is simply using your product name as a hashtag so that customers that are looking for your products will be able to easily find your product and visit your website to make the purchase. If you understand that then, you can create a post with a hashtag of food such as pasta or spaghetti so that anybody that is looking to pasta will be able to see your post and visit your restaurant. Also, if you are a coffee shop, you could post images with the hashtag coffee.

Now using this type of hashtags is good, but however, you can narrow them down to increase your chances of Engagement and to increase your target audience. For instance, instead of using the hashtag coffee, you could use the hashtag latte art for photos while showing your barista artistic talent. Instead of using the hashtag van, you could use the hashtag Volkswagen van. Instead of targeting people that are looking for a van, you should target Volkswagen lovers.

Lifestyle Hashtags

The next one is a lifestyle. Lifestyle hashtags are similar to product hashtags in which you can use your post to be able to connect to your customers and your target audience that share a similar lifestyle. To market to your customer base, you need to think of their hobbies and their lifestyle. If you are in the travel niche, then you can create travel content with travel-related hashtags like well-traveled.

Event hashtags

The next one is the event hashtag. This event hashtag will allow you to connect with other participants in an event so that you guys can form connections now invent #dodon't necessarily have to other participants in an event so that you guys can form connections now these hashtags don't necessarily have to be about an actual event like a community, a product launch or a seminar. It could be something simple as a holiday or a worldwide celebration. If your business is taking part in a particular event, you could create a hashtag for it to notify your followers.

If there is an annual event that your company normally partakes in you, you could use a hashtag to gather awareness for the events and give your donators and followers an insight into what the events look like.

Location hashtags

The next one is the location hashtag. Now with the name of a location, you could simply create a hashtag out of it to a target audience in that specific location. This type of hashtag is going to be beneficial if you are a local based business because it will help you to be able to connect with your local customers and unique sense of community in that niche.

You can use a specific location hashtag to get your business known in a specific city. For instance, if you are a local business owner, you could use the hashtag of your town to allow your post to be seen by the local customers, which the town has started to interact with the potential customers that are already using the hashtag. In summary, the main type of hashtag that you could use on your Instagram post is campaign hashtags, content hashtags, Brand hashtags and trending hashtags.

Now one important question that you need to understand when it comes to using hashtags is many hashtags you should use. Now unlike Twitter on Facebook that people are more hospitable to hashtag fatigue. Instagram users typically like to engage with hashtags. The more hashtags, the more the interactions that it will generate for you. Now, this doesn't mean that you have to type out every post that you create with a maximum number of hashtags that is allowed. Do not declutter your post with too many hashtags so that it will not dilute your message. It is best to include only 45 hashtags on your Instagram post and don't forget that you should use relevant hashtags that to your post and to your brand.

You don't want to use a hashtag just to gain visibility, because it will confuse your followers with your message and make your account look like spam so don't just include the hashtag Superbowl or Justin Bieber in your post if your post has nothing to do with those hashtags. Those hashtags will only discredit your brand in the eyes of your followers. Now, no matter how many hashtags you are using, try as much as possible to hide them so that they don't declutter your caption. The hashtag is not an attractive element of a post, so try as much as possible to hide them by cloning them in the comments section below the post, where they won't be visible after other users have let their comment unless the user select the view or comment option.

Also, you can separate the hashtag from your caption with a few lines of thought. Instagram allows captions that appear after three lines. So that it won't be visible to the users except if they click on the symbol option.

Branded hashtags

The next two are going to talk about his branded hashtags. Branded hashtag is simply unique hashtags that you create for yourself consist of your company's tagline slogan and it will help people to be able to associate and recognize your business. The company KitKat uses the hashtag to have a break, which many people can recognize as the slogan for the company. The company uses the hashtag consistently on all their social media channels to encourage their customers to use as well.

So here are some specific things that you need to keep in mind when using Brand and campaign-specific hashtags. You need to make sure that all your hashtags are unique and memorable you need to keep your branded hashtags are consistent across all your social media platform and make sure that you always use the hashtag, you need to keep your business hashtag relatively short and make them easy to remember and spell. You also need to make campaign hashtags for your social contest and promotions to generate awareness of your marketing campaign.

You also want to continually monitor your campaign and your branded hashtag, so that you can respond to users that are using them.

So some of the few things that you have to consider when creating a brand hashtag is to make it unique to your brand and to keep it brief and easy to spell. If your hashtag is too long or too complex, your followers will have difficulty trying to understand what it says, and they will not want to search for it or use it themselves because it takes too much time to type. You also want your branded hashtag to be memorable and to be short. If your branded hashtag is short and memorable, it will be easier for your followers to remember it.

Use something very easy for your followers to remember than something that spells out exactly what your message is. So instead of using something like #we have a wide selection of flavors, you could use something like #55 flavors or #10 flavors. You don't want to use a hashtag that has words like off or right next to another word. As it makes it difficult to read your hashtag. A simple thing to do will be to search for all the hashtags that you are considering.

Look up the hashtag on every social media channel to see the result that the hashtag will bring up. If the hashtag has already been used by another brand, then you want to avoid the hashtag altogether so that your users don't get confused with another type of content that is not related to your brand. If the hashtag brings up a wide range of content or is far too common, then you should narrow it down for something more unique and simplistic.

Chapter 16

− − − − − ❦❧ − − − − −

Instagram ad campaigns

Successfully creating and launching an ad campaign on Instagram might sound a little scary. It is quite easy if you know what you need to do. In this section, you will learn about the different things that you need to do to attain this objective.

Step One: Research

The first step is to find the inspiration for your Instagram ads by analyzing the things that others in your niche or your industry are doing. Before you create an ad campaign, you need to check what your competitors are doing. You need to spend some time researching the kind of ads they are running, the call-to-actions they use, and the engagement they are able to get.

One of the easiest ways to do this research is to view your competitor's Instagram handle and go through their mobile website. Now, you need to go through their product page and check the specific products. If that specific Instagram account uses Facebook pixel for remarketing, then once you return to your Instagram page, you will start to see their ads on your feed along with the products you searched for. Remarketing is a strategy that targets users with specific ads related to the products they searched for previously. If you repeat these steps with different competitors, it will give you an idea about the type of ads they are running. Also, it is a great way to find some inspiration and ideas to design your own campaign.

Step Two: Campaign Objective

There are different campaign objectives that Instagram offers, and it is given in the form of a pre-made list. The objective that you choose from this list helps optimize the ads and determines how you pay for the same. For instance, if your aim is to gain more followers, then the click-through on the ads will not be your primary priority. The different campaign objectives that you can choose on Instagram are as follows:

Brand awareness helps you reach the audience who are likely to pay attention to your ads and increases the overall awareness of your business.

Reach - Select this objective to increase the reach of your ads.

Traffic - It is ideal to opt for this objective to increase the drive the traffic to your website or the app store (if you have an app).

App installs - Directing traffic to the app store so that they can install or purchase your app.

Engagement – Engagement is important to increase the number of people who see and engage with your page or posts. It includes comments, shares, likes and, responses you receive.

Video views - As the name suggests, it is to promote the number of views the videos you post garner.

Conversion - To convert your audience into paying customers or to make any other similar valuable action.

If your marketing objective is to sell products or to run a remarketing campaign, then it is a good idea to install Facebook pixel. It is a small code that you can place on your business website to track the visitors and any other conversions. When you use Facebook pixel, whenever someone clicks on the Instagram ad, they visit the website and make a purchase, and the pixel shows a conversion. Then this conversion is matched against all those who click on your Instagram ad to see the sales or conversions you have made with a specific ad.

Step Three: Targeting

Instagram ad targeting helps you find the best audience to whom you can advertise a specific ad to. It helps you target those who are likely to perform or take the action that you mentioned in your campaign objective. For instance, if your business sells quirky socks, you will obviously want to target all those people who are likely to make a purchase. It's a great thing that Instagram ads have similar targeting options Facebook ads. You have different targeting options like location, demographics, behavior, interests, and much more.

At the primary level, your campaign needs a specific geographical region (country), gender (if it is a gender-specific product or service) and ideal age group. For instance, you can have a campaign that targets men and women between the ages of 18 to 40 who live in metropolitan cities. Try to be as specific with this as possible while you are targeting your audience. The greater the reach of the targeting ads, the better your chances of attaining conversions or obtaining your campaign goal.

Instagram also offers the option of creating custom audiences to reach all those who have interacted with your business in the past or with similar businesses.

Step Four: Creative

The fourth step is to build your Instagram ads creative. This is partially a science and an art in itself. Before you start, you need to think about your objective, the audience you are reaching and the kind of message you must deliver to encourage your audience to engage with the ad. Instagram offers different types of ad formats to choose from and they are photo, carousel, slideshow, and video ads.

Photo ads

You can use these ads to tell the story of your brand and feature different products by using visual imagery that's engaging. If you are just getting started with using ads on Instagram, then this is the safest and the easiest option to start with. Not only are they easy to set up but are easy to run as well.

Carousel ads

If you want to strategically showcase various products or multiple uses of a given product, then opt for this ad format. This format of ad allows the user to swipe to see more images and includes a call-to-action button that will direct them to a landing page to learn more. For instance, a restaurant can use this type of ads to showcase all the different ingredients used to prepare a tasty meal. Once the viewer swipes through all the images, you can use a call-to-action button that will direct users to a reservation page or something similar.

Video ads

A video ad can last for up to 60 seconds. Ensure that your ad is great and that you use the first 30 seconds wisely. This is the time frame within which users will want to engage with the business. When you are designing these ads, you need to create content that integrates well into your follower's feed.

Slideshow ads

You can create a simple video ad using a series of stills. This is a good type of ad, if you don't want to spend a lot of time creating video content for your business.

Businesses also tend to use user-generated content. If you want to promote a product using ads on Instagram, try to include some real-life situations or testimonials that your audience can relate to.

Step Five: Create the Ad

Now, it is time to create your Instagram ad and here are the steps that you need to follow.

The first thing that you need to do is link the Instagram account to your Facebook page. Go to the Settings option on your Facebook page and select the "Instagram Ads" option from the menu. Then, you need to click on "add" to get started and you will need to enter your Instagram login details to get started.

The next step is to open the Facebook Ads Manager and click on the "+Create Campaign" option in the top-left corner of the screen. You need to select the campaign objective in this step.

Once you select an objective, you need to create your Ad Set. You can define your target audience and set your budget in this step. While selecting your budget- there are two options to choose from. The options are daily budget and a lifetime budget. The daily budget option allows you to run the ad throughout the day, meaning that Instagram's algorithm will automatically pace your spending in a given day. The lifetime budget option specifies the time for which you want to run the ad for. This option will pace your spending budget throughout the duration or lifetime of the ad. It is a good idea to start with a small ad budget and you can expand if the ad performs well.

Once you set your budget, you need to select the number of images you wish to use and choose an ad format accordingly. After you select the option, you need to upload all the visuals you want to use and add the relevant text. Include a headline and text caption to your ads.

Step Six: Tracking

You will need to edit and constantly optimize your ad campaign on Instagram to generate the best results. There are different tools that you can use to track the performance of your ads on Instagram. The tools that you use will depend on the size of your business and the number of ads you wish to run. Use Power Editor if you want to manage multiple campaigns or if you want precise control over the advertising campaigns. If you are part of a large business team, then use Facebook's Ad Manager. If you are just starting out with Instagram marketing, then use Ads Manager.

Step Six: Tools to Use

The list of social media tools that you can make use of is endless; you might need some help to figure out the best options that are available. Following are some of the most helpful social media tools:

Mention - This can be thought of as the Google alerts for social media. Mention is considered one of the best tools that can help you monitor the presence of your brand on the World Wide Web. Mention also has certain features that let you respond to the mentions that have been made to your brand and to share the news that you might have come across with the industry.

Buffer - This is a really powerful analytical tool that integrates social media publishing in it. Buffer is a helpful social media tool that helps send your updates to the giants of social networking platforms such as LinkedIn, Instagram, Facebook, Twitter, Google+, and many more. This tool comes with an analytic system that is inbuilt and lets you understand the reason why particular posts tend to be working better than the other posts and also the best possible time for making any particular publication based upon the requirements of your audience. Not just this, it also lets you collaborate with your team and keep the account updated with fresh content regularly.

Feedly- Feedly is a content discovery tool. You won't just find good content, you can also share your findings with your audience without trouble. You get to subscribe to the RSS feeds to help keep in tune with all the recent updates on the industry blogs as well as news sites. If you are interested in a topic, then Feedly can be made use of for tracking related content.

Zapier - This is a platform that acts as a connector for all the various services that you make use of individually and lets you synchronize them all to make your work simpler. For instance, if your team usually makes use of HipChat for keeping in touch then by making use of Zapier you will be able to set up the option for automatic notifications within HipChat rooms for any new updates. You will be able to connect all the various apps that you are making use of. If all your apps are integrated on a common platform then your work gets much simpler.

Bottlenose - Bottlenose now comes with a new feature that has a real-time search engine that consolidates all the information from social networking sites and various groups and displays the resultant information in an order or algorithmic importance. The result of all this work is a stream of content that has already been marked from most to least important. When you have information that is already arranged according to your needs, your work gets simpler. You can also share any of the search results. You can also integrate Buffer and Bottlenose for adding any additional content and resources that can be utilized on a later date, if you don't want to overwhelm your followers.

Quintly - This is a really powerful tool that can be made use of for obtaining detailed analytics of social media and helps you keep a track of your business on social media platforms such as Facebook, Twitter, YouTube, Google+, LinkedIn and Instagram as well. Quintly also helps you to benchmark those features that help you compare your performance with those of your competitors in the industry and also against the industry averages. The Quintly dashboard also provides for customization so that you can simply focus on the stats that matter more to you when compared to the rest.

Use these different apps to track your performance on Instagram.

Chapter 17

— — — — — ❧❦❧ — — — — —

Different ways to make money on instagram

One of the neat things about Instagram is that there are a lot of different ways that you can earn money through this platform. While this guidebook has spent a lot of time talking about how businesses can grow their following and earn customers, the same tips can be used for individuals who are looking to earn money online. A business may decide to just sell their own products online to customers and make a profit that way, but there are other methods that small businesses (depending on who they are) and individuals can use to earn a very nice income online from all the hard work they have done to gain followers and a good reputation on this platform. Let's take a look at some of the different ways that you can potentially make money on Instagram.

Affiliate Marketing

The first option is to work as an affiliate marketer. Basically, with this option, you are going to promote a product for a company and then get paid for each sale. This is something that is really popular with bloggers because they work on getting their website set up, and then they can write articles about a product, or sell advertising space, and then they make money on any sales through their links. You can do the same thing with Instagram as well.

When you want to work with affiliate marketing with Instagram, you need to post attractive images of the products you choose and try to drive sales through the affiliate URL. You will get this affiliate link through the company you choose to advertise with. Just make sure that you are going with an affiliate that offers high-quality products so you don't send your followers substandard products. And check that you will actually earn a decent commission on each one.

Once you get your affiliate URL, add it to the captions of the posts you are promoting or even in the bio if you plan to stick with this affiliate for some time. It is also possible to use the bitly extension to help shorten the address or you can customize your affiliate link. It is also possible for you to hook up the Instagram profile and blog so that when people decide to purchase through the link at all, you will get the sale.

If you have a good following on Instagram already, then this method of making money can be pretty easy. You just need to find a product that goes with the theme of your page and then advertise it to your customers. Make sure that the product is high-quality so that your customers are happy with the recommendations that you give.

Create a Sponsored Post

Instagram users that have a following that is pretty engaged have the ability to earn some money through the platform simply by creating sponsored content that is original and that various brands can use. To keep it simple, a piece of sponsored product through Instagram could be a video or a picture that is going to highlight a brand/specific product. Include branded hashtags, @mentions and links in the posts.

While most brands don't really need a formal brand ambassadorship for the creators of this kind of content, it is pretty common for some of these brands to find certain influencers to help them come up with new content over and over again. However, you must make sure that the brands and the products that you use are a good fit for the image that you worked so hard to create on Instagram. Show followers how this brand is already fitting into your lifestyle so they can implement it as well.

Sell Pictures

This one is one that may seem obvious, but it can be a great way for photographers to showcase some of the work that you do. If you are an amateur or professional photographer, you will find that Instagram is the perfect way to advertise and even sell your shots. You can choose to sell your services to big agencies or even to individuals who may need the pictures for their websites or other needs.

If you are posting some of the pictures that you want to sell on your profile, make sure that each of them has a watermark on them. This makes it hard for customers to take the pictures without paying you first. You can also use captions to help list out the details of selling those pictures so there isn't any confusion coming up with it at all.

To make this one work, take the time to keep your presence on Instagram active. This ensures that the right people and the right accounts are following. This is also a good place to put in the right hashtags so that people are able to find your shots. You may even want to take the time to get some engagement and conversations started with big agencies in the photography world who can help you grow even more.

Promote Your Services, Products, or Business

If you already run a business, then Instagram can be a good way to market and promote your business. For example, if you already sell some products, use Instagram to post shots of the products, ones that the customer can't already find on a website. Some other ways that you can promote your business through Instagram include:

•Behind the scenes: These are very popular on Instagram. Show your followers what it takes to make the products you sell. Show them some of your employees working. Show something that the follower usually won't be able to see because it is unique and makes them feel like they are part of your inner circle.

•Pictures from your customers: If you pick out a good hashtag and share it with your customers, they will start to use it with some of their own pictures. You can then use this content to help promote your business even more.

•Exclusive offers and infographics: You can take the time to market your services through Instagram with some exclusive offers and infographics of your products. This works really well if the offers are ones the customer wouldn't be able to find anywhere else.

Sell Advertising Space on Your Page

If you have a large enough following, you may be able to get other brands and companies interested in buying advertising on your profile. They will use this as a way to gain access to your followers in order to increase their own followers, sell a product, or increase their own brand awareness. This is the perfect opportunity for you to make some money from all the hard work that you have done for your own page.

There are many different ways that you can do this. You can offer to let them do a video and then post it as your story, promote a post on your profile, or use any of the other ad options above. You can then charge for the type of space they decide to use, the amount of time they want to advertise for, and how big of an audience you are promoting them in front of.

Become a Brand Ambassador

This is something that is becoming really popular with MLM companies. There is so much competition on Twitter and Facebook that many are turning to use Instagram as a new way to promote their products and get followers that they may not be able to find through other means. And because of the visual aspects of the platform, these ambassadors can really showcase some of the products through pictures and videos.

There are many companies that you can choose from when it comes to being a brand ambassador. Since you have already taken some time to build up your audience and you have a good following, so if you can find a good product to advertise to your followers, you can make a good amount of money. You have to pick out a product that your followers will enjoy, ones that go with the theme of your profile to enhance your potential profits.

As you can see, there are many different options that you can choose from when you want to make some money through your Instagram account. All of the different methods make it perfect no matter what your interests are. After you have some time to build up your own audience and you have quite a few followers already looking at your profile and looking to you for advice, you can leverage this in order to make some money through this social media platform.

Chapter 18

Influencers

When it comes to Instagram marketing, one of the biggest markets is the influencer market. Making sure that you use Instagram influencers for marketing your product or for growing your page can help you tremendously when it comes to building your brand or making you more recognized. That being said, there are specific ground rules to look at when it comes to finding the right Instagram marketing for your needs. So in this chapter, we will talk about what to look out for when hiring Instagram influencers and how to get the best return from it. With that being said, let us talk about how to find the right influencer for your niche and how to go about advertising with them.

How to find the right influencer?

One of the things to look out for when looking for influencers is if they have a following. Not many people realize this, but having a massive following does not equal a good return. For instance, as you know, many people can buy Instagram followers who are not engaged and will not react to any post, which is why when you look out for Instagram influencers, do you look for accounts that have a big following and get a ton of engagement? You can check the engagement by going online and looking at the engagement calculator. There are many calculators online that will tell you what the engagement rate is for a specific account. If you are looking to get a good deal and a good return on your investment, then make sure that you look for accounts that have at least a 2 % engagement rate. The 2 % engagement rate is for accounts that have at least fifty thousand followers to a million followers.

Once you have checked if the account has the right number of following, and the engagement rate is reasonable, then you can proceed with the negotiation and figuring out the right price for your shoutout. Keep in mind that the average rate for a shoutout is around $40 with a story swipe up. If an account below a million is asking for more than $40 for a story shoutout, chances are, they do not know what they are talking about, and you should look for other accounts. This is true for most of the niches; however, if you are in the makeup niche, then the prices will be a little bit higher.

To find out the right price for your niche, asked many influencers what their rates are, and they will give you the cost. Once you've got the price, average out all the influencers' rates and go from there. Make sure that when you are looking for influencers, you are looking for influencers in your niche. One of the worst things you can do is for you to start looking for influencers who are not in your niche. The truth is they will gladly take your money, but you will not get any return from it. Overall, make sure that you are looking for people who are in your niche.

Finally, the last thing to remember when looking for Instagram influencers is how open they are with you. If they are in it to grab your money and are not willing to negotiate the price, then there is a chance that they will not be the type of person you will want to work with. Most of the time, influencers will level with you and come out with a better price, which is why it is so crucial that you negotiate when looking for influencers and getting the best bang for your buck. If you are not negotiating the price, then you are leaving money on the table. Let us avoid that. These are the basic rules for finding the right influencers. Make sure that you use all the advice provided to you in this section, as it will help you to save a lot of money but, more specifically, get a better return on your investment.

Why should you use influencers?

Many people might be wondering why is it so crucial for them to hire an influencer and promote their product or their page. The truth is that Instagram influencers can be a fantastic tool when it comes to growing your page or your business. The great thing about Instagram influencers is that they have a broad engaged audience that will be ready to buy your products or start following you. This is something you can't rule out in regards to growing your business. Make sure that you use Instagram influencers, especially in the beginning, as they are very crucial for your growth. More often than not, you will not have an idea of how to market your page using Instagram ads. Granted, we have given you the tools for it, but that does not mean that you will be successful from the get-go. What Instagram influencers can do is give you the warm traffic that is ready to follow you or buy from you. Once you have gotten enough sales or enough followers, you will have a better chance of being successful with Instagram ads. The more deals you have in your pixel, the better the chances of being successful in your Instagram ads. Influencer marketing can facilitate that for you.

Moreover, in the beginning, you will have a better return on investment if you use Instagram influencers. Instagram influencers are straightforward to use and can be very reliable, which is why you should not ignore this and utilize it in the beginning, and even when you are more successful. To this day, many businesses like Nike use Instagram influencers to grow their page and business, so do not rule out the possibility of Instagram influencers. The reason that they work is that they have a warm audience ready to buy, an audience that trusts their word. Also, they have spent years and years growing their page, so they know what they are talking about.

Shoutout for a shoutout

If you are not aware of this method, then let me clarify it for you. This method requires you to give a person shoutout, and in return, they give you a shoutout. This is a great way to grow your page or to get more sales without spending a lot of money. This method has been used by many people to get a ton of deals on their page and to grow their page without spending a lot of money. If you do not have a lot of money to start with, then this method can work significantly for you when it comes to influencer marketing. The great thing about influencer marketing is that you do not need a lot of capital to get started. You can have no money and still see great results, which is why you must use Instagram marketing to work toward your advantage. In this instance, you can see that having no money makes no difference when it comes to Instagram influencer marketing, as he or she can do something called a shoutout for a shoutout. However, there are specific rules to this method, so let us talk about it. The first thing you need to make sure when doing a shoutout for a shoutout is that you both need to have a similar following.

Do not expect a page with a million followers to give you a shoutout when you only have a thousand followers. If you only have a thousand followers, then make sure that you partner up with someone who has two thousand followers or at least close to it. Now, if you are wondering how the returns will come from someone who only has a thousand followers, then let me tell you that it will be pretty good. This method, although it will not work as well as someone who has a million followers, will slowly yield you a good return, and you are a free investment.

You will indeed get some followers and some sales. This is for people who do not have any money and yet want to grow their Instagram page. If you are in that bucket, then make sure they use this method by messaging a lot of people, with the same following, to give you a shoutout. One thing you need to make sure is that the person you were going to do a shoutout for does not have any fake followers. The best way to check that out is to ask them their "top countries by follows." If most of them are from India or China, then chances are, they have bought the followers. You do not want someone who has a lot of bot followers.

Chapter 19

––––– ❧☙❧☙ –––––

How to track your success

With all that time you've invested into making your Instagram profile and marketing campaigns look awesome, you'll want to know if all your efforts have indeed paid off. If your campaigns are as successful as you hoped it would be, you should learn to track how well it has lived up to the goals you set before you launch your advertising campaign to begin with.

Think about this scenario for a minute. You're sitting at the office, going through your company's social media content and responding to comments from customers. Your manager comes over and says that they want a report on how the brand's Instagram profile has been performing over the past three months. What would you do to provide this detailed report? Going back to your Instagram metrics will help you track and measure your efforts.

How to Start Tracking Your Success

Metrics and tools provided by social media platforms make life a lot easier for marketers who need valuable information and data to help them keep track of how successful their social media profiles are doing online. There are several ways you could track the performance of your ad campaigns:

• How Many Followers You've Gained: Big numbers always get any brand excited, especially if they are organic followers. Big numbers always mean that you're doing something right, doesn't it? That your campaign is working the way that you hoped it would. Well, in a way, yes, but what's more important is to track how much of an impact your content is having on these followers. Switching your focus from how many people are following you to how much reach your content is getting is a lot more valuable. Having a bigger reach means your audience is engaged with the content that you're providing, which is always a good thing as opposed to them aimlessly scrolling through your content without taking any real action.

• How Much Engagement You're Getting Per Follower: A metric which is going to be helpful in determining your campaign's success is how much engagement you are getting per follower that you have. This will help you determine which of your content is making an impact and resonating with your audience, encouraging them to interact with your brand. To monitor this, what you'll want to keep a lookout for is the average amount of likes that you're getting per post. Also, keep tabs on the comments that you receive and activities such as how many people are visiting your profile and clicking on your website. Engagement rates can be calculated on a weekly or even a monthly basis, depending on how often you are posting content on your profile.

•   How Each Individual Post Is Performing: There's a lot of focus that goes into your post activity, and there's a good reason for it. Think of it this way, if your audience numbers are growing, but your content doesn't seem to be making much of an impact despite that growth, that could be a good indication that something needs to be changed. Reviewing the impressions, comments, likes, and reposts is a good way to track and understand how each post on your profile is performing. Once you have the statistics and necessary figures, compare that to the details of another post you have done. Determine which one has performed better and why it did. These valuable insights can help you create much better content going down the road.

•   How Your Instagram Stories Content Is Performing: Stories are great to show your audience that there's more to your brand than just making products to sell to them. It's great for giving your audience a sneak peek behind the scenes, letting them see what your brand is up to and what inspires your team at work every day. Your audience can interact with your Instagram Stories and express their interest in your content, and for a business, you'll get to observe the replies that come in, the interactions you get, how many views you receive, the reach, and the navigation. The navigation tool is especially useful in this scenario because it lets you see if your audience is simply tapping through your content or watching it all the way through. If they are breezing through your story and tapping through way too fast, that's an indication that they're not engaged enough in your content. These metrics can reveal a lot of insightful information about how your post is performing and what you can do moving forward to improve your content for better engagement.

• How Many Comments You're Receiving: This metric can be an indicator of how engaging your Instagram content is. Comments are a much stronger indicator than likes are because it takes a lot more time and effort to write a thoughtful comment on a post than it does to like it. TrackMaven looked into it and found that brands received an average of 18.54 likes per picture per 1,000 followers. However, they only averaged 0.63 comments, which is a significantly lower number. When your audience takes the time to comment on your content, that means it resonated and spoke to them. They connected with it enough to want to leave a remark, whether positive or negative. At least, it evoked some form of emotion with them, and that's what you want to aim for, a content which sparks an emotion or reaction. If you barely receive any comments on your content or the number of comments you've been receiving lately is on the decline, that could be an indication that your audience isn't connecting as well with your content as you hoped.

• How Your Hashtags Are Doing: Hashtags and Instagram are like two peas in a pod. You'll hardly ever see one without the other. Not only do hashtags help to bring in more engagement and make your post more discoverable, but you can also even use hashtags to track which ones are getting you the most engagement for your post. Instagram is one of the few platforms out there which encourage the use of multiple hashtags (although you still shouldn't use too many). Keeping track of your hashtags and putting together a list of which ones generally draw in the most likes when you use them will help you determine your most effective hashtags. These are going to be the ones that you want to start using most often since they bring in the most traffic. Keeping tabs on hashtags which perform well will also give you a much better idea about what type of content you should be focusing on and which ones your audience wants to see more of. When it comes to content planning, this is going to be a big help during your brainstorming sessions. If at any time you find your hashtags aren't drawing in a lot of likes, review them and see what needs to be changed.

• How Much Referral Traffic You're Receiving: This metric will give you a good indication of how much website your traffic is getting from your Instagram profile. If you want to track your return on investments (ROI), this is how you do it. It is entirely possible to track your social media's ROI, and in fact, that is what you should be doing to keep tabs on just how successful your marketing campaigns are. Instagram posed a challenge for marketers when it came to tracking ROI because of how the app does not allow your clickable links to be included within posts. To combat that setback, marketers had to turn to UTM parameters to do the trick. UTM parameters are the tags which you add onto a URL. These tags will then give Google Analytics more information about the link. Adding these UTM parameters to the links that your brand shares on Instagram will enable you to accurately track your campaigns and determine which traffic is coming as a direct result of your Instagram content. URLs tend to be quite long too, so using a URL shortener like Bitly.com helps you include these links into your captions too. Also, you might want to think about including these shorter links into your bio section, given that Instagram allows for one clickable link to be placed within your profile.

Understanding Instagram Insights

This is Instagram's native analytics tool. It helps provide marketers with data on their followers, including details about the demographics of these followers, what actions they have taken, as well as how well a piece of content is performing on the social media site. With the information on hand, marketers will be able to measure campaign performance, compare content to see what's working and what isn't, and to keep tabs on how individual posts are performing.

The Insights feature is only available if you have an Instagram Business account, which is why it is recommended that you get one if you're using this platform to promote your brand. You'll instantly gain access to Insights the minute you switch to a business profile, and you won't be able to view any sort of data at all if your profile remains personal. On the Instagram app, you will find the Insights data located at three different sections. If you want to access Insights directly from your profile page, what you would need to do is look at the upper-right hand corner of your mobile phone screen, and then tap the bar graph icon at the top.

The main Insights home page will provide you with a summary overview of the data from the content which you have posted over the past seven days. You will be able to view details such as how many followers you gained over the past seven days, and how much engagement you received per post during that same period.

Insights is an extremely useful feature because it enables you to see important details, including:

•   The behavior of your followers

•   Gender

- Age

- Where your followers are located

- How many times they are online in a day

- Filter your content according to metric, timeframe, and type of content

- The number of engagements you received on your profile

- The number of impressions you received

- The ratio of engagement and reach per post

- What your best performing and worst performing content was

- Number of profile visits

- Number of website clicks

- Number of user accounts which have started following your profile

- View your Instagram Stories metrics

Chapter 20

————— ✲❧❦✲ —————

Common mistakes to avoid when marketing on instagram and the best tips for growing your instagram business

Many beginners are excited to bring their business onto Instagram and share some of their products and services with others online. Instagram is great to use and it is good that you are excited, but you need to make sure that you are doing it all in the right way. There are some mistakes that you could make that would drive away the potential customers and could make all of that hard work that you are doing go to waste. Some of the common mistakes that you should avoid with Instagram include:

Combining your business and personal profiles

Sometimes it is tempting to combine the personal and business profiles on Instagram together, but this is going to take away from the professionalism of your page and can sometimes confuse other people about what the page is all about. If you want to have a personal page that shows your daily life and all the cool things that you do and see, then set this up separate from the business page that you are trying to create.

Your business page should only have stuff that has to do with your business on it. This helps your customers to know what to expect and what kinds of products and services that you offer. There is nothing wrong with using a personal account for some of your personal life stories, but this should never combine with your professional or business page.

Ignoring the idea of sponsored posts

If you would like to be able to gain a lot of exposure for your business page, going with sponsored posts can be a great way to do this. In order to leverage your sponsored post and get all the benefits, you must find some accounts on Instagram that are more influential and which have quite a few followers already in place; you also want to make sure that these sites that you are going with will have the same target demographic and niche that you want to work with as well. Then you need to get in touch with some of these users and find a way to convince them that it is a good idea to promote some of your content on their news feed.

Now, this can be a hard task to get done. What do you need to do in order to get these people who have influential accounts to take the sponsored posts, especially if they already have lots of people asking the same thing? For the most part, you should check the bio of the accounts that you want to work on because these are usually going to mention whether they accept these sponsored posts or not and they will include their contact details to help make it easier to communicate with the parties that are interested. If you see something like "Open to Business Enquiries" or "Accepts Sponsored Posts Requests" in the bio, make sure to email your details to the account that you are interested in and ask to see what their pricing structure is; you are also able to do some negotiations if you would like.

It is going to cost you a little bit of money to use this technique, but it is one that has been proven to add thousands of new followers to your account in just a short amount of time. There are many marketers on Instagram that have used this strategy to reach out to a lot of customers who are not already their followers. As a beginner, you may feel that you shouldn't spend the money on this, but considering the amount of followers it can add to your Instagram page, it is well worth your time and money.

Improper use of hashtags

Hashtags can be an important tool that you can use on Instagram, but you need to make sure that you are using them and using them properly. If you are sending out Instagram posts without a hashtag, you are really missing out on an opportunity to get some new users.

On Instagram, you are allowed to add up to 30 of these hashtags so go ahead and use a few. You don't want to go overboard and you probably don't need to use all 30 because it does look a bit spammy and can make you lose some of your credibility. But there is nothing wrong with adding in two or three of these with each post is going to help you to see some results and bring in more of your customers.

Forgetting to respond to user comments

It is easy to get caught up in all the things that you have to do to keep your business running, but if you want to interact with your customers and make them feel valuable, you need to respond to the comments that others leave on your posts. Even if it is something as simple as thanking them for responding or you answer some of their questions, this shows the customer that they are important. Also, make sure to be there not only before the sale but afterward as well. Some customers have questions after they make a purchase and no one wants to feel like they are just a number because you ignore their questions or their concerns.

Checking your account a few times a day to look at the comments and respond as needed. You don't need to be on all the time and customers don't expect you to be there instantly all the time, but having a regular schedule for checking in on the account and assisting your customers can help you see better results.

An incomplete bio

Inside of Instagram, you will get a small space to write out some details about your business and the brand that you are working with. This is an important part of your business because it is going to help to show you as a professional in the industry and gives potential followers a little look into what you provide.

As a business, you need to fill out your whole profile, including the bio. People are not going to follow you if the profile is not fully complete because it shows that you didn't really value this information or helping out the customer. Another mistake that beginners can make? Forgetting to place their website link inside of the bio. You will not be able to place this link with your pictures

The best tips for growing your instagram business account

Now that we have had some time to learn what Instagram is all about and all of the great ways that it is able to help us to add to our marketing plan without having to spend a lot of extra money on a social media expert. But even though we need some of the basics, what are some of the things that you are able to do in order to make yourself stand out on Instagram so that your potential customers would choose you over someone else. Some of the best tips that you can do in order to help grow your Instagram business account include:

- Connect Facebook and Instagram together: these two social media sites are actually connected and when you let them work together, you will find that they can be really powerful tools. Make sure that Instagram and Facebook are connected so that you can get the best from both of them and boost some of the marketing efforts. You can even add in a tab for Instagram on your Facebook page so that when you post something on Instagram, it will automatically link up with the Facebook and send it over, saving you time.

- Create your strategy: as a business owner, you need to make sure that you have a good brand strategy that is going to help your business to grow. You will want to make sure that whatever strategy you start to use on Instagram is going to keep the focus on the brand that you have built and how that brand sees the world. Instagram is great for sharing videos and photos so make sure that when you connect the business with your followers, make sure that it stays consistent with your brand rather than straying away or showing things that just don't go together.

- Use your brand or company name in hashtags: the hashtags that you pick don't have to be complicated. If you already have a pretty good following on

Instagram, or your brand name is well known, go ahead and use this as one of your hashtags. This will make it easier for your followers to find you because they can just search the name and find some of your posts.

- Make a follower famous: it is not just about your followers checking out your posts, it is about how you interact with your followers. Take the time to look over the pages of your followers and then like and share some of their posts. This helps to show the customers that you really appreciate them because you are acknowledging their cool posts and sharing them with others on your page. Be careful with this one though because some may be personal and you should always ask for permission beforehand if you are unsure whether they would like it shared or not.

- Be creative with the pictures: it is not enough to just take a few pictures of your products or services and then call it good. You need to get a bit creative. There are thousands of pictures of food or sweaters and so on, how are you going to make your pictures draw the attention of the customers that you want? You can use filters, different angles, changing the lighting, and some of the other tricks on photography to help you out. you don't need to hire a professional photography to do this, but you should be a bit creative with what you are doing.

- Work on videos: a new feature that you are able to find with Instagram is that now you can add videos to your postings. This is a new way to interact with your customers, telling them about some of the products, bringing up rules about a promotion, or doing something else that is creative. Just like with the photos that you post, the videos need to have something to do with the business, but it is fine to be a bit creative with this.

- Think about how to show your products: remember that as a business, you need to make sure that you are showcasing some of the products that you sell. Show these products in a bunch of different ways. This is a mobile site so be creative when showing it off, but many times businesses see success when they show the products in real life, such as something wearing the sweater on a walk rather than just having it lay there.

- Post some good videos (or you): if you are the CEO of your business, this means you need to post a few videos of yourself. This is meant to make the top executive of the company look personable. Make some short and even some quirky videos of the CEO to add to Instagram. Showing some of your hobbies outside of work, for example, can be a lot of fun.

- Partner with some other brands: this can be beneficial for both you and for the other brands that you decide to work with on this promotion. If the two of you are reaching for similar customers but are different products, it can make it easier to find customers that both of you can use. Partner up with a few other brands and have them post some of your products on their feeds while you do the same for them.

- Post on a consistent basis: it is not going to do well for your business if you just post for a few days here and there, ignore the profile for awhile, come back for a week, and then ignore it again, keeping up on this same cycle for the next few years. If you want to find more followers and get more customers, you need to post with some consistency. You can even post some of the same things on Instagram more than once, just make sure that you find a good rhythm to when you post. Sure there will be days when you miss out because you get busy, but make sure to keep up with this as much as possible.

- Track your results: how are you supposed to know if what you are doing is successful if you aren't keeping track of what is going on with analytics and other tracking tools. You should use some of the tracking tools that are available through Instagram and monitor when is the best time for you to post, what your followers like the most, and other things that make it easier for you to get better results in the future.

- Host a photo contest: there are many options that you can stick with when it comes to having a photo contents. The first option is to have your followers post some pictures of them using your products, and then have a vote on which ones are the best with the winner getting a prize. Sometimes you can post one of your own pictures and have your followers like and share that picture to be entered for a prize as well. Videos can work in much the same way. You can mess around with this one a bit to see what you are able to figure out for terms and prizes, but this is a great way to get people to interact a bit more on your page and to share your products even more.

Conclusion

----- ❧❦❧ -----

Marketing businesses have never been this easy with the advent of the Internet. Business persons not only find it convenient to market their brands over the Internet, but they also find it affordable. YouTube is one of the leading social media pages out there. With millions of people accessing it on a daily basis, it means that it stands as a great platform to market your brand. Just like Facebook, people expect to communicate with brands in a natural way. Therefore, the marketing strategies that you employ will make a difference in your campaign. Unique marketing strategies that you use will definitely make you a loveable brand among your audience.

One of the most important considerations that should be remembered is the fact that the message is very important. What you tell your audience about your product or service will give them an overall picture of your brand. Crafting the right message will, therefore, have a positive impact on your audience. As had been recommended, you need to keep it short. Your message should also be clear. If your audience cannot figure out exactly what you are selling, then you need to redraft your message again.

With regards to improving your video quality, it also begins by working on your content. Besides this, you should take the time to learn more about the essentials required in producing great videos. For instance, if you lack the experience in shooting videos, you can always turn to an expert for assistance. They have the experience that will transform your idea into a must-watch type of video. Equally, you need to invest in purchasing the right equipment that will get you the results you need.

Think outside the box when it comes to creating your YouTube video. Think about the expectations that your customers have in mind. Create videos that not only meet their expectations but surpass them. You need your clients to keep coming to your YouTube channel. This implies that you have to captivate them with your content. The strategies that have been discussed in this book should help you in becoming a good marketer on YouTube.

Another thing worth recalling is the fact that there are various ways to use YouTube for your business. Before rushing in to use YouTube to promote your business, you should first consider why it is important for your business. For instance, the platform could be used to market specific products and services that you offer. Alternatively, it could also be used in promoting your company in general. Your YouTube use will have an impact on the marketing strategies that you would adopt. Hence, the purpose of YouTube should be carefully determined at the early stages of your marketing campaign.

Most importantly, you need to evaluate how your YouTube marketing strategy is working out. This calls for the use of YouTube analytic tools. These tools will help you gauge the effectiveness of the videos that you upload. For instance, the subscriber rate will give you an insight into whether the content resonates with your audience or not. A higher subscriber rate implies that your audiences love your videos. On the contrary, a low subscriber rate will mean that your content needs some adjustment. Consequently, you should resort back to the tips that will help you in improving your video content.

Equally, there are specific things that you should not forget about when marketing your brand on YouTube. These essentials will determine whether or not your marketing efforts will pay off. For instance, a simple mistake like forgetting to post regularly will destroy your online presence. As a YouTube marketer, you need to embrace the idea of having evergreen content on your channel. Your customers need access to content that is always fresh. If you must post videos that are outdated, edit them and update them where necessary. Also, you need to understand that there are other things that you should not be doing on YouTube. Keeping your channel private, for example, is a huge mistake. It will cost you the entire marketing campaign. You will realize it when it is too late, and your competitors have pushed you out of the industry.

it should also come to your attention that your followers have other social media pages that they often use. this implies that you need to have an online presence on those pages where your prospects are active. post your youtube videos here and market them appropriately. the fact that you are uploading content to your youtube channel doesn't mean that you are limited. focus on getting your promotional message to as many social pages. in the end, you will increase your reach.

Social media is the singular, most powerful tool in reaching out to a large number of people. If you do not make it a part of your marketing strategy, especially if you are a small business venture, then you will find yourself facing a huge loss in the Digital World of Today, where everything runs on hashtagging and commenting on a post.

Instagram is a mobile photography platform where you must make use of pictures to tell your customers who you are, what you sell and why they should try your product. A picture is indeed worth a thousand words – keep them fun, interactive and cool so that your customer base grows day by day. Use all your social media accounts, from Facebook to Tumblr to promote your brand – interact with your customers and analyze the trending tags in the market to examine what they want and plan your business model accordingly.

Remember that the key to making your Instagram activity effective is engagement and reach. As important as gaining followers is, it's as important to maintain them. This can be achieved with quality content and interaction with your followers.

Make sure that you are consistent in updating your profile and keep things interesting, but relevant to your brand.

If you keep all these fundamental tips in mind, you're on track for success on instagram. Good luck!

www.ingramcontent.com/pod-product-compliance
Lightning Source LLC
Chambersburg PA
CBHW071313210326
41597CB00015B/1218